living
organic

living
organic

easy steps to an organic
family lifestyle

Adrienne Clarke, Helen Porter,
Helen Quested, and Patricia Thomas

SOURCEBOOKS, INC.
NAPERVILLE, ILLINOIS

Designer: Bet Ayer
Editor: Lesley Wilson

Sourcebooks, Inc.
P.O. Box 4410, Naperville, Illinois 60567–4410

TEL: (630) 961–3900
FAX: (630) 961–2168

Printed and bound in Italy by Amadeus

1 2 3 4 5 6 7 8 9

ISBN: 1–57071–680–3

Acknowledgements

The editor would like to thank all at Green Baby for their
photographs on pages 214, 228, 252, and 257. Thanks
also to Sarah Ratty for the selection of her clothes on
page 100 (photography by Ben Gold,) and to Auro
natural paints, who kindly allowed us to reproduce
images from their catalog on pages 89 and 117.

Images supplied by Environmental Images: pp.8, 114,
127, 246, photography by V. Miles; pp.65, 218, 235, 263
by D. Christelis; p.85 by R. Roberts; p.97 by C
Macpherson; p.106 by A. Gazidis; p.110 by M.
Wijnbergh; p.135 by B. Rogers; p.140 C. Westwood;
p.151 by C. Smith; pp.169, 175 by G Burns; p.183 by E.
Maynard.

Images supplied by Retna Pictures Ltd.: p.196 photography by P. Wysocki; p.211 by J. Powell; p.223, by J.
Acheson

Images supplied by the Organic Picture Library:
p.122, photography by G. Wilkinson

contents

Foreword by Nora Pouillon

As chef and owner of *Restaurant Nora*, I've made a commitment to living organically. *Restaurant Nora* is the first restaurant in the United States to be certified organic by a respected organic certifier, Oregon Tilth. It took two years but I felt that it was important to bring an increased awareness and credibility to organic food.

Born in Vienna, Austria, part of my childhood was spent on a farm, where I learned the importance of fresh, healthy food. When I came to the United States in 1965, I was astonished at the increased rate of heart disease and cancer here, and realized that the underlying cause of the sickness must be connected with what we eat and drink. Upon further research, I learned about the terrible depletion of the nutrients in our soil due to pesticides, and was shocked by the ubiquitous use of antibiotics and growth hormones in livestock. Certain that I didn't want to eat food that was raised in this "conventional" manner, I made a conscious choice to live organically and create a venue to offer delicious, well-balanced organic food to the public.

When *Restaurant Nora* opened its doors in Washington, D.C., in 1979, I was challenged to find organic produce and meats, let alone olive oil and fresh herbs. Today it's heartening to visit our grocery stores and see organically grown produce. Now the choice to buy healthier fruit and vegetables is ours, and organic food enjoys the support of many environmental organizations. Growth and acceptance of the organic lifestyle is also visible in my restaurant—after twenty-two years, we're busier than ever!

Organic living has matured from a hippie ideal to a sensible lifestyle choice. Choosing organic foods is choosing to have a sustainable lifestyle. In *Restaurant Nora* I try to subtly educate my guests about the philosophy behind organics by including my suppliers and seasonal availability of food on the menu. Through fresh, delicious dishes I've tried to show that organic food doesn't mean sacrificing taste.

This book is a practical, thoughtful guide to making decisions that will empower you and your family to lead healthier lives. With earth-friendly alternatives for every part of your home, this book shows how small changes in your own household will lead to an improved quality of life. Start with changes that can be built upon over time—decide to buy only organic apples or organic lettuce, then add another item like dairy products.

I try to inspire people to bring the organic lifestyle into their homes and in this book you'll find that living organically isn't difficult. It is a choice that will improve both your well-being and the future of the planet. Enjoy!

organic

food and drink

Why organic?

Organic food has come a long way since the days when it had a reputation for being grubby, eccentric-looking, and usually found lurking in the dark recesses of health food shops.

Today everyone wants a bite of the organic cherry. Demand is growing at up to 50 percent per year, and big business is muscling in where once only earnest idealists dared to tread. Supermarkets, who not so long ago sniffily dismissed organic food as "niche," are rushing to stock their shelves with it. Multinational food companies, including Nestlé, are promoting their new organic lines. In addition, a new breed of organic supermarkets and juice bars frequented by wheatgrass-sipping celebrities, have helped give the organic image a designer makeover.

But the organic food revolution isn't being driven by multinationals, supermarkets, or design gurus—this quiet revolution is driven by consumers in search of food they can trust (to use a phrase from the organic movement).

In the last ten years, intensive farming methods have given us Alar in American apples, BSE in British beef, dioxins in Belgian animal products—and much more besides. The newest food drama—genetically modified food—is just beginning to play. And each new scare reveals just how far removed food production has become from what we would like to imagine is natural.

Food you can trust

As one food scare follows another, it's easy to see the attraction of a food production system that prides itself on integrity and traceability and has, at its heart, a commitment to human health, animal welfare, and the environment. The way organic food is certified demands a clear audit trail from the field to the shop shelf. A good organic butcher, for instance, could tell you which farm he gets his beef from. And if you went back to the farmer, he'd be able to tell you which fields that particular animal grazed in, who its parents were—even what it ate for its last breakfast. As one organic farmer put it, "I could show you every certificate of births, marriages and deaths here."

The crowds who flock to farmers' markets, or buy their food directly from organic producers and community supported farms, know exactly where their food has come from. They can ask everything they want to know about the way crops and animals were raised—and the farmer has to look them in the eye to reply. For many people, it's worth paying the premium price that most organic food commands for that reassurance alone.

War and peas

Sixty years ago, organic wasn't an issue. It was simply the way most food was produced. But the post-war demand for high volumes of cheap food, coupled with the development of potent pesticides (a spin-off of chemical warfare research) set food production on a new course.

Traditionally, farmers fed the natural fertility of the soil with manure, crop rotation, and nitrogen-fixing plants like peas, beans, and clover. Good husbandry was the key to healthy animals. The ironically named "green revolution" allowed farmers to throw away the old rule books and harness the power of chemicals to write the new rules as they went along.

It seemed that there was a chemical solution for everything. Nitrate fertilizers produced quick-growing, high-yielding crops. Antibiotic growth promoters did the same thing for animals. Pesticides negated the need for crop rotations to keep pests at bay, so farms that raised heterogenous crops began to disappear from the landscape, replaced by vast monoculture systems. As the land was pushed into intensive production, so too was livestock with the emergence of factory farms for pigs and poultry. There was a new emphasis on breeding animals that would grow fast and, in the case of diary cows, give high milk yields. Pushed beyond their natural limits and living in cramped conditions, intensively farmed animals needed a daily dose of antibiotics to keep diseases in check.

Three generations down the line there is mounting evidence that the environment, farm animals, and human health are all paying a high price for cheap food.

A healthy choice?

People choose organic food for a myriad of reasons—but health concerns and the belief that organic food is better for us top the polls every time. These concerns include the wish to avoid chemical residues in food and a belief that organically-grown food is nutritionally more sound.

The nutritional benefits of organic food may be debatable, but there is no doubt that eating organic reduces your exposure to pesticides. Conventionally grown food crops are sprayed with a cocktail of chemicals both while they're growing and after their harvest.

HIT OR MYTH

Pesticides don't wash off

Scrubbing or peeling fresh fruit and vegetables removes some, but not all, pesticide residues. You can buy products especially designed to wash off pesticide residues and other contaminants, however, there is no way to remove systemic pesticides which are absorbed into the flesh of the plant.

SEE HOW IT GROWS

The organic boom

• *Worldwide organic sales topped $20 billion in 2000. Analysts predict the market will reach $100 billion within the next ten years. Biggest growth areas for organics are in the U.S. and Japan.*

• *In 2000 the U.S. organic market was worth $10 billion—that's expected to double by the year 2004.*

Source: IFOAM

Government monitoring programs regularly turn up pesticide residues in a range of conventionally grown foods. Although residues are generally well below the officially prescribed "safe" limits, between one and two percent of produce tested goes over the limit in every survey.

The idea that foods contain pesticide residues at all, however minute, is enough to concern some people. Respected scientists, including White House advisor John Wargo, think they might well have cause for concern. Very little is known about "the cocktail effect," that is, the long-term health effects of absorbing tiny amounts of a multitude of different pesticides along with other pollutants from food, water, and the atmosphere. Preliminary research in the U.S. has confirmed what some have long suspected—that the combined effect of several different chemicals is far greater than the sum of their parts. Yet current monitoring programs and pesticide approval mechanisms don't take this into account.

Some people are concerned that national pesticides monitoring programs are not comprehensive enough and that they are seriously underestimating pesticide residue levels.

The official line is that the short-term health effects of eating foods with an unacceptably high pesticide load don't amount to more than a mild stomach upset. Long-term, nobody knows for sure. Many pesticides have been linked with cancer, immune deficiencies, nerve damage, and fertility problems. Seventy-one known carcinogens are sprayed on food crops.

Among the most suspect pesticide groups are organochlorines (OCs) and organophosphates (OPs). These are the biproducts of chemical warfare research during World War II, and they were developed at a time when the pressure to produce cheap food overrode safety concerns and testing and approval methods were less stringent. Today there are still huge gaps in the official safety data for OPs and OCs, so farmers are using these highly toxic chemicals without full knowledge of what their health effects may be.

However, pesticide residues in food are just the tip of the iceberg. Official reassurances about the stringent regulation and monitoring of pesticides and their use ring hollow when you realize that no amount of legislation can confine these potent poisons to the farm. Up to 90 percent of pesticides fail to reach their target. Spread by spray drift, vaporization, run-off, and leaching through the soil, pesticides routinely contaminate our food, air, drinking water, and even rainwater. It's a widely accepted fact that we all have pesticide residues in our bodies.

The number of active chemical ingredients used in pesticide products has snowballed from a few dozen in the 1950s to today's level of around six hundred. Ninety percent of these toxic chemicals are used in agriculture.

Some pesticides degrade fairly quickly. Others classed as Persistent Organic Pollutants (POPs) accumulate in body fat of people and animals. It can be passed on to the consumer in milk and meat, and nursing mothers pass pesticide residues on to their babies through their milk. The notorious organochlorine DDT, which inspired Rachel Carson's book *Silent Spring*, has been banned for agricultural use for years. Yet it still turns up in human and animal milk.

Carried in the atmosphere, pesticides accumulate near the Earth's poles—DDT has been found in the body fat of arctic penguins. Atrazine, the most widely used weedkiller in the U.S., is regularly found in rainwater. Lindane, has just been found in several well-known brands of chocolate.

A number of POP chemicals, including atrazine and the organochlorine pesticides lindane and endosulfan, have been linked with increased birth defects, sexual abnormalities, and declining sperm counts. Disturbing new research suggests that babies exposed to low levels of these chemicals while they are in the womb could suffer life-long health problems.

> **DID YOU KNOW?**
>
> **Let us spray**
> • *Every year, U.S. farmers use more than nine hundred million pounds of pesticides.*

International concern over the threat to human and animal health posed by these endocrine disrupters or "gender-benders" led to a United Nations agreement to control POPs, due to be finalized in 2001. But concerned scientists and international campaigners, including the Worldwide Fund for Nature, are now calling for an immediate ban.

What about the wildlife?

Despite all this, conventional farmers are using more, not less, pesticide. In a nutshell, intensive farming has become chemical-dependent, and, like any other dependency, farmers soon discover they need to boost the dose in order to register an effect. Bugs and weeds quickly develop resistance to pesticides, so farmers resort to higher doses or to new, stronger pesticides.

U.S. farmers now use ten times more insecticide than they did in 1945. Yet over the same time span, crop losses from insect damage have nearly doubled. If this continues, the outlook for the environment is bleak. By wiping out hedges and species-rich, traditional hay meadows, monoculture farming systems have destroyed wildlife habitats. Pesticides take vital links out of the food chain, for instance, by poisoning and killing the insects on which birds feed. In addition, the beneficial microorganisms and worms essential for a healthy soil are unable to tolerate regular doses of pesticides. Once they're squeezed out, the soil is leached of nutrients—effectively it becomes no more use than a sponge—and dependent on artificial fertilizers.

The United Nations Food and Agriculture Organization (FAO) estimates that 75 percent of the genetic resources for food and farming have been lost within the last century.

DID YOU KNOW?

Water worries

• *According to a 1998 EPA report, agriculture is the biggest polluter of America's rivers and streams, fouling more than 173,000 miles of waterways with chemicals, erosion, and animal waste runoff from livestock production.*

• *Nitrate pollutes drinking water supplies in forty U.S. states. In 1994 about five hundred thousand people in the U.S. drank tap water that officially violated the nitrate maximum contaminant limit.*

• *"So extensive is the agricultural pollution of the Mississippi River—the main drainage conduit for the U.S. cornbelt—that a "dead zone" the size of New Jersey forms each summer in the Gulf of Mexico, the river's terminus."*

• *In their study "Same As It Ever Was," Environmental Working Group reported that in twenty-eight of the twenty-nine cities tested, weed killers (herbicides) were found in tap water.*

(Sources: Pesticide & Toxic Chemical News, Pesticides Trust, Worldwatch Institute's "State of the World 1998 Report," and Environmental Working Group)

Water

Nitrates from fertilizer, pesticides, slurry, and silage effluent can all pollute water courses, posing a serious threat to the aquatic life of rivers and streams, and in some cases to human health. The potentially fatal "blue baby syndrome" (the baby turns blue around the mouth, hands, and feet) is associated with overexposure to nitrate, and there is some evidence linking nitrate to cancer.

We're all paying extra on our water bills to cover the cost of cleaning up contaminated water to make it fit to drink. Still, it seems consumers aren't convinced by official reassurances that tap water today is safer than ever. Mineral water sales have increased despite reassurances that 99.8 percent of drinking water meets stringent safety tests.

Bugs and drugs

It seems madness to risk human lives for the sake of a few pennies off the price of a pound of bacon—but that is just what we are doing. The routine use of antibiotics on factory farms is a major feature in the erosion of the power of these life-saving drugs in human medicine.

Antibiotics are part of the daily diet down on the factory-farm, especially for pigs and poultry. They are used as growth-promoters in animal feed to push animals to reach their slaughter weight up to 10 percent faster. Nearly half of all antibiotics used in the U.S. are given to animals. And 80 percent of those are used as growth promoters.

Antibiotics are also used prophylactically, to protect animals from the bugs like *Salmonella* and *Campylobacter* which thrive in dirty, over-crowded conditions.

Down on the farm, this encourages the development of "super-bugs," or antibiotic-resistant bacteria, that go on to infect people and spread potentially untreatable diseases.

In 1999 the European Union banned four antibiotic growth promoters which were related to the antibiotics used in human medicine. Yet in the U.S., nineteen different drugs are still used as growth promoters—and at least seven of these are ones used in human medicine.

There's evidence that antibiotics are losing the battle against *Salmonella* and *Campylobacter*—the two bugs responsible for most food poisoning. A new strain of *Salmonella* has emerged which is already resistant to five antibiotics.

Animal farm

The routine use of antibiotics props up factory farming. Without antibiotics, even meat industry spokespeople admit that many intensive livestock farms would be overrun with disease. As news filters out of the appalling conditions under which the majority of pigs and broiler chickens (those raised for meat) are kept, it's hardly surprising that consumers are beginning to seek out meat farmed under more humane conditions. Piglets are naturally sociable, lively creatures. When kept in overcrowded, indoor units young pigs are unable to express their natural behavior by rooting and foraging—and start biting their companions' tails in frustration. Instead of giving the animals more space and a stimulating environment, some farmers dock their tails and cut their teeth.

The same twisted logic justifies debeaking chickens to stop them from pecking at each other in similarly crowded conditions. The other main welfare issue for broiler chickens is that they have been selectively bred to grow twice as fast as they did thirty-five years ago. Their muscles grow quickly, but their legs, lungs and heart are unable to keep pace. According to Compassion in World Farming, millions of chickens each year are left barely able to walk, millions more die of heart disease.

Dairy cows on intensive farms are suffering similar problems. Selectively bred to pump out maximum yields and milked for all they're worth, few dairy cows last longer than five years. Dairy farmers in the U.S. can use the controversial genetically-engineered hormone, BST, to squeeze another 10 to 15 percent milk from their cows. BST is banned in Canada and the European Union because of concerns over its effect on human and animal health. BST milk is mixed and processed with the "ordinary" milk supply and there is no legal requirement to label it. Perhaps it's no coincidence that consumer demand for organic dairy produce is growing fast.

GM moods

Finally, buying organic is the only sure way to avoid foods produced using GM technology. Developments in genetically modified (GM) crops have distilled consumer concerns over the way our food is produced. Battered by a series of food scares, European consumers have not swallowed GM companies' line that the new technology will help feed the world, improve the environment and, eventually, offer a whole raft of new and exciting foods.

Rather, consumer concerns have focused on the safety of GM foods and their potential to harm wildlife, the environment, and human health. With all the evidence stacked against pesticides, it's hardly surprising that people are rejecting a technology designed to work hand in hand with pesticides.

In the U.S., where some fifty million acres of crops were planted with gene-altered seeds in 2000, and where there's no requirement to label GM food, many consumers were intitially more accepting. But, following two U.S. studies reporting that GM corn poses a serious threat to monarch butterflies, U.S. consumer opinion is beginning to turn against biotechnology.

Mounting pressure has arisen for the Food Development Agency (FDA) to adopt safety testing for GM foods, following the revelation in September 2000 that nearly three hundred corn products, including popular brands of tortillas, taco shells, and nacho chips, were recalled after tests revealed they were contaminated with a GM-corn called StarLink which has not been approved for human consumption. Consumer confidence was rocked further when it was revealed that StarLink could provoke allergic reactions. In addition, the contaminated corn products were found after tests by a coalition of environmental groups, and not by the FDA.

So what is organic?

The previous section looked at what organic food isn't. This section takes a more detailed look at the people who grow it, the way they farm, and what makes organic food so special.

Cutting out chemicals on the farm

If going organic was simply a case of cutting out the chemicals and raising prices, we'd see a flood of farmers going for organic certification. But organic food is governed by a strict set of rules that cover every aspect of food production—from what cows are allowed to eat, to the number of permitted additives in a hamburger.

Farmers have to manage their land organically for a minimum of two years before it is eligible for organic certification. Once certified by one of their country's independent bodies, farmers must keep detailed records and brace themselves for regular inspections and thorough audits. In addition, they pay an annual fee, usually based on a percentage of the farm income, to stay certified.

Without a chemical crutch, organic farmers work on developing a healthy, fertile soil using tried and tested natural methods. They feed the soil with manure, natural fertilizers (such as seaweed and rock potash), and "green manures" (cover crops like alfalfa and red clover or fava beans) that trap valuable nitrogen in their roots. Rye is widely used as a green manure/cover crop—but is not in fact a nitrogen fixer. Many organic farms support a mix of livestock and crops—the animal manure feeds the crops, and at least some of the crops will be grown to feed the animals. This self-sustaining approach is harder for bigger, less diverse organic farms to maintain.

A vital soil which supports healthy plants is an organic farmer's first line of defense against pests and diseases. Crop rotations ensure that the soil is not exhausted by one particular crop and that diseases peculiar to certain crops don't build up in the soil.

The pesticide-free environment and the wide variety of crops grown on most organic farms encourage beneficial insects and other wildlife to act as natural predators of crop pests. For instance, organic growers do all they can—including planting their favorite flowers—to encourage ladybugs and hoverflies, which feed on aphids. A new approach is to bring in "biological controls" (insect and nematode predators) to deal with the really troublesome pests like slugs.

The organic alternative to chemical weedkillers is hard work. However, weeds can be kept in check by planting crops in certain ways and by "mulching" and some weeding can be done mechanically and by using flame-throwers. Smaller producers find there's no natural and effective alternative to back-breaking, painstaking weeding by hand.

Happy hens, contented cows

High standards of animal welfare are enshrined in most organic standards. Organic livestock live the way we would like to imagine all farm animals do. Hens live in small groups, free to peck about outside all day, cows graze on clover-rich pastures, and sociable pigs live together in groups, with space to root and wallow as much as they like. Central to organic livestock production is the premise that animals should be free to express their natural behavior. In practice, that means giving them plenty of space, a natural diet, and shunning the cruel excesses of factory farming.

The routine use of antibiotics, wormers, and other drugs is banned—as are mutilations like debeaking chickens and docking piglets' tails. Organic farmers only resort to antibiotics and other conventional treatments when an animal is sick, and many organic farmers use homeopathic remedies. Native breeds of animals are popular with organic farmers because they are naturally suited to the regional climate and conditions.

On organic farms, new-born animals are kept with their mothers for much longer than on factory-farms. The animals also eat organic and GM-free—with most standards specifying a diet that is between 85 percent to 90 percent organic.

Because they grow at their natural rate, organically raised animals take roughly twice as long to mature as their chemically enhanced counterparts. When it comes to slaughter, welfare is the priority again. The emphasis is in keeping travel time to the slaughterhouse and the amount of time that animals are kept there to an absolute minimum.

Inevitably, animal welfare standards do vary from country to country and between different certifying bodies. Standards for organic meat are only just being developed in the U.S. (For more on this see "How do I know it's organic?" and individual sections under "What's on the menu?").

Wild things

One of the things that strikes first-time visitors to an organic farm is the noise. While birdsong and the hum of insects are increasingly rare sounds in our countryside today, they are very much in evidence on well-managed organic farms.

The diverse nature of organic farms makes them a haven for wildlife. Hedgerows, wide field margins, mixed grasses, and a wide variety of crops all provide habitats for a range of rare plant species and wildlife. A recent study found that even the center of

THE FACTS

Farmers at risk

According to the World Health Organization, three million people a year suffer acute pesticide poisoning, and about three hundred thousand people a year die as a result of accidental pesticide poisoning, mostly in the developing world.

organic fields were full of life. Farmers encourage this by leaving a "beetle-bank"—an uncultivated strip of land—in the center of the field. The traditional hay meadows which are still a feature of many organic farms support up to sixty plant species, compared with a maximum of five in a silage field. And, of course, there are no pesticides or herbicides to upset the delicate balance of the farm's ecosystem.

International studies have confirmed that organic farming methods boost biodiversity, and many conservation and wildlife organizations have thrown their weight behind organic farmers for this reason.

By growing a wide variety of produce, including many "heirloom" varieties, organic farmers are also helping to preserve our valuable genetic pool of food crops; this pool has been dangerously depleted over the years by conventional agriculture's narrow choice of crops. In addition, organic farming methods have a low impact on the wider environment. They don't pollute water courses or the atmosphere with toxic chemicals.

How do I know it's organic?

Because the label tells you so. The problem for consumers is that there is a muddling proliferation of organic labels—characterized by strange symbols and ugly acronyms —each representing slightly different shades of organic. While every country has its own mix of certifying bodies and accompanying labels, there are two which are internationally recognized:

Demeter The Greek goddess of agriculture is the international symbol of the Bio-Dynamic Agricultural Association (BDAA). Biodynamics adds a cosmic dimension to practical organics. Cynics dismiss biodynamic practices—such as planting with the phases of the moon, and sprinkling the soil with crystals and homeopathic solutions— but it's gaining more converts, especially in wine production.

IFOAM Accredited It's estimated between forty and 50 percent of organic products worldwide now carry this seal. Introduced in 1999 by the International Federation of Organic Agriculture Movements (IFOAM), which represents the worldwide organic community, the IFOAM seal should help make life easier for globe-trotting consumers. Basically, organic certifying bodies who are already accredited IFOAM members can apply for the seal. Seventeen different certification bodies have already done so, and another six are in the pipeline. Look for the IFOAM seal alongside the individual certifiers' logo.

In the United States organic food producers are bracing themselves for a major shake-up as the National Organic Standards Board, part of the U.S. Department of Agriculture (USDA), nears the end of a long, tortuous route to developing the United

FAKING IT

It's a sure indication that organic is about to hit the big-time when some less scrupulous dealers have been caught trying to pass off fake organic foods. How do you spot the genuine article?

- *Buy direct from the producer when you can.*
- *Look for the organic certification body's unique symbol and code number before you buy.*
- *Most organic produce is sold prepackaged to avoid confusion with conventional foods. Shopkeepers selling loose food as "organic" must be able to provide proof of certification to their customers. If in doubt—ask!*

States' first national organic standards. Once the standards become law, probably in 2002, all food labeled "organic" will have to comply. Hopefully, from this date on, consumers will find it much easier to buy organic with confidence, and the legal standards set will ensure a more stringent approach to organic production overall.

Meanwhile, some forty different agencies across the U.S. already certify organic food producers. Of these, eleven are state-run. The others are private companies, growers' cooperatives, and charities.

Standards vary slightly between certifiers, but they are all based on earlier guidelines issued by the National Organic Standards Board. According to the Organic Consumers Association, they are nearly all operating at a very high standard that consumers can trust. Two of the biggest and best known certification bodies are Californian Certified Organic Farmers and Oregon Tilth.

In practice, many organic farmers go above and beyond the baseline standards. There are, however, occasional tales of farmers who've been turned down by the more stringent certifying bodies who shop around for a less demanding certifier.

With so many different standards and certifiers, the quality and integrity of organic food has become a contentious issue. The worry for consumers is that unscrupulous retailers can seek out organic food produced under the less strict regimes, pay less for it, but still change the consumer top dollar. Consumers then end up paying more for food that is less organic than they thought. One effect of this might be that the producers and certifiers who truly are committed to the principles of organic farming will find themselves sidelined as an expensive option.

Farmers and growers who are in the process of converting to an organic system can't sell their produce as organic. Some retailers, including a few supermarkets, sell this under an "in-conversion" label. It's worth supporting farmers who are going through this tough transitional period if you can.

There are also many small-scale growers and farmers who are more-or-less organic, but for one reason or another have never bothered getting the official organic stamp. They're the sort of people who might sell through farmers' markets and their own farm stands. If you're convinced that they are genuine and that their produce has been raised with high standards, there's a persuasive argument for supporting them.

So, what is the freshest, tastiest food produced in the most sustainable way? Is it the food grown and harvested just up the road by a farmer whose methods you trust and with whom you can deal with directly (but who isn't necessarily certified organic)? Or is it the certified organic food that is grown thousands of miles away and subject to all the same transport, packaging, and distribution concerns as most conventional produce?

There's no easy answer and, generally, all but the most dedicated purists adopt a pick and mix attitude to sustainable shopping. After all, not many of us are prepared to make the ultimate sacrifice—chocolate—for a point of principle!

Why does it cost so much?

Talk to any organic producer and it soon becomes clear just how much more labor-intensive organic agriculture is compared to chemical-dependent farming. Also, just about everything organic takes a lot longer to produce. If you're buying imported produce then that, too, impacts on price.

Comparing organic with intensively produced foods is not to compare like with like. There's a world of difference between, say, an organic carrot and a chemically raised one, between organic pork raised outdoors and meat from a factory farm, and between the natural richness of organic ice cream and cheap alternatives that are full of artificial additives and air. On the whole, if you compare organic food to other premium quality foods, you will see that the price differential isn't significant.

Food from intensive farming is artificially cheap. Organic proponents point out that producers internalize all their costs so that we don't have to pay extra in taxes or water rates to clean up their agricultural pollution and related healthcare costs.

It's widely agreed that about 30 percent extra is a fair premium to pay for organic food, since the organic premium reflects the true cost of producing food with a care for the environment and human health. Of course, not all organic options are more expensive. There is high demand and an adequate supply of organic milk and yogurt which has brought prices for these products in line with their non-organic equivalents. However, for other foods, organics are in such high demand and supply is so limited that some retailers are charging well over 30 percent more for them. As demand for organic food grows, and the supply improves, we can expect to see the price of other foods leveling out.

CASE STUDY

Looking At the Peaches—Camille Sears of Terra Bona Organics, Ojaj, California

Californian fruit farmer Camille Sears didn't have to look far for the evidence to convince her that growing organic was an environmentally-sound option. In her day-job as an atmospheric scientist, she was all too aware of the problems wrought by environmental pollution. Closer to home, in the fertile, orange-growing district of Ojaj, she has seen more than enough of the effects of chemical-dependent agriculture.

Camille says, "I never considered the conventional farming approach, as I've seen first hand the problems caused by this method. There are local concerns with pesticide drift and groundwater contamination from nitrate fertilizers. These concerns become compounded as many of the farms in our area are adjacent to residential areas."

Since buying her orchard just four years ago, Camille has planted more than one thousand fruit trees, including mandarins, peaches, plums, figs, and pears.

Customers at health food stores in Southern California can't get enough of her sun-ripened fruits: "They take as much as we can get to them, and I've been told that our fruit tastes better than that grown by most other farms," says Camille.

Camille's fruit is about 10 to 20 percent more expensive than conventionally-grown fruit. But then, conventional farmers don't have to hand-weed young citrus trees. Also, Camille routinely sacrifices a proportion of her crop to pests. Terra Bona's only "pesticides" are gopher traps and limited soap sprays for aphids. Soil fertility is boosted by applications of compost, seaweed, and fish-based sprays for the citrus, and "green manure" cover-crops like clover.

Camille prefers to sell her fruit locally, and she has plans to try Community Supported Agriculture (CSA) and to investigate selling through farmers' markets or her own farm stand.

What's on the menu?

Shopping for organic food used to mean long afternoons trekking up muddy farm tracks. Today, with organic food on everybody's doorstep, the challenge is no longer where to find it but where to start.

Popular demand has boosted the quality, range, and availability of organic food in ways that even the most optimistic organic pioneers wouldn't have dared to imagine just a few years ago. Organic is fast becoming a gold standard for premium foods—particularly for dairy foods, vegetables, meat, and chocolate.

While mass-market producers pick varieties of crops and livestock that will grow fast, look uniform, and give the maximum yield, organic farmers and growers tend to choose more traditional, native breeds that offer more flavor. Grown at their natural pace, organic livestock and crops take roughly twice as long to mature as chemically farmed produce, allowing their full flavor and texture to develop.

Where to buy

Supermarkets Supermarkets, which once struggled to offer the odd bag of organic carrots, can now stock up to nine hundred lines of organic produce from around the world, with consistent supply all year round. The quantity and quality of organic products vary from store to store. Generally they are good for dairy, dried, and canned goods, and convenience foods, but offer a poor selection of meat. Fresh produce is often highly packaged, ruining any good environmental intentions. A couple of recent surveys concluded that supermarkets were over-charging for organics. Currently, chain supermarkets are not geared to deal with small, local, organic producers.

Specialty shops, organic supermarkets, health food stores, and delis These are well-established in the U.S., with chains like Wild Oats and Whole Foods, and there are independent organic delis springing up all over. The best of these stock a bigger and more imaginative range than you'd find in supermarkets, and they endeavor to support specialist local producers. Their staffs are likely to be knowledgeable and enthusiastic about organics. In the worst case, low turnover means stale produce. Prices can be surprisingly competitive.

Community Supported Agriculture (CSA) These farms require more commitment—you pay the farmer in advance for a share of produce throughout the growing season and share the risks. If crops fail, your weekly box of seasonal farm produce stays empty, but if there's a bumper harvest then you can prepare to feast. As its name suggests, CSA enables consumers to develop close links with local farms. Some CSA farms even offer people the chance to work for some or all of their share of the produce—and you can't get much closer to your food than that.

What's on the menu?

Fruits and vegetables

Although not all organic produce tastes markedly different, the best organic fruit and vegetables are a wake-up call to the taste buds. Their fresh, intense flavor and natural sweetness are rarely encountered in chemically produced foods. Top chefs and restaurateurs rave about the superior taste and cooking quality of organic vegetables.

The secret is in the soil. Organic fruit and vegetables are raised in healthy soil and without artificial fertilizers and pesticides. Crops grow more slowly, absorb less water ,and take in more nutrients than those grown with nitrate fertilizers. This, plus the plants' natural struggle to grow without a chemical crutch, can boost the flavor and nutritional value of well-grown organic fruits and vegetables.

To root out the freshest and tastiest fruit and vegetables there are, try and buy locally and in season. In summer and autumn you'll have many choices, but in the late-spring "hungry gap," when stored vegetables begin to run out and the new season's produce has yet to appear, even the most dedicated supporters of local food will buy imported produce for a bit of variety.

Wherever you shop, follow your nose and use your common sense. If organic

HIT OR MYTH

Organic food is more nutritious

A study by Rutgers University comparing organically and conventionally grown food found that many essential trace elements were at a very low level in the conventional produce, whereas they were several times higher in their organically grown counterparts.

Groundbreaking new research from Copenhagen University suggests that organic food may be better at protecting us from cancer. Researchers found high levels of a potent group of antioxidants called phenolic compounds in organic crops. According to the researchers, phenolic compounds are ten times more efficient at mopping up cancer-causing free radicals in the body than other antioxidants like vitamins C and E.

Most research confirms that organically grown crops are higher in vitamin C. They also have lower nitrate levels and, consequently, lower water content, as artificial nitrate fertilizers encourage plants to take in more water.

Despite more than three hundred studies worldwide comparing the nutritional value of organic and conventional produce, even organic enthusiasts agree that more definitive research is needed in this area.

produce looks good and smells good (and we're not just talking peaches because organic potatoes can smell delicious), then it's likely to taste good. Don't worry about the odd blemish or irregular shapes—they're a sure sign that it's been grown naturally— but obviously avoid anything that looks dull, damaged, or old.

Conventional growers have access to a battery of chemical solutions to produce uniform, perfect looking fruit and vegetables year round that keep "fresh" for weeks. But, once these crops have been picked, no chemical fix can stop their nutritional value from deteriorating in storage. Untreated organic produce doesn't keep as long, which means it will come to market sooner and you will eat it fresh and get the maximum nutritional benefit. Precisely because it is untreated, some organic produce needs a little extra care.

Root vegetables, onions, and garlic Carrots win hands-down against conventional ones for their delicious, sweet flavor. Potatoes similarly have a more pronounced taste and robust texture.

In spring, potatoes, onions, and garlic heed nature's call and start sprouting. Keeping them somewhere cool and dark helps delay the process, but by late spring if you want sproutless organic spuds, you'll probably have to pay top dollar for imported ones until the first domestically grown, new potatoes arrive. Celery head, rutabaga, and carrots keep well in the fridge. Don't be tempted to scrub the earth off roots until you're ready to use them—it helps to preserve them.

Squash Organic growers liven up autumn with glossy-skinned, sweet-fleshed pumpkins and squashes in colors and shapes that you wouldn't believe. Look out for butternut, acorn, and kabochas.

Salads and leafy greens Spicy oriental salads are popular with organic growers—great to perk up your palate and salad bowl. And if you thought

HIT OR MYTH

Do organic farmers use any pesticides?

Yes. When it's a matter of life and death for their crops and all else has failed, organic farmers are allowed to use a very limited number of naturally derived pesticides. Their use is severely restricted, and farmers have to get clearance from their organic certifying body. Organic farmers can only use the following:

Copper salts Used on fungal diseases, particularly potato blight. However, because there are concerns over copper's potential to harm earthworms it may be banned.

Sulfur Used to control some fungal diseases.

Rotenone Pyrethrum Plant extracts, used only as a last resort as they can harm beneficial insects as well as pests.

Soft soap Aphid control.

Weedkillers and synthetic pesticides are not allowed.

lettuce, cucumbers, and celery were dull, flavorless things fit only for garnish, then try the organic versions and think again. Organic green celery is especially tasty!

Fresh leafy vegetables and salads keep best in the fridge. If you find the odd bug or slug lurking in the outside leaves, just flick them off and look on it as a guarantee that your produce is pesticide free.

Vegetable fruits Good organic tomatoes have a concentrated "real tomato" flavor and are juicy, but not watery. Avocados are creamy and seem less prone to dark-spotting and fibrous flesh than the conventionally grown fruit.

Frozen vegetables Peas, green beans, corn, mixed vegetables, and even French fries are now widely available and reasonably priced.

Apples and pears These fruits are difficult to grow organically, so there is not a lot of variety around. If you can find them they are generally good; apples keep well.

Soft and stone fruit Peaches and nectarines are often of the prized, white-fleshed varieties, bursting with flavor and dripping with juice. The best are left on the tree to ripen in the sun, but that makes the delicate fruit difficult to transport without bruising or crushing. By the time they reach you, they may be the worse for wear and will need to be eaten quickly. If you must keep them, try putting them on a plate in the fridge or turn them into ice cream, fruit syrups, and sauces.

Citrus fruits Extra juicy and a must for cooks who want peel that is free of chemicals and wax. They won't last long in the fruit bowl but will keep weeks in the fridge.

Bananas Ultra-creamy and well-flavored. Organic suppliers have had problems getting bananas to the consumer at the right stage of ripeness. Conventional growers pick and ship them green, and then flush them with ethylene gas to ripen. To ripen organic bananas, seal them in a plastic bag and let their naturally produced ethylene get to work. Controversially, some organic standards now allow the artificial use of ethylene.

Meats

The quality of life enjoyed by animals on organic farms is reflected in the superb quality of meat they produce. Animals grow at their natural rate, generally taking twice as long to mature. This results in more flavorful meat.

Much of the organic meat (including poultry) from small producers is hung after slaughter (pork for at least a week, beef for up to three weeks). This traditional butchery further improves the flavor and texture of the meat. Higher-volume organic meat suppliers who stock supermarkets rarely do this, so you'll notice less difference in their meats. Modern organic farmers crossbreed full-flavored native animals with leaner foreign breeds to get the ideal balance of flavor and leanness.

Inevitably, all of this comes at a price. Organic meat is considerably more expensive—the best chicken costs about four times more than the cheapest supermarket bird. But the difference is so pronounced that converts say it's worth eating meat less often in order to be able to afford to buy organic.

If you're used to conventional meat, your taste buds and teeth are in for a surprise. Organic butchers tell of new customers who thought there was something wrong with their meat because it tasted, well, so "meaty"—and they had to chew it. That's not to say you should grin and bear it if you are sold tough organic meat (and there is some around). Just be prepared for a pleasantly chewy texture.

For the best price and expert advice on organic meat, try buying directly from the farm or a specialist butcher. Even some of the smallest farms have websites with ordering facilities. CSA farms can also be a reliable source of quality meat.

It's best to assume that organic meat won't keep as long as conventionally grown

HIT OR MYTH

Dishing the dirt on *E. Coli*

The late 1990s saw the beginnings of a backlash against organics with highly publicized claims from some quarters that organic farmers' liberal use of manure meant that the food they produced was up to forty times more likely to be contaminated with E. Coli than conventionally produced food. These claims turned out to be based on a very imaginative interpretation of U.S. government statistics and were quickly discredited.

More to the point, at a conference focusing on the safety and quality of organic food in the summer of 2000, the influential UN Food and Agriculture Organization concluded that, far from increasing the risk, "organic farming potentially reduces the risk of E. Coli infection." Its conclusion was based on research from Cornell University that found that cows fed mainly on hay and grass (which organic animals are) generate less than one percent of the E. Coli found in grain fed animals.

In addition, the U.S. Center for Disease Control (CDC) identifies the main source for human infection with E. Coli as meat contaminated during slaughter. Organic standards require that any manure brought into the farm must be composted—a process which kills harmful bacteria.

So, all the evidence points to poor hygiene in slaughterhouses and unnatural diets on the farm being the prime suspects in cases of E. Coli poisoning—and not well-managed, organic manure heaps. You need to thoroughly clean organic produce before using it, just the same as you would any other food.)

meats—after all, it's not laced with preservatives and antibiotics to keep the bugs at bay. Aim for a maximum of three days in the fridge.

Chicken With organic chicken, more than with any other meat, you get more for your money because the high water content of conventional birds causes them to shrink dramatically in the oven. A small, four-pound, organic chicken will comfortably feed six healthy appetites, with some left over.

The quality of organic chicken is variable, depending on which organic certifier stamped it. Some certifying bodies have very loose standards on poultry and egg production which allow a greater degree of crowding. Again, this is more likely to apply to the high-volume producers who supply supermarkets. It's worth shopping around to find chicken stamped by an organic body which insists on high standards of animal welfare. Or find out for yourself by talking direct to the farmer.

Lamb Organic farmers are not allowed to use organophosphate sheep dips, or the regular doses of antibiotics which other farmers rely on to keep their flocks worm free. As a result, organic sheep farmers tend to keep fewer sheep per acre. Beyond that, there's not such a dramatic difference in farming methods, yet organic lamb is highly flavorful. Organic farmers have learned to extend their lambing season to meet the demand, but the flavor of new season, spring lamb remains something special and worth seeking out.

Beef Most organic beef comes from "suckler herds," where the calf stays with its mother for up to a year. Once weaned, calves graze on an organic diet made up mostly of grass, silage, and hay.

Again, the difference in taste will come from using native breeds, raising them naturally, and not slaughtering them until they are twenty to twenty-four months old, twice as long as conventionally farmed animals live. Whether you get good organic beef depends very much on the skills of the farmer and the butcher. Dark, purplish red meat is a sign of mature beef hung for a decent time. Grass-fed animals have creamy yellow fat.

Pork, bacon, and ham The quality of good organic pork is incomparable to that produced from intensive systems, and the difference is delicious: lip-smacking flavor, crispy crackling, and melt-in-your-mouth fat. Organic farmers shun the cruel practices of intensive pig farming we've already cataloged.

Bacon and ham is equally tasty, and it is not pumped up with water as is often the case with conventional meat. The difference is very clear when you cook organic bacon—it sizzles in the pan, smells wonderful, and doesn't end up swimming in fatty white emulsion.

Some organic standards now allow nitrites to be used for curing meat, although many producers still prefer not to use them. The justification for allowing nitrites is that they inhibit the growth of potentially dangerous bacteria in the meat. They also give bacon and ham that distinctive pink tinge. Critics argue that nitrites are potential carcinogens and that there is no place for such suspect preservatives in organic food. If you want nitrite-free organic meat, check the ingredients label for nitrites.

Sausages, burgers, etc. Traditionally, organic farmers have made their own sausages. Now you can buy sausages, burgers, and novelty shapes for kids in most supermarkets. Usually, these have a very high meat content, although there's nothing to stop a producer from padding sausages with fillers like rusk. (Just check that it's organic rusk.) As with all processed foods, up to 5 percent non-organic ingredients are allowed.

Fish This is a new and important class of organic food, but one with which organic standards bodies are still grappling. Farming the seas has become as industrial and intensive as anything that the agribusiness does on dry land and the consequences are just as dire leaving us with polluted waters, and resulting in perilously depleted fish stocks.

Conventional fish farms are bathed in pesticides, which are used to treat lice infestations and prevent weed-build up. Like their land-based colleagues, organic fish farmers do not use pesticides, routine antibiotics, or artificial color to produce pink-fleshed salmon and the trout, and stocking densities are lower. Organic trout has firm, creamy flesh and a fresh, earthy taste.

So far there are only a few sources of organic fish, but it's worth trying specialist suppliers. If you draw a blank, then the next best thing is to find yourself an environmentally aware fishmonger.

Dairy and eggs

Cows' milk, like human breast milk, is a sensitive environmental indicator—if there are any pesticides and pollutants about, you'll find them floating in your cereal. Lindane, dioxins, and even the banned pesticide DDT regularly turn up in routine tests of conventional milk.

Milk The creamy sweetness of organic milk is the not-so-secret ingredient which gives all of the dairy products described here the flavor and quality that makes chefs and consumers enthuse about it—and it has helped put them on top of the organic shopping list. The difference is outstanding in unhomogenised whole milk, but less so in skim, 2 percent, or 1 percent, and the more widely sold, homogenized whole milk versions. Cream is also available.

Butter A real star churn, organic butter is soft, creamy, and much more tasty than most conventional butters. The flavor of organic cream shines through. It is widely available and priced about the same as other premium butters.

HINTS AND TIPS

Stan Frankenthaler, award-winning chef-owner of Salamander, Cambridge, Massachusetts

"We use between 35 and 75 percent organic ingredients. Root vegetables, greens, and dairy are especially good. We also buy organic canned tomatoes and flour which affects a lot of different foods we make. Even organic canned tomatoes are more flavorful, they never seem to be watery and there is a real benefit to using them. I find organic dairy products more flavorful and richer in body—organic butter especially.

Not only is it good to have regionally based food and agriculture for the economy. If you're buying food from close by it can be riper and more special. Local strawberries don't travel well, but because they don't have to travel far they're wonderful.

We buy from a lot of farmers who might not be certified organic but are farming in a sustainable way.

Organic farmers tend to use traditional varieties and heirloom varieties—you get a broader range with many more types of melons, or many more types of apples and interesting squashes.

In the States now it's really hard to buy anything that you can be sure is GMO-free unless it is certified organic."

Cheese   You name it, and there's sure to be an organic version of it, from the international "big-cheeses" like feta, parmesan, and brie, to regional favorites. Some are produced on a fairly large scale by organic dairies, others are hand-made on the farm. About half are produced with raw (unpasteurized) milk. Sheep and goat's milk cheeses are available too. Some organic standards specify vegetarian rennet. All organic cheeses use non-GM rennet. There are some wonderful cheeses, but it's worth shopping around and doing your own taste test as the quality depends very much on the skill of individual cheesemakers.

Yogurt   This is one of the bestselling organic foods. It is widely available and often priced the same as conventional products. There is a huge range, from lovely, lumpy, creamy-crusted yogurts made and sold by small, independent dairies, to the smooth and tasty products of bigger scale production. The range of organic yogurts available matches that of conventional yogurts, with low-fat, full-fat, "Greek-style," and brightly packaged lunchbox-size containers available. The big difference is the quality of ingredients. As you'd expect, organic yogurts are made with organic milk, fruits, and sugar, and no artificial additives. They are generally lower in sugar than conventional yogurts—but there's no guarantee. Low-fat, low–calorie versions do not contain artificial sweeteners. Up to 5 percent non-organic ingredients are allowed.

Ice cream and frozen yogurt   This is generally gorgeous. You'll think it's the best homemade ice cream you've ever had! With no artificial additives—you get real vanilla instead of synthesized vanillin—organic ice cream is made as it should be with simple ingredients: eggs, cream, milk, sugar, and natural flavorings. Cheap ice cream is fluffed up with a lot of air, but organic ice cream makers keep air content to a minimum. Up to 5 percent non-organic ingredients are allowed. The price is equivalent to other premium ice creams.

Eggs   Organic standards bodies haven't quite cracked this one yet. Some have very high standards about animal welfare, while other standards are very vague. Generally, though, hens are kept in smaller flocks, are free to peck on organic pastures, and have a minimum of 70 percent organic diet. Producers are not allowed to put food coloring in the hens' feed to give egg yolks that "natural" yellow—as most conventional producers do. The yolk color and taste of organic eggs changes with the season. So does availability—hens need a lot of persuading to lay in winter. Organic eggs are expensive, but the best ones, with thick shells and lovely rich yolks, are worth it.

If you have trouble finding a good organic supply, at least try and find a producer

HINTS AND TIPS

Is organic food GM free?

The risk of accidental contamination of organic crops by GM pollen means that it can't be guaranteed GM-free. But organic food production is the only system which bans the use of genetically modified organisms at every stage—from animal feed to food processing.

whose chickens are truly "free-range" as many small farmers and smallholders' are. Don't be afraid to ask how the hens are fed and raised, and look for small groups of hens pecking around outside with plenty of space and greenery.

The larder

The meteoric rise of organics means that today you can leave dusty brown rice and gritty lentils on the shelf and buy tasty, top-quality organic alternatives for just about any of your cupboard essentials. And the range of convenience foods and sweet and savory snacks is growing by the day—and is certainly too wide to catalog here. Here are some pointers to help you decide how to stock your larder.

Rice, grains and cereals, corn and soy The huge global demand for these staple crops means they are heavily doused with pesticides. Pesticide residues are routinely detected, especially in rice and wheat, and this is particularly discouraging if you prefer whole grains, whole wheat bread, whole wheat pasta, and rice. These are also the most likely crops to follow corn and soy into widescale GM commercial growing.

If these issues concern you, choose organic rice, soy, wheat, and grain products, and, for the most part, you'll discover finer tasting versions of otherwise bland foods. Organic risotto rice (*arborio*, *Carnaroli*, or *Vialone Nano*) is especially prized for its excellent cooking quality and nutty flavor. If you've only had conventional polenta and wondered what all the fuss was about, try the sunny-colored organic version, and you'll discover polenta really does taste of something.

Pasta and noodles There is a staggering choice of organically grown plain and egg pastas of every size, shape, and color—including a better than average selection of wheat-free and gluten-free pastas for people on restricted diets.

Flour Once just sold by a few specialist millers, there are now organic options offered by most big commercial millers. They are widely available and have similar keeping and cooking qualities to conventional flours. If you're a home baker, treat yourself to some fresh, stone-ground, whole wheat flour from one of the traditional millers. You will notice a difference. Some bigger millers include "flour improvers" in organic flour—generally vitamin C—but it irks those in search of unadulterated food.

Beans and legumes Canned varieties are generally good and rarely contain added salt or sugar. The quality of dried beans is less consistent—there are some tough ones about, usually victims of long storage and low turnover. Make sure you buy dried beans and legumes long before their sell dates and from a source with high turnover.

Other canned goods The best organic canned tomatoes are so good that you can eat them straight from the tin—and they make a great base for quick salsas. Baked beans, sweetened with apple juice or molasses, generally taste and look altogether too wholesome to convince kids, but it is worth a try.

Nuts and seeds Whether conventional or organic, nuts with a high oil content—for example, pinenuts and walnuts—go rancid very quickly. The same advice applies to dried legumes such as peanuts. Conventional nuts are fumigated in storage to prevent growth of aflatoxins (carcinogens which are produced by molds in storage). Organic producers must rely on optimum storage conditions, so it's worth choosing your supplier carefully.

Dried herbs and spices Many conventional dried herbs and spices are irradiated, as well as being treated with the usual range of pesticides. So, if you don't fancy gamma-rayed garam masala, choose organic.

Dried fruit Buying organic avoids the noxious preservative, sulfur dioxide, that is widely used on conventional dried fruit. Sulfur dioxide can cause acute allergic reactions in some people. Unsulfured, organic dried fruits—especially apricots—are darker but flavorful.

Chocolate Just for the taste! High cocoa solids content is around 70 percent, plus strictly limited organic ingredients make for a sublime, guilt-free treat. Leading organic brands are also "fair-trade"—so you're supporting better conditions for plantation workers, and minimizing your own (and their) exposure to some of the most harmful pesticides. The organochlorine lindane is routinely used on conventional crops and turns up regularly in tests on chocolate.

Processed foods, including biscuits, sweets, savory snacks, breakfast cereals and ready-made meals Organic refers to the way food has been produced, but it doesn't guarantee that the end result will be healthy, tasty, or nutritious. Many of the foods in this ever-expanding category are great, but others are just as over-packaged, high in sugar, salt, and fat, and low on taste and nutritional value as their conventional counterparts. Up to 5 percent nonorganic ingredients are allowed. Read the label and exercise your common sense.

Drinks

Tea, coffee, and cocoa Altruism, more than any other factor, drives people to pay more for an organic cuppa. All these crops are intensively grown, with liberal doses of organochlorine pesticides, and it's the plantation workers, not Western consumers, who suffer as a result. By the time coffee, tea, and cocoa have been processed and end up in your cup, it is rare for even the most persistent pesticides to filter through.

Organic standards insist on sustainable farming and do not allow deforestation—a major environmental problem associated with conventional plantations. Some brands take it one step further by also adopting fair-trade principles which ensure a better deal and quality of life for workers.

A wide range of teas and coffees are sold, from instant coffee and standard tea bags to the finest arabica coffee beans, healthy green teas, and single-estate teas. There is less choice of cocoa powder, but what there is, is deliciously deep and dark flavored—and it makes fantastic cakes.

Organic fruit and herbal teas are good for a clean-tasting, refreshing change. Despite their "natural" image, conventional teas can be host to synthetic flavorings.

Do organic tea and coffee taste better? Not necessarily, but you can't beat drinking with a clear conscience!

Juices Organic orange, apple, grapefruit, and vegetable juices are sold widely. Freshly squeezed orange juice is wonderful—like bottled sunshine in the middle of winter. The quality of concentrated juice is also good and more economical. Some apple juices are pressed from single varieties and so have unique characteristics. Most pack a fruity punch. Organic carrot juice is inextricably linked with hippies in many people's minds, but it has a dedicated following and is worth trying if you're in need of a tonic.

Sodas and spritzers There is a sparkling array of natural alternatives to the chemical-filled drinks that kids crave. Organic sodas and lemonade are less sweet than their conventional competitors (they will still rot your teeth) and about twice the price. There are some delicious spritzers and sophisticated fruit cordials that are made purely of organic fruit and sugar, which will appeal to adults as much as—if not more than—kids.

Beer The growing thirst for organic beer has been stumped by the limited supply of organically grown hops. Conventional hop growers use highly suspect organophosphates along with the usual doses of pesticides. Fans of organic beer declare it fresh and full flavored.

Wine This was once a bit of a joke, but now even the biggest wine snobs admit that there are some classy organic wines, mostly from the cellars of Californian vineyards. You don't have to be a wine buff to enjoy a good bottle of organic wine. It's widely sold through all the usual outlets, as well as through some excellent mail-order specialists and is only marginally more expensive than a conventional tipple.

With wine, the term "organic" usually refers only to the way grapes have been grown and not to the wine-making process—though the organic standards bodies are working on this. Although organic wine makers can use sulfites to stabilize the wine, they keep levels to a minimum. This helps explain why converts to organic wine say it doesn't give them a hangover. Interestingly, viticulture is one area of cultivation where it's widely acknowledged that the lower yields produced by organic methods result in a better quality grape. Some of the best vineyards have long grown their grapes with the minimum amount of pesticides, and interest in organic viticulture is growing.

Spirits Had enough of chemical cocktails? Try stocking your cabinet with organic gin, vodka, whisky, calvados, grappa, and port. They are all out there, although not so widely available. Only one company in Kentucky makes organic vodka for instance, but specialist suppliers should be able to help.

CASE STUDY

Best Cellars: Organic Wine from Bonterra Vineyards, California

Bonterra is one of a steady flow of wineries switching to organic, but this is no heady idealist's dream—Bonterra is owned by one of the U.S.'s biggest wineries, the Fetzer Vineyards Brown Forman Corporation. The tide turned for Fetzer when their winemakers tried fruit from the organic garden of the then company president Jim Fetzer. According to the story, the winemakers were so impressed with the intense flavor of the fruits that they were inspired to start experimenting with organic grapes. Bonterra now grows its own certified organic grapes on seven hundred acres in Mendocino County, and its certified suppliers across the county grow a total of fifteen hundred acres. Bonterra has picked up an array of awards and accolades and a reputation for making wines with pure, concentrated flavors.

Robert Blue, who oversees all winemaking for Bonterra Vineyards says, "These wines represent a commitment to wine quality. While ensuring the safety of workers and preservation of land and water resources, we're making wines that are a reflection of Old World tradition, nurtured from the good earth."

The four seasons

Buying fresh, local, organic food puts you back in touch with the seasons. In spring you can look forward to the first of the new season's potatoes and tender, baby vegetables. In summer luscious, sun-ripened peaches and strawberries are a treat. During the cold months, there are big-flavored, vitamin-packed roots and greens to sustain you.

Skilled organic farmers grow a fantastic range of fruits and vegetables, including heirloom and "gourmet" varieties that are rarely seen elsewhere, to supply their customers with produce year round.

This section guides you through the seasons, with notes on what's available and ideas for quick and tasty ways of cooking with fresh organic produce. The best thing about good organic food is that it doesn't need much improving—cooked simply, its natural flavor shines.

Many of the more common vegetables—such as celery, turnips, and beets—have been left on the shelf in the rush to grab "exotic," imported produce. But, as more and more cooks are discovering, there is good reason why these "old-fashioned" vegetables stood the test of time—cooked sympathetically they're delicious. Besides, if you're not used to it, some of the unfamiliar but wonderful produce that turns up in the farmers' market or comes direct from the farm can pose quite a culinary challenge. Ever wondered what to do with kohlrabi? What are those strange nobbly vegetables that you've seen at the farmers' market but just can't identify? Help is at hand now with hot tips and great recipe ideas, including some from the most innovative chefs that are working with seasonal organic produce every day.

Spring

Early in the season, the "hungry gap" begins to bite. Roots and onions kept in storage over the winter start to run out and deteriorate, and early crops are not yet ready for harvesting.

Potatoes are thin on the ground, but by late spring you'll get delicious, waxy new potatoes. In milder areas, spring also brings creamy-headed cauliflowers.

There's no shortage of greens—from the traditional collards (spring greens), to cabbage, kale, and oriental salad greens with evocative names like "emeralds in the snow," and peppery leaves that are guaranteed to spice up spring salads and stir-fries.

Oriental salad dressing

This warming dressing is delicious on raw and cooked greens and stir-fries—and just the job for blasting off a spring cold: 7 tablespoons olive oil, 1 tablespoon sesame oil, 2 tablespoons rice or white wine vinegar, 1 teaspoon of fresh grated ginger root, 1 clove garlic, 1 teaspoon honey, 2 teaspoons soy sauce, pinch black pepper. Pop it all in the blender, whiz, and adjust seasoning to taste.

Once deemed fit only for cattle, curly kale has spruced up its image as skilled organic growers choose newer varieties and only pick the young, tender leaves. Some dramatic lookers include dark red Russian kale and Italian black Cavolo Nero, which is actually very dark green. Kale and other dark leafy greens like savoy cabbage and collards (spring greens) are ideal candidates for stir-frying, they carry strong flavors well too.

Preparation: Strip bigger leaves off their tough central stalks and blanch in boiling water for about three minutes. Drain and rinse with cold water to retain color. Squeeze out excess water, roll leaves up, and slice across into ribbons. Stir-fry with garlic, spring onions, and chopped chili until tender. Add a can of chopped tomatoes and some black pepper, and serve as a side dish. Serve with polenta for a great contrast of colors and flavors.

Or: Cook baby leaves in plenty of boiling water until tender. Drain, return to the pan and stir in prepared mustard, salt and pepper to taste. Top with a generous pat of butter. Also wonderful in the classic British bubble and squeak (see Winter) or in American hash.

Or: Soup it up. Shred dark leafy greens and add to hearty stews and soups ten minutes before the end of cooking time. This is especially good in soups with chickpeas or white beans.

Quick Italian bean soup

Fry 2 sticks chopped celery, 2 cloves crushed garlic, and 1 finely chopped onion in olive oil, add 14 oz can cannellini beans (or soak 4 oz dry weight beans overnight and boil in fresh water for about an hour), 1 bay leaf, and 4 cups hot vegetable stock. Simmer until the celery is tender, then add 6 oz shredded greens (kale, cabbage, collards, or chard) and chopped, fresh herbs to taste.

Simmer until greens are tender and season. To serve, put one slice of day-old or lightly toasted country bread in the bottom of each bowl, drizzle with extra virgin olive oil and heap soup on top, sprinkle with freshly grated parmesan. Chopped bacon or chorizo sausage tastes great in this soup.

Fava (broad) beans, sold fresh in their pods, come in late spring. Generally, beans in their pods yield about a third of their weight in beans. If you've only ever had them gray, wrinkled, and over-cooked, forgive and forget—and try this.

Preparation: Pop the beans out of their pods and drop into boiling water for a couple of minutes. Drain and as soon as they're cool enough to handle, slip the beans out of their tough outer jackets to reveal bright green, tender nuggets that taste pea-fresh. Eat just like this.

Or: These beans are delicious with Mediterranean flavors such as garlic, lemon juice, fruity olive oil, and especially with thyme. They are delicious in risotto, added near the end so they keep their fresh color. They are good, too, in frittatas with potatoes and greens (see summer recipes).

Or: Fry chopped onion and garlic in a little olive oil, add shelled beans and fresh (or canned) chopped tomatoes, and chopped, fresh thyme. Warm through. Lovely as a warm salad, piled on to couscous, or as an accompaniment to all sorts of things, especially good with new potatoes and spring lamb. If serving with lamb, try adding lots of chopped fresh mint instead of thyme.

HINTS AND TIPS

Fresh greens keep best if they are sealed in a food-quality plastic bags in a fridge, but if you want to try something different, some independent organic shops and kitchenware specialists sell polythene bags impregnated with a Japanese stone powder which, it's claimed, naturally slows down the aging process and will keep carrots, for instance, "fresh" for up to a month.

DID YOU KNOW?

Chemical preservatives and waxes used on "fresh" fruits and vegetables:

• *Skins of citrus fruits, apples, and pears are routinely waxed with petroleum-based substances or shellac (beetle extract), which effectively seals in any surface pesticides.*

• *After their harvest, most apples are dipped in fungicide—carbendazim and/or metalaxyl.*

• *Sprout-suppressants used on potatoes include chlorpropham, tecnazene, and thiabendazole.*

• *In the U.S., produce that's been treated postharvest is labeled.*

Sources: Central Science Laboratory, MAFF U.K., Pesticides Trust

Broad bean and olive pâté

In a food processor, blend together 1 pound broad beans shelled and skinned as described above, grated rind and juice of one lemon, two garlic cloves peeled, 5 oz pitted green olives, 2 teaspoons chopped fresh thyme, 2 oz grated pecorino or parmesan cheese. With the motor running, slowly add fruity olive oil until the pâté is the consistency you like. Add black pepper to taste and serve with chunky Italian bread or crostini, lemon wedges, and mixed olives. Serves four to six as a starter or a snack.

RECIPE

Purple-sprouting broccoli is a real treat. Although many home gardeners grow it, commercially it's rarely sold outside farmers' markets and CSA farms. If you see it, snap it up—it's the vegetable queen of spring (unless you're lucky enough to find organic asparagus). Both the succulent purple spears and the stems, trimmed and sliced into batons, are delicious.

Preparation: Overcooked broccoli loses its delicate flavor and gorgeous color and turns into a mush. Drop into plenty of boiling water, cook quickly, and drain immediately. This is a pot worth watching!

Or: Delicious topped with butter and black pepper or a simple tomato sauce.

Or: Broccoli livens up all kinds of spring dishes—especially stir-fries and risottos. It goes well with nuts and cheese, especially blue cheese. Try a risotto based on broccoli, leeks, pine nuts, and a creamy blue cheese like dolcelatte or gorgonzola.

Or: Make a quick pasta dish. Steam broccoli and rinse in cold water. Meanwhile cook pasta until al dente, rinse through with hot water. Return pasta to the pan with the broccoli, drizzle with your best olive oil, and add grated lemon rind, shavings of parmesan, flakes of sea salt and freshly-ground black pepper. Add kalamata olives, slivered almonds, pine nuts, or chopped walnuts for a more substantial supper.

Summer

Summertime, and suddenly the eating is easy. Organic growers are still harvesting new potatoes and fava (broad) beans, but they're also pulling up sweet new root crops including carrots, baby beets, and tender turnips. You can use fresh beet roots and turnip tops just like spinach. Baby turnips are tender so there's no need to peel them because they're tasty simply trimmed and steamed whole with baby carrots.

Tomatoes, sweet peppers, zucchini, and eggplant are ripening, ready for an autumn abundance. They're all delicious when gently roasted with olive oil, garlic, and herbs (rosemary or basil especially) either in the oven or on the grill.

There's no better encouragement to eat your greens than the sight of a vegetable box full of glossy Swiss chard, summer spinach, and salad greens such as purple lollo rosso, frisee, watercress, and mixed bags of European and spicy oriental salad greens.

Swiss chard or beet greens Striking-looking, dark green, rumpled leaves sit on white or ruby-colored stems. Rainbow chard has white, red, pink, and yellow stems. Baby leaves are good in salads. Strip larger leaves off of their midribs and you can use them like spinach. Save the stems and try them stir-fried or lightly steamed and served with butter or cheese sauce as a side dish.

NORA'S BEET VINAIGRETTE

This summer recipe comes from one of America's organic pioneers Nora Pouillon, award-winning chef and owner of Nora's and Asia Nora in Washington D.C. Nora's was the first certified organic restaurant in the U.S.

4 large shallots, peeled
1 teaspoon olive oil
Sea salt and freshly ground black pepper to taste
4 small beets/about 1 pound, greens trimmed
⅛ teaspoon caraway seeds
1 tablespoon red wine vinegar
¾ cup water
½ cup canola oil

Preheat the oven to 400°F.

Put the shallots in a small, non-reactive baking dish. Dress with 1 tsp of olive oil and season with salt and pepper. Cover with aluminum foil and roast 30–40 minutes or until soft.

Steam or boil the beets 15–20 minutes in a small saucepan. Peel the beets while still warm and put them in the blender with the roasted shallots, caraway seeds, salt, pepper, vinegar, and just enough water to cover the blades.

Purée the ingredients and, with the machine running, add the oil in a thin stream, blending until emulsified. Add more water, if necessary, to thin the vinaigrette to the consistency of heavy cream.

RECIPE

Summer greens frittata

Drop 4 medium potatoes, chopped into bite-sized chunks and 4 oz broad beans (out of their pods) into a pan of boiling water. Cook for about five minutes, until the potatoes are just tender. Drain and rinse in cold water.

Heat about 2 tablespoons of olive oil in a large, heavy frying pan, add potatoes and leave to fry gently until just golden.

Meanwhile, pop beans out of their tough outer skins. Chop a bunch of spring onions and add the onions and the beans to pan with potatoes. Add 14 oz Swiss chard or spinach, washed, stripped off stalks, and shredded—don't worry if they swamp the pan, they'll soon cook down.

Lightly beat 6 large eggs, 1 tablespoon each of chopped fresh mint and parsley, salt and pepper together in a bowl until well mixed. As soon as the greens have cooked down in the pan, add the egg mixture. Tilt the pan so that the egg mixture spreads evenly around and cook until the egg is just set.

Slip the pan under a broiler until the top of the frittata is spotted and golden brown. Quarter and serve with fresh tomato salad or ratatouille and chunky bread. Good hot, cold, or sliced in sandwiches. Serves four.

HINTS AND TIPS

Susan Spicer, award-winning chef at Bayona restaurant, New Orleans

"About a third of the produce that I buy is organic and most of it comes from one local farmer who calls me on Saturday and delivers once a week. I like hearing from him about what he's growing, about his methods and how he keeps his plants healthy without having to resort to "organic pesticides."

I think the main reason that organics taste better is that they're grown for flavor and "richness" in nutrients and not so much for looks or durability. Even lettuces tend to have more texture—lots of crunch and taste. We do, however, find the occasional "wildlife" among the lettuces and such!"

Preparation: Spinach and chard go well in curries. For a quick side dish, fry mustard seeds, cumin, coriander powder, chopped garlic, chili, and onions in a little olive oil, add chunks of parboiled potatoes and shredded chard or spinach, and cook until potatoes start to color and greens have wilted. Serve with yogurt and chopped fresh mint or coriander.

Or: Good too on pizzas or in savory pies mixed with pine nuts and blue cheese.

Or: Spinach forms the basis of the classic Greek dish, spanokopita. Basically, this is filo pastry filled with spring onions, wilted spinach or chard and bound together with beaten eggs, feta cheese, parsley,

and nutmeg. Brush with butter and baked until the pastry is crisp and golden.

A green glut Surplus salads make great soup. Fry chopped onions, leeks, and chopped, peeled potatoes (or equivalent amount of long-grain rice). Add hot stock and simmer until potatoes or rice are tender. Throw in a few handfuls of mixed, shredded salads—preferably including some sorrel, Asian greens or watercress for a bit of "oomph"—and take off the heat as soon as the greens wilt. Food process until smooth. Return to the pan. Add grated nutmeg, salt and pepper, and a swirl of cream.

Beet Sweet, earthy, and an entirely different proposition than the pre-cooked, vinegared, and vac-packed variety. Adventurous growers produce pretty golden and crimson beets.

Preparation: Wrap in foil and bake, or boil whole until tender and then peel. Good hot or cold combined with horseradish or sour cream and herbs, or in salads with oranges, nuts, and Belgian endive (chicory).

Or: Pureed with sour cream, dill or chives, and plenty of black pepper, beets make a beautiful side dish to serve with game, strong cheeses, and other robust-flavors.

Or: Beets' main claim to fame is as the star of the classic Eastern European soup, borscht. Recipes for borscht abound. It's easy to make, a feast for the eyes and the stomach—and surprisingly popular with children.

Summer fruits Sun-ripened, soft fruits like raspberries and strawberries just aren't designed to be kept. Eat as many as you can fresh (that shouldn't be too difficult!), and then try bottling a bit of sunshine to keep you going through winter.

RECIPE

Fruit syrup
Wash and drain the fruit and put in a large pan. For blackcurrants add 1 cup of water for each cup of fruit. Other berries are fine undiluted. Cook over low heat until the juices run. Crush the fruit with a potato masher. Bring the fruit rapidly to a boil, simmer for one minute, and then remove from heat. Put in a jelly bag and leave to drain overnight. Measure the juice into a large pan and add 1½ cups sugar for each 2½ cups juice. Heat very gently, stirring constantly until the just sugar dissolves. Pour into sterilized bottles, and seal. The syrup will keep in the fridge for about six weeks. If you want to keep it longer, freeze in cartons or ice-cube trays. Dilute five parts water to one part syrup for a delicious vitamin-packed drink, or use undiluted to flavor milkshakes, pour on ice cream, or add to cocktails.

Cheats' ice cream

Use any summer fruit to make a purée (blackcurrants, plums, peaches, and other stone fruit need gentle cooking first to soften). Whiz the fruit in a blender and then push through a sieve to get a really smooth puree. Sweeten to taste, add a squeeze of lemon or cranberry juice to lift the flavor, and stir into softly whipped cream (or half whipped cream half yogurt if you're counting calories). As a rule of thumb, measure the puree and use about half that amount of cream. If you have an ice cream maker, follow the manufacturer's instructions from here. Otherwise, pour into a shallow freezing container and freeze on the coldest setting. Just as the ice cream is beginning to firm-up (between two and four hours), take it out of the freezer, tip into a bowl, and beat until smooth to break up the ice crystals. Return to the freezer until firm.

Autumn

As summer fades into autumn, organic growers reap a glowing harvest of richly colored vegetables. Deep red tomatoes and sweet peppers join dark green and orange squash, glossy purple eggplants, and golden sweet corn. There are still green salads in abundance and Florence fennel. Kohlrabi appears late in the season. In abundant contrast to the lean pickings of spring, you might find yourself wondering what to do with a glut of juicy tomatoes, sweet peppers, and squashes.

Kohlrabi It looks like an extra from a "vegetable mutants from outer space" B-movie. Shiny green or purple spheres with protruding tentacle-like leafy stems. Tastes somewhere between a cabbage and a peppery turnip. Fans, including innovative U.S. chef Stan Frankenthaler, eat small ones raw. Larger kohlrabi can be tough and fibrous.
Preparation: Tasty peeled, boiled, sliced, and fried in butter with a sprinkling of brown sugar or chopped dates. This works well for turnips too.
Or: Useful in soups and stockpots.

HINTS AND TIPS

Stan Frankenthaler is the award-winning chef-owner of Salamander restaurant in Cambridge, Massachusetts
"I love rutabagas (swedes) in curries. They have such a sweetness of their own that is a great addition to a spicy curry; try adding some coconut milk too."

Florence fennel A pale green swollen bulb with feathery leaves and delicate licorice flavor.
Preparation: Crunchy and refreshing, eat raw in salads.
Or: Good in rich stews and French cassoulet.
Or: Goes well with cheese: steamed and sprinkled with parmesan, or in a gratin, smothered in béchamel sauce.
Or: Delicious braised in vegetable or chicken stock, with tomatoes and black olives.
Or: Classic in combination with fish or chicken.

HINTS AND TIPS

Homemade vegetable stock

Save clean, undamaged potato and other root vegetable peelings, chunks of uncooked, left-over vegetables, celery leaves, broccoli stalks, trimmed leek greens, parsley, and coriander stalks in a plastic bag in the fridge. At the end of the week, put all these and any root vegetables or squash you want to use up (chopped into rough chunks) into a stockpot, or your biggest pan. Include at least two sticks of celery and a few carrots. Throw in a whole onion studded with a few cloves, a whole head of garlic sliced in half crossways, about a tablespoon of whole black peppercorns, a pinch each of thyme and salt, a little grated nutmeg, and some bay leaves. Experiment with different combinations of fresh and dried herbs and vegetables. Cover the lot with cold water, bring to a boil, and simmer until the vegetables are very soft and the stock is really flavorsome. Leave to cool and then strain well. If you do not plan to use it immediately, freeze it. Use in soups, risottos, and gravies.

Squash The catchall name covers a wide variety of vegetables, ranging from Halloween pumpkins to spaghetti squash and dark green Kabochas that are prized for their sweet, nutty flesh. Generally, smaller squash have the best flavor, although you can make perfectly good soup from a Halloween pumpkin. If stored somewhere dry, most squashes keep well into winter.

Preparation: Spaghetti squash, unravels its flesh into "spaghetti" as it cooks. Great fun, but not very tasty on its own. Drop big hunks of the flesh into boiling water, and leave it in the pan just long enough to "unravel." Drain and toss in olive oil or butter and lots of fresh chopped herbs and seasoning. Alternatively, serve with a pasta sauce.

Or: The easiest way to prepare the flesh of tough-skinned squashes for soups and pies is to roast the squash whole. Remember to prick with a fork before roasting. It's ready when the skin crumples and you can feel the soft flesh beneath. Slice in half, scoop out the fibrous bits and seeds, and discard them. Scoop the tasty flesh out of its skin and use in your recipe.

Or: Squashes make beautifully colored, velvety soup. Flavor with cinnamon and nutmeg—or spice it up with chili, fresh ginger, cumin, and coriander.

Or: Save the seeds. Wash, dry, and roast or fry with olive oil and soy sauce or your favorite spices. Delicious sprinkled on soup, incorporated into breads, or just to nibble.

Or: Try a savory pumpkin pie filled with feta or goat cheese and caramelized onions and flavored with thyme or sage.

Or: Squash is delicious roasted. Cut in half with your sharpest knife, scoop out seeds and fibers, and then cut the squash into wedges. Brush with olive oil and sprinkle with sea salt and fresh herbs before roasting. It is lovely stirred into risotto.

Tomatoes If you see ripe-to-bursting organic tomatoes being sold cheaply, snap up a box. With their intense flavor and low water content, they roast like a dream.

RECIPE

Oven-roasted tomato sauce

Quarter large tomatoes, then halve the quarters. Halve cherry tomatoes, if using these. Spread these in single layers in roasting pans, poke in some garlic cloves and sliced onion or shallots, and add a generous amount of your favorite fresh herbs (basil leaves, sprigs of rosemary, and thyme are all good.) Sprinkle with black pepper and flakes of sea salt, drizzle with olive oil, and a little honey, if you want. Toss it all around and roast in a moderate oven, turning tomatoes about every half hour, until the ones on the outside edges are just beginning to blacken and the remaining tomatoes have reduced to a juicy, caramelized sauce. It's worth making lots to freeze. The sauce is delicious stirred through cooked pasta, in risottos, on pizza, or as a side dish with eggs or polenta.

RECIPE

Oven-dried tomatoes

All the taste and a fraction of the cost of trendy sun-dried tomatoes. Halve tomatoes, scoop out, and discard the centers. Arrange tomatoes cut side down on baking sheets lined with nonstick parchment paper. Brush with olive oil. Cook in coolest oven until wrinkled, chewy, and thoroughly dried (up to eight hours.) Packed into clean jars with a sprig of fresh rosemary for extra flavor and covered in olive oil, they'll keep well.

RECIPE

Ratatouille

In a large, covered pan, fry 3 medium, sliced onions in olive oil until transparent. Add 3 cloves of chopped garlic; 3 medium, sliced eggplant; 4 medium, sliced zucchini; and 3 medium, sliced sweet peppers. Replace lid and cook gently for 10 minutes. Add 1¼ pounds fresh tomatoes, skinned and chopped; 2 bay leaves; 1 tablespoon coriander seeds, and salt and pepper to taste. Cook gently for another 45 minutes until vegetables are tender. Add chopped fresh parsley and basil and a splash of extra-virgin olive oil. Good hot or cold with lamb, eggs, cheese, or pasta.

Winter

Winter brings heaps of vitamin-packed root vegetables, some, like parsnips and Brussels sprouts with their flavors intensified by a blast of frost. All are ideal fodder for comforting casseroles and roasts. Squashes are still in store. Oriental salads, Belgian endive, kale, and white and red cabbage keep the greens end up.

Brussels sprouts Well-known victims of overcooking, there are plenty of good things to do with Brussels sprouts. They're much better under- rather than over-cooked. *Preparation:* Slice and stir-fry. Good with chestnuts and a little hazelnut or sesame oil. *Or:* Lightly cook and add to root mashes or hashes.

Or: In her classic *Four Seasons Cookery Book*, Margaret Costa suggests lightly cooking sprouts and blending to a puree with a little cream. Reheat the puree with more cream and a little butter, and season with salt, freshly ground pepper, and grated nutmeg. "You'll be astonished by its beauty and how good it tastes."

Belgian endive (chicory) Tightly-packed white cones of chicory are a great standby for winter salads.
Preparation: Belgian endive's slightly bitter taste is complemented by sweet beets, roasted root vegetables, or orange in salads.
Good, too, fried or baked in a gratin (blanch in boiling water for about 5 minutes first).

Salsify and scorzerona A long, tapered root with a mild parsnip flavor. Salsify has creamy-colored skin, scorzerona has black skin.
Preparation: Clean and boil whole until tender. Rinse in cold water and rub the skins off. Slice the roots, coat in flour that has been seasoned with salt, pepper, and nutmeg and fry gently. Serve with lemon wedges and a crunchy salad.

Jerusalem artichokes Although they are no relation to the gourmet globe artichoke, these knobbly roots are just as delicious in their own way. When they are cooked they have a soft texture and a sweet flavor a bit like chestnuts.
Preparation Scrub and roast or sauté as you would potatoes.
Or: Tasty with almonds and garlic.

Palestine soup

RECIPE

Blanch 1¼ pound Jerusalem artichokes in boiling water for a couple of minutes. Drain, rinse, peel, and slice. Fry in 2 oz butter with 1 chopped onion, 2 finely chopped cloves of garlic, and 2 chopped sticks celery. Add 4 cups stock and simmer until artichoke is tender. Blend, return to pan and add cream, chopped parsley, and salt and pepper to taste. Serve with a sprinkling of toasted almonds.

Celery root White-fleshed, swollen stems with tangled roots and strong celery flavor.

Classic French salad, celeriac remoulade

RECIPE

Peel and grate 1¼ pound peeld and grated celeriac and put in cold water with a squeeze of lemon juice to stop the celery root discoloring. Mix 1 teaspoon Dijon mustard with 3 to 4 tablespoons mayonnaise. Drain the celery root (celeriac) and add that too. Add chopped fresh herbs and 3 teaspoons chopped capers (optional).

Rutabaga This has a delicate sweet flavor and cheery color.

Root vegetables All the roots—carrots, parsnips, turnips, sweet potatoes, celery root, and rutabagas—have very individual characteristics, but much in common when it comes to cooking them. Basically, anything you can do with a potato, you can do with other roots, from chips to mashes.

Preparation: Cut into matchsticks and stir-fry. Cooked like this, root vegetables caramelize very quickly—the resulting sweetness appeals to children.

Or: Do the mash. Either on their own or half-and-half with potatoes. Flavor with fresh herbs, garlic, spices, cheese, chopped bacon, or mustard. Throw some chopped cooking apple into the pan with celeriac or parsnips a few minutes before taking off the heat, mash together, and sprinkle with some grated nutmeg. Add shredded greens or leeks. For a fresh flavor, mash in extra virgin olive oil; for a more traditional mash, use butter and cream or milk. Use potato or root mashes to top winter pies and casseroles. Fry mixed mash and greens together to make a colorful hash. Or go for an exotic version with chopped fresh coriander and chilies.

Or: Make "Rooty sausages." Mix mashed roots with crumbly cheese, egg yolk, and plenty of seasoning (especially if you're using one of the milder roots like turnip). Leave to cool, then with floured hands, shape into "sausages." Dip in lightly beaten egg white, then bread crumbs, and fry in a shallow pan or bake at 400°F.

Or: Roast chunks of mixed root vegetables in olive oil, and discover why chefs and clever home cooks rave about organic roots—they're gorgeous. Serve hot with traditional roasts, with couscous and spicy sauce, polenta, or even at room temperature with Belgian endive as a winter salad.

Or: All the roots make wonderful, warming soups in their own right.

DID YOU KNOW?

In 1998 Swissair became the first air carrier to serve organic food to passengers. The change came after surveys showed that customers wanted food that is "fresh and natural."

Future food

In August 2000, movers and shakers from all parts of the organic world gathered in Switzerland for their first international conference of the new millenium. Topping the bill were discussions on organics in the supermarket and organic-processed food.

That's an indication of how dramatically things have changed—organic is hitting the big time, and going mainstream. It's never been easier to buy organic food, and the choice of products is amazing. It's turning up on the menu in the most unlikely places too—from fast-food restaurants to municipal nurseries, from company cafeterias to airline meals.

Whether this is good news depends very much upon your outlook. Today you can buy organic food without adjusting your lifestyle. A few years ago, buying organic meant picking up a box of freshly harvested vegetables from a local farmer, but now you can eat organic without a morsel of fresh food passing your lips. You can stock up at the supermarket on frozen dinners, sweet treats, and a car load of highly packaged, globally sourced goodies. Many of these products mirror their conventional counterparts so closely that your neighbor in the checkout queue would never guess that you were saving the world with your shopping—unless they got a peek at your receipt. The inflated prices are a dead giveaway.

On one hand, it's reasonable to argue that if you're choosing organic over conventional food—whether it be prepared meals or freshly dug carrots from the farmer down the road—then you are still doing your bit to support organic farming and all its associated benefits. But with all the predictions pointing to processed food as the biggest growth area for organic food in the future, and with the market dominated by supermarket sales, the lines are drawn for a battle over the heart and soul of organics.

Many pioneers of the organic movement fear that the drive to push organic food into the mainstream could be at the expense of the principles of providing wholesome, fresh food and supporting local economies. They argue that the pressure to meet consumers' insatiable appetite for organics has already led to some supermarket chains shopping around for large-scale producers who meet the least stringent organic standards at the most competitive prices.

Farmers and growers who are committed to producing their food with the highest organic standards risk being left on the shelf by the corporate buyers because they are too expensive. This is already an issue with pork and chicken where there is a huge gap between animal welfare standards from one organic label to the next.

It's inevitable, too, that increasing organic production means that the old truism about organic growers choosing interesting heirloom varieties and crops for flavor will not necessarily hold true any more. Just like any other supermarket suppliers, organic producers need to grow fruit and vegetables that can withstand the rigors of a supermarket distribution chain; shelf life and appearance will become top priorities.

Supermarkets and the major food companies who are developing their own organic lines vigorously counter all this by arguing that they would be shooting themselves in the foot if they did anything to undermine consumer confidence in the integrity of organic produce. They stress the close links and supportive relationships that they are cultivating with their organic suppliers.

While organic standards are still evolving in the U.S., this is certainly going to be an issue for consumers to watch in future.

Developing alongside the swelling supermarket demand for organics, initiatives like farmers' markets and Community Supported Agriculture offer a glimpse into a more sustainable future. As well as throwing a lifeline to struggling small farmers, projects like these are helping to re-awaken shoppers' jaded tastebuds and an appreciation of the rich variety of local food—and the people who produce it.

Farmers' markets started in the U.S. and have successfully taken root across the U.K. too in the last few years. Not just popular with consumers, farmers' markets have won the enthusiastic support of enlightened local authorities who recognize their potential to aid urban regeneration by drawing life back into town and city centers. At the last count there were 2,863 across the U.S.

Initiatives like Chefs Collaborative 2000 in the U.S. are successfully forging closer links between consumers and local food producers. Many of the American chefs interviewed for this book—including Stan Frankenthaler and Nora Pouillon—are members of Chefs Collaborative. This group of chefs, restaurateurs, and other culinary professionals promote sustainable cuisine by teaching children, supporting local farmers, educating each other, and inspiring their customers to choose healthy foods. In practical terms this translates into shopping at farmers' markets, buying directly from local farmers and growers, and encouraging their customers to do the same. Some take an even more active role. For example, Stan Frankenthaler was one of the driving forces behind Chicago's organic farmers' market.

The growing success of Community Supported Agriculture in the U.S.—where numbers have snowballed from sixty such farms in 1990 to more than one thousand today—offers hope of a more sustainable future for our food. It all boils down to how much thought we give our food and whether a generation raised on the convenience of supermarkets and year-round availability of produce can break the habit. With all the excitement over organic food, it's easy to forget that only a tiny portion of the land is farmed organically. The area of land under organic production in the U.S. is just one fifth of one percent.

Increased demand for organic food has led to all sorts of optimistic forecasts for organic farming. The Organic Consumers Association, for instance, predicts that 10 percent of U.S. agriculture will be organic by 2010. Although organic groups and farmers' advisory services report a huge upsurge in interest from farmers considering going organic, the truth is that converting a conventional farming system to organic requires a lot of hard work and capital in the early years.

The most potent tool we have is the money in our pockets. To quote Bernward Geier, the executive director of the International Federation of Organic Agriculture Movements (IFOAM), "It's only the individual consumer who can make a change. It's already started, and every person who buys organic food makes a difference—to the landscape and the environment, to keeping rural communities alive, and all the other benefits that come with organic farming."

DID YOU KNOW?

It's wild on the organic farm

A 2000 report comparing the levels of wildlife between organic and conventional farms found organic farms buzzing with life.

Organic farms have

• Five times as many wild plants, including a greater number of rare and threatened species.

• Roughly one and a half times as many of the insects which birds feed off, and at least three times as many butterflies.

• 40 percent more birds.

Source: The Biodiversity Benefits of Organic Farming, Soil Association U.K.

Get fresh

At a glance guide to seasonal vegetables and fruits. This gives you an idea of the range of produce you might find at a farmers' market or in your box of vegetables if you buy direct from the grower.

spring

Vegetables
arrugula
asparagus
    (late in season)
beets
broccoli
Brussels sprouts
cabbages
carrots
cauliflowers
celery root
collards (spring greens)
fava (broad) beans
garlic
globe artichokes
Jerusalem artichokes
kale
leeks
onions
oriental greens
parsnips
new potatoes
    (late in season)
pumpkins and squash
rutabagas
salsify
tomatillos
turnips

Fruit
apples
kumquats
rhubarb

summer

Vegetables
asparagus
beets
bush beans
cabbages
carrots
cauliflowers
celery
chard
chili peppers
eggplants
fava (broad) beans
Florence fennel
garlic
globe artichokes
green sprouting
kohlrabi
leeks
mooli
okra
oriental greens
peas
pole beans
radishes
shallots
spinach
sweet corn
sweet peppers
sweet potatoes
tomatillos
tomatoes
turnips
watercress
zucchinis

Fruit
blackberries
black and red currants
blueberries
cherries
figs
gooseberries
loganberries
melons
peaches
plums
raspberries
strawberries

fall

Vegetables
arrugula
beets
broccoli
cabbage
carrots
cauliflower
celeriac
celery
chard
chicory
cucumbers
eggplants (aubergines)
Florence fennel
garlic
green sprouting
Jerusalem artichokes
kohlrabi
leeks
lettuce
mooli
parsnips
potatoes
onions
oriental greens
pumpkins
radishes
rutabagas
spinach
squash
sweet corn
sweet peppers
sweet potatoes
tomatoes
tomatillos
turnips
watercress
zucchinis

Fruit
apples
blackberries
cranberries
dates
guavas
pears
plums

winter

Vegetables
arrugula
Jerusalem artichokes
beets
Belgian endive
broccoli
Brussel sprouts
cabbages
carrots
celeriac
chard
chestnuts
endive
garlic
green sprouting
kale
kohlrabi
leeks
mooli
onions
oriental greens
parsnips
potatoes
pumpkins
rutabagas
salsify
spinach
sprout tops
squash
turnips

Fruit
apples
citrus
guava
kumquats
pears
pomegranates

10 steps to
eating organic

1. Look at your larder—think about the foods you eat the most and experiment with some organic alternatives.

2. Try one of the organic options where you'll really notice a taste difference. Carrots, tomatoes, yogurt, bananas, peaches, chicken, or pork are all good bets.

3. Indulge in organic luxury—chocolate, wine, or ice cream.

4. Find out what's being produced organically near you—and try some. You'll be amazed how many organic enterprises there are around. Watch out for local cheeses, preserves, and snacks, as well as meats and vegetables. Local organic groups should be able to help put you in touch with local growers and producers.

5. Check out shopping alternatives. Skip the supermarket for a week and support farmers' markets, natural food stores, and specialty organic shops.

6. Think about joining a Community Supported Farm. It's the best way to support local, organic farmers and to get fresh produce for yourself, although it doesn't suit everyone. Many run trial offers.

7. Grow your own. Once you get a taste for organic food, it's hard to go back to buying chemically produced alternatives. Why not save some money and get the freshest food possible by growing a few things at home—even if it's just a few herbs or tomatoes in pots.

8. Make a commitment to buy a certain number of organic items a week.

9. Visit an organic farm and see for yourself the difference that you're helping to make.

10. Keep yourself informed—check out some of the contacts we suggest in the resouce section at the back of this book.

Resource material

To dig deeper into organic issues use the following contacts. Some websites are outside the U.S. but they are useful and informative regardless of where you live.

International Federation of Organic Agriculture Movements (IFOAM)
Okozentrum Imsbach
D-66636 Tholey-Theley
Germany
Tel: 001-49-6853-919890
www.ifoam.org
IFOAM's website has comprehensive links to organic organizations around the world.

Organic Trade Association
PO Box 547
74 Fairview Street
Greenfield, MA 01302
Tel: 413 774-7511
Fax: 413 774-6432
www.ota.com

Organic Consumers Association
6101 Cliff Estate Rd.
Little Marais, MN 55614
Tel: 218 226-4164
Fax: 218 226-4157
www.purefood.org
Packed with info about organics, useful links and an international news archive.

The Organic Alliance
400 Selby Avenue, Suite T,
St. Paul, MN 55102
www.organic.org

Biodynamic Farming and Gardening Association, Inc.
Building 1002B, Thoreau Center
The Presidio,
P.O. Box 29135
San Francisco, CA 94129-0135
Tel: 888 516-7797
Fax: 415 561-7796
www.biodynamics.com
Website includes searchable databases of Community Supported Agriculture farms throughout the U.S.

USDA's National Organic Program
www.ams.usda.gov/nop

For more information
on food and farming issues

Center for Science in the Public Interest (CSPI)
1875 Connecticut Avenue NW, Suite 300
Washington, D.C. 20009
Tel: 202 332-110
Fax: 202 265-4954
www.cspinet.org

Fair Trade Online
www.transfair.ca
Fair Trade Online has been developed by TransFair Canada to provide information about the fair trade movement to producers, suppliers, students, and the movement itself.

TransFair Canada (Fair TradeMark Canada)
323 Chapel St., 2nd floor
Ottawa, Ontario
Canada K1N 7Z2
Tel: 613 563-3351
Fax: 613 237-5969
Toll free: 1-888-663-FAIR

Chefs Collaborative
282 Moody Street, Suite 207
Waltham, MA 02453
Tel: 781 736-0635
Fax: 781 642-0307
www.chefnet.com/cc2000

Mothers and Others
Mothers & Others for a Livable Planet
40 West 20th Street
New York NY, 10011-4211
www.mothers.org/mothers

Greenpeace
Greenpeace USA
702 H Street NW, Suite 300
Washington, DC 20001
Tel: 1-800-324-0959
www.greenpeaceusa.org

Environmental Working Group
1718 Connecticut Ave NW, Suite 600,
Washington DC 20009
www.ewg.org
*Excellent investigative material on U.S. food and
farming. Plus very unappetizing lowdown on pesticides
in everyday foods.*

Stop POPs
www.stoppops.org
A campaign to ban persistent organic pollutants

Panna – Pesticides Action Network North America
49 Powell St., Suite 500
San Francisco, CA 94102
Tel: 415 981-1771
Fax: 415 981-1991
www.panna.org

Worldwide Fund for Nature
WWF Canada
245 Eglinton Avenue East, Suite 410
Toronto, Ontario
Canada M4P 3J1
Tel: 1-800-26-PANDA

WWF US
1250 Twenty-Fourth Street, N.W.
P.O. Box 97180
Washington DC 20037
Tel: 1-800-CALL-WWF
www.worldwildlife.org

For information on where to buy
organic food and drink

Farmers' markets
To find one near you go to:
www.ams.usda.gov/farmersmarkets

Canadian & US Food Co-op Directory
www.prairienet.org/co-op/directory
*Includes many organic and natural foods buying
co-ops.*

*Also see Biodynamic Farming and Gardening
Association details for locating CSAs.*

Some companies that deliver across the US

Eco-Organics USA Home Delivery Club
Tel: 1-888-ECO-ORGANICS
www.eco-organics.com

Diamond Organics
Tel: 1-888-ORGANIC
www.diamondorganics.com

Organic Wine Company
1592 Union Street, #350
San Fransisco, CA 94123
Tel: Toll Free 1-888-ECO-WINE
Fax: 415 256-8883
www.ecowine.com

organic

home

Introduction

Create an organic home and you'll enjoy a haven, a place to relax and rejuvenate your energies in healthy, inspiring surroundings. Decorated, or built from scratch, using natural materials that are low in chemicals, an organic home offers a sanctuary that will live and breathe with its inhabitants.

What an organic home is not, is a "one size fits all" solution. While some people build new homes using natural and organic materials such as straw bales or earth, others prefer to find creative ways to improve an existing home. Each individual or family has different needs that require different approaches. For example, a family with a child who is allergic to wool can't install an organic wool carpet.

Nor is creating an organic home going to be an overnight transformation. Just as the word "organic" implies a natural, gentle process, you should start with what's most easily achievable and carry on making changes as and when it's comfortable. Unless you are badly affected by chemicals and have little choice but to make major and expensive alterations to your home, move gradually towards a healthier home. For example, you can start by cutting down the amount of waste that your home produces. Try to buy clothes that are made from natural or organic fabrics. Use kinder cosmetics and cleaning products. Finally, choose better products when it's the next time to decorate. And remember that laughter, lightness, and an individual touch will do more for a healthy home than a grim determination to eliminate every single chemical in the house!

DID YOU KNOW?

Bank on a healthier life
People interested in healthier ways of living are now turning to ethical investments. It is possible to arrange virtually all your finances—from bank accounts to pensions—on an ethical and environmental footing. Some banks allow investments to be directed to specific interests, such as organic farming. Credit cards issued by charities mean that they benefit every time you use the card.

Healthy housekeeping

Cleanliness might be next to godliness, but overdoing housework won't do your health any favors. Scientists suspect that our love affair with domestic products is responsible for sky-rocketing asthma rates, since ultracleanliness and antibacterial cleaners eliminate germs that help children build up healthy immunity.

It's hard to resist the clamor of cleaning product promotions, all claiming to be crucial for a hygienic home. But indoor air quality expert, Quade Stahl, is skeptical; he knows that the chemical residues from cleaners can pollute the air inside our homes, and he believes that persuasive advertising is turning us into chronic over-cleaners. "People are sold a lot of new products—one to clean windows, another for this, another for that—they have twenty to fifty products when two or three would do the job just as well," says Stahl.

Conscious cleaning

Cleaning a healthy home doesn't need complex ingredients; going right back to basics, salt, baking soda, white vinegar, and fresh lemon juice will clean a house safely and cheaply. But the prospect of squeezing lemons every time the toilet needs a scrub does not appeal to most people, so ready-made cleaners with dramatically fewer chemicals and natural ingredients are proving winners with health-minded home-makers. These are widely available from organic and natural products stores and even some supermarkets, and range from toilet cleaners and laundry liquid to dishwasher tablets and fabric softeners.

Smell alone sets these natural cleaners apart from the others. Instead of the synthetic fragrances that mask chemical odors, natural cleaners use essential oils from plants. As eco-interior designer Victoria Schomer says, "Don't think that if it doesn't go into our bodies it's OK—if you smell something, its molecules are in your nose and therefore in your body!" And forget lurid colors, too—natural cleaners come as they are. After all, since when did being baby pink or sky blue make a laundry liquid wash any better?

Where the differences are not so clear-cut is in their environmental claims. Amid the plethora of products claiming to be biodegradable, it's easy to forget that no product is truly environmentally friendly—some are just less unfriendly than others. So while many cleaners meet criteria for "primary" degradation—that is, the time it takes for the product to lose its main characteristic such as its washing action—they may still remain in the environment for years. "Greener" products aim for complete biodegradability.

Healthy spaces

Like people, homes grow sluggish and need re-invigorating. The ancient oriental art of feng shui has become so fashionable that it's hard to escape the earnest but often impractical advice—there's not much you can do if your toilet is inauspiciously sited! But it does have many useful things to say about "space clearing"—keeping a home's energy vibrant and healthy. Lighting a candle, ringing a bell, or burning incense sticks in parts of the home that feel cheerless are easy ways to encourage positive energy to flow.

HIT OR MYTH

Bacteria are bad for our health

Bacteria found in soil can transform harmful chemicals into useful compounds that can be turned into drugs. Indeed, far from being our enemy, some bacteria are being used to nurse the sick back to health, cut asthma rates, and clean up toxic pollution.

The war waged in homes against germs—fueled by the advertising tactics of manufacturers who persuade us that we need to protect our families against "deadly" bacteria—could be doing long-term harm. "Dousing everything we touch with antibacterial soaps...can upset the natural balance of microorganisms in and around us, leaving behind only the 'superbugs,'" says physician and microbiologist Dr. Stuart Levy.

Everyday household germs may even give a baby's immune system the exercise it needs to develop normally. Exposure to germs during the first year of life is vital for developing antibodies that will fight off infections later in life.

Even the mundane spring cleaning is an opportunity for some powerful space clearing. Remove any clutter that doesn't lift your energies, and vow only to buy products in the future that will enhance the home (a noble ambition most of us fall short of, judging by the junk hidden away in our cupboards and lofts). Meanwhile, for continued good energy, try to keep on top of household repairs, bill paying, and letter writing—and do your best to keep the house consistently clean and tidy.

In the laundry

At least the Romans had no illusions when they used ammonia from rotting urine to wash their clothes. Beneath the soft blue colors and tempting fragrances of today's laundry cleaners lie harsh synthetic ingredients, including optical brighteners which give clothes a "whiter than white" appearance, without actually making them any cleaner, and set unrealistic standards in the process. Detergents (or "surfactants") reduce the surface tension of the water so it can penetrate the fabric better, and dissolve grease—qualities that can be toxic to wildlife in rivers and streams.

Natural laundry products do away with the artifice—no optical brighteners or artificial colors here. Instead of petroleum-based surfactants, they use soap, which quickly becomes harmless in streams and rivers and degrades completely within three to eight days, and natural surfactants based on sugars or vegetable oils, both of which biodegrade much faster than petroleum versions. To create softer water—which makes soap and detergent more effective—natural products use ingredients such as baking soda, and steer clear of the phosphates which have been added to conventional laundry products since the 1940s. Many manufacturers are now removing these because they can cause toxic algal blooms in waterways.

HINTS AND TIPS

Washing the blues away

• *Wash clothes less often—modern washing machines make the job so easy that we're washing more frequently than we need to and using more chemical cleaners.*

• *As a general rule, washing powder contains less detergent than the liquid equivalent.*

• *Enzymes added to detergents to deal with certain stains, such as chocolate and milk, and used in some natural products, can cause skin irritation.*

Washing balls These plastic spheres and discs use magnetic technology to prevent a calcium crust from building up in washing machines and dishwashers. This means that less detergent is needed. Others contain pellets (for which refills are available) made from ionic crystals and salts that dissolve in water to release ionized oxygen, which activate water molecules so they clean fabric without the need for detergents.

Their makers claim these devices are cheaper per wash than normal cleaners, don't fade bright colors or damage fibers, and don't need a second rinse cycle, thereby saving energy and money. Testing has shown that the detergent-free balls were no better than water at shifting stubborn stains, but they do freshen clothes and are said to kill bacteria so they can be used on lightly-soiled clothes.

Bleach Mainstream washing agents often include bleach as a matter of course, so it gets used whether the clothes need it or not. Because only about one in five washes is a white wash, much goes to waste. Manufacturers have moved away from the harshest bleaches, although the commonly-used alternative bleach perborate—often described on packaging as "active oxygen" or "oxygen bleach"—needs other chemicals present to work and can damage plants.

Alternatives to using harsh bleaches include percarbonate, made from soda and oxygenated water (and which comes separately so it's used only when needed); boiling white cottons; applying lemon juice; drying clothes in sunlight, or adding 4 ounces (½ cup) of borax (a naturally-occurring mineral with no toxic fumes, available from grocery stores and drugstores) to a full load of washing.

Natural stain removers As advertisers are fond of telling us, tough stains need tough action—but we don't need to resort to chemical solutions. Natural citrus solvents, for example, readily shift stains and will remove grease, ink, oil, and pet soil from fabrics, carpets, and upholstery.

- For fruit and vegetable stains, bleach colorfast fabrics, or if color may be affected, try a little lemon juice or vinegar. Remove spinach stains by rubbing the affected area with a raw potato, and then wash in warm soapy water.

- To remove red wine stains, sprinkle with baking soda or cornstarch. When the powder becomes stained and sticky, brush off and add more powder, repeating the process until most of the stain is gone. Put a last application of powder on, then leave the stain for a couple of hours before washing. This method works on fruit stains too.

- Remove ink marks on white fabric by immediately sprinkling with salt and then rubbing with a cut lemon and rinsing off. For stains on colored fabrics, soak immediately in slightly warm milk.

HINTS AND TIPS

Your water

Find out from your water company how hard your water is so you can adjust the amount of washing agent you use—lightly soiled fabric washed in soft water areas requires less than dirtier clothes washed in hard water areas.

• Soak rust stains with lemon juice, rub with salt, and dry in the sun before washing.

• Rub grass stains with glycerin, leave on for an hour, then wash.

• For blood, chocolate, mud, coffee, mildew, and urine stains, dissolve ½ cup borax in two cups of water and sponge on to a stain or pre-treat before washing.

Fabric softeners and conditioners There's no need to use these if clothes are dried outdoors. If that's not possible, add 9 ounces white vinegar or 2 ounces (¼ cup) baking soda during the final rinse in the washing machine, or buy detergents based on vegetables and natural scents.

Dry cleaning An average dry cleaner generates 20–50 gallons of waste containing solvent every month, and uses chemicals such as perchloroethylene, which could be carcinogenic. A handful have switched to "wet-cleaning," which uses special biodegradable detergents, dramatically lowers the amount of petroleum-based solvents needed, and is said to produce no odors or hazardous wastes.

Kitchen and bathroom

Chemicals are the last thing you want around food, particularly if you're making the effort to eat organic foods, and bathrooms are prime spots for overpowering air fresheners and harsh cleaners.

Dishes Automatic dishwasher cleaning agents rely on chemical cleaning power to compensate for the fact that water jets are less effective than a person using a scrubbing brush.

Natural dishwashing agents are made from vegetable-based detergents and are enhanced with essential oils and botanical ingredients, such as the healing herb calendula, or whey, a natural by-product of cheese-making, which soften skin and prevent it from drying.

HINTS AND TIPS

Cleaning solutions

• *You'll get good service out of natural brushes and scourers, and many people find them more attractive than plastic scrubbers. Wooden dishwashing brushes with natural bristles come with replaceable heads, which means that you get more life out of one handle.*

• *Bicarbonate of soda removes grease from pots, pans, and other utensils, but rinse in hot water before drying and don't use on aluminum and enamelled pots.*

• *Forget chemical drain-openers. Natural versions use bacteria to break down fats, oils, and organic matter. Or pour ½ cup of baking soda followed by ½ cup vinegar down the drain, plug it for a minute or two then unplug and run hot water for a few minutes.*

The natural tablets on the market do not contain phosphonates or chlorine bleaching agents. Instead they use sugar-based detergents, natural water softeners, and enzymes (to break down protein stains).

Surfaces It's amazing how effective water is, but we've lost faith in it with the bewildering array of cleaning products. Try simply wetting dirty surfaces then wiping up after a few minutes. So-called "miracle" micro-fiber cloths tackle chrome, wood, plastic, marble, tiles, and glass using only water as a solvent, claiming to do away with the need for cleaning agents altogether. Their makers put this down to ultra-small fibers that allow the cloth to absorb and accumulate more dust and dirt particles than normal cloth, and static electricity and capillary action that draws dirt and grease up, trapping it in the fabric.

When something stronger is called for, natural, multi-purpose cleaners use alcohol, sugar- and vegetable-based detergents, or the abrasive action of chalk or clay. Scrubbing with simple bicarbonate of soda, followed by a hot water rinse, will eliminate germs cheaply and naturally.

Mold, which can cause coughs and allergies, only grows where it's wet, so the best defense against it is to keep the bathroom (and the rest of the house) dry and well ventilated, and achieve a relative humidity of less than 60%. Avoid carpeting bathrooms, and fix leaks immediately. To clean mold, treat the affected area with a mix of borax and water in a spray bottle.

Floors A mop version of the microfibre cloth can be used dry, to attract dust and dirt particles, or damp for dirtier floors. Use cleaners based on linseed oil which keep baked tiles, stone and linoleum clean and polished. For linoleum, also try 9 ounces white vinegar and 1¾ pints water. For anything else, use soapy water and a soft cloth.

Ovens If you wipe the oven out regularly, harsh oven cleaners won't be necessary, but for intractable grime, mix 1 ounce (2 tablespoons) liquid dish soap, and ½ ounce (1 tablespoon) borax in a spray bottle. Spray the dirty areas and leave for an hour before scrubbing.

HINTS AND TIPS

Nature's air fresheners

• *Commercial potpourri may contain chemical fragrances and colors. Making your own natural version is easy—there's no set recipe, so try combinations of citrus peel, dried rose petals, pine cones, attractive twigs, and cinnamon sticks, and then boost their natural scent with essential oils.*

• *Grow herbs around the home—lavender and rosemary scent the air when you waft your hand through them.*

Glass and chrome Clean glass and mirrors with a mixture of 50% vinegar and 50% water in a spray bottle. Microfiber glass cleaning cloths need just a mist of water to clean easily and effectively. Use apple cider vinegar to polish chrome taps.

Toilet Incredibly, the toilet seat is more hygienic than most other surfaces in the home, including kitchen chopping boards and sinks—probably because toilet seats are too dry for bacteria to thrive. Researchers found that even before they introduced disinfectant, toilet seats were always cleaner than chopping boards, which had three times as many bacteria. Fluid wrung from dishcloths had a million times more germs.

Natural toilet cleaners avoid corrosive acids, bleach, and garish colors that give the impression of cleanliness but can upset the action of septic tanks. Instead they use food acids, such as vinegar and citric acid, and plant oils to disinfect and decalcify. For a homemade cleaner, use lemon juice or vinegar which are both simple and effective, and remove limescale. Just add a dash of tea tree oil to disinfect. Don't mix toilet cleaners with bleach—the combination can release poisonous gases.

Air fresheners The powerful air fresheners we use to tackle toilet smells don't really freshen the air, they just add more chemicals to mask odors and often release irritating and toxic chemicals in the process. Herbal water sprays give a fresh, clean smell—boil cinnamon and cloves in water, and put the resulting solution in a spray bottle—or use an essential oil burner.

Hand cleaners Soap made from plant oils comes in delicious scents. For a heavy-duty clean, use products with vegetable- or sugar-based detergents, natural abrasives such as wood powder or pumice, and natural solvents including citrus oil. Olive oil and granulated sugar will help to remove fruit stains on hands—rub well into skin and leave on a few minutes before washing.

Dusting and polishing

The happy jumble of furniture, ornaments, books, and electrical appliances in living areas demands regular dusting and polishing. Used dry, microfiber cloths make wonderful dusters; their static effect draws dust and tiny particles to the cloth, thus eliminating the need for chemicals.

HINTS AND TIPS

Candle wax

Remove melted wax from a candle-holder by running a hair dryer over it to melt the wax, which can then be wiped off.

Everyone dreads polishing, but at least natural brass, silver, and furniture polishes get the job done without chemicals. Try the following Do-it-yourself ideas:

Polish furniture with a mixture of one part lemon juice and two parts olive oil, or with a plant- or beeswax-based product.

Silver stains can be removed, says Johns Hopkins professor Jerome Kruger, by wrapping the object in aluminum foil (save clean, used pieces of foil for this) so that it fits snugly with the object in at least one place. Make a few cuts in the foil to let liquid seep in. Place in a large glass, enamel, or stainless steel pot and cover with a solution of 4–5 tablespoons of baking soda per quart of water. Simmer gently for 30 minutes. Remove the foil, rinse the silver, and dry it thoroughly.

Soft furnishings

The household where nothing ever gets spilled is a rare one, so choose carpet, rugs, and upholstery fabrics in darker colors and patterns to reduce the amount of cleaning needed in future. Install mats for wiping shoes—or take shoes off at the door—to reduce the amount of dirt being brought in to the house. Another strategy is to buy furnishings that can be washed, instead of having to be dry cleaned—even some rugs can be cleaned in a washing machine. Protect sofas and chairs with an attractive throw—any stains it picks up can easily be washed out.

If the inevitable happens, rub spills promptly with a vinegar and water solution, sponge with water, and dab dry. Pour salt on red wine spills and vacuum when dry; soda water may also remove stains.

If you do need to have your carpet cleaned, hire a carpet-cleaning service that uses steam to clean instead of detergents, or take an idea from interior designer Victoria Schomer, who rents a carpet-cleaning machine and uses a natural citrus-solvent cleaner, thus avoiding the chemicals used by commercial carpet cleaners. She says, "It's strong, safe, I don't need much of it, and there's not much residue left on the carpet—if there is, I can just go over it again."

DID YOU KNOW?

Death by sauna

The millions of bugs that infest the antique treasures in Britain's stately homes could face death by sauna, if trials of a slow-heating oven are successful. The oven destroys bugs such as the carpet mite without the need for toxic insecticides, and because it heats up so slowly, the valuable objects are not damaged.

Fighting pests

No one wants bugs in their home—but critter control can come at a price. Using bug spray in the home may increase the risk of developing Parkinson's disease; a study has found that Parkinson's patients are more than two times as likely to have been exposed to insecticides in the home.

The safest way to deal with pests is not to invite them indoors in the first place. Keep your kitchen clean, so that spilled food, grease, and fat doesn't attract them; keep jars and containers tightly closed. Pests depend on water for survival so fix leaky plumbing, dry out wet materials, and don't let water build up anywhere.

HINTS AND TIPS

Alternative insceticides

• *Forget smelly moth repellents, which can contain the chemical paradichlorobenzene, also used in air fresheners. A sachet containing lavender flowers or cedar chips will keep moths at bay naturally—sew the lavender and cedar inside a muslin or cheesecloth "envelope" or scatter the cedar chips in the wardrobe. If you can't find cedar chips, use cedar essential oil. Do the same for shoes—a sachet inserted in smelly shoes will freshen them up and help them hold their shape at the same time.*
• *Growing pennyroyal near doorways will stop ants from entering the house, while a pot of basil in the kitchen will keep flies away.*

Pet hates

Love pets, but hate the fleas they bring? Animals hate them too, and it's their welfare that should be top priority, so don't persist with a product if it's clearly not working—try another treatment from the arsenal of natural flea killers, which includes shampoos, sprays, and flea collars.

Frequent treatment, on every front, is the secret to beating fleas. Natural shampoo can be supplemented by powders and herbal sprays between washes, while herbal flea collars fight fleas with natural repellents (such as pennyroyal and eucalyptus oils) and can be renewed with a few drops of oil.

Borax or pyrethrum powder will kill fleas harboring in carpets, alternatively swap carpet for a wooden floor. And feed pets a healthy diet—the healthier the pet, the more resistant it will be to fleas.

Pet allergens tend to gather more in synthetic pillows than feather ones, probably because feather pillows are encased in tightly woven fabric that not only stops feathers from escaping but keeps dust and pet allergens out. Synthetic pillows also harbor more house dust mite allergens than feather pillows. Allergen-proof covers may be a more affordable option than feathers.

CASE STUDY
Clean thinking

Peter Malaise is somewhat of a guru at Ecover, a maker of environmentally sound cleaning products. It's not a description he's comfortable with, but his role as concept manager means he keeps his finger on society's pulse, providing inspiration for new products that are kinder to the environment and easier on people's health.

He's well qualified for the role; he's been a pioneer in the field for twenty-five years, joining Ecover in 1991. He is enthusiastic—at home, he uses natural paints, has very few plastics, and he wears natural materials.

At work, Malaise enjoys a people-friendly environment. In keeping with its philosophy of health—Ecover products contain just 2% petrochemical ingredients compared to conventional cleaners with as much as 98%—the company has built an ecological factory. Featuring a grass-covered roof and outdoor eating areas; natural, colorful materials; a wooden floor; and plenty of natural light indoors—it makes for a pleasant working day.

The company's principles extend to transport; employees are encouraged to bike or car-pool. In Peter's case that's impractical, as he lives thirty miles from the factory, so he drives a small, fuel-efficient company car.

Malaise has done a lot of thinking about the future. He foresees a time when products are not just biodegradable but compostable, and when worthless agricultural waste, such as straw and citrus pulp, is made into useful ingredients instead of being thrown away. Also on the horizon is technology that cleans by physical means, potentially making cleaning substances redundant, but this prospect does not deter Malaise: "We have to be flexible."

While he'd love to see the company making totally organic products, to do so now, he explains, would take valuable ingredients away from organic food production. When the organic movement has grown and strengthened, and more "second hand" ingredients are available, only then will the company make its move.

Natural beauty

What you put on your skin affects your health—as eighteenth-century Europeans who powdered their faces with deadly white lead discovered when the poison not only destroyed their looks but in some cases even proved fatal.

Modern toiletries and cosmetics seem harmless by comparison, but their petrochemical-based ingredients, synthetic fragrances, and colors can have undesirable effects. As much as 60% of what's applied to the skin enters the body via blood vessels beneath the skin.

Those in the know say that if you wouldn't want to eat it, don't put it on your skin. "Whatever you're putting on your skin will have an effect internally," says natural beauty therapist Claire Besent. "Anything you put on your skin has to be processed by the liver." Why treat the body to organic food then feed it from the outside with chemicals?

Cosmetic culprits

The American Academy of Dermatology claims that up to 10 percent of us may have an adverse reaction to a cosmetic product in our lifetime—these are mainly women, because they tend to use more cosmetics. Skin irritations show up within a few days, although allergic reactions can take a week to ten days to manifest. What bothers women most are moisturizers or sunscreens, make-up ingredients, perfume, hair care products, and nail products, while men tend to suffer from after-shave, cologne, and shampoos. Permanent hair dyes and antiperspirants are other common irritants.

Much of the blame can be laid at the door of the more than five thousand fragrances used liberally in beauty products, but they are not the only culprits, says Claire Besent. "Alcohol will affect the pH of skin," she explains, "and a lot of chemicals come from petroleum, such as propylene glycol which was originally designed for antifreeze for the car."

Sodium lauryl sulfate (SLS) and its slightly milder cousins sodium laureth sulfate (SLES) and ammonium lauryl sulfate are commonly-used detergents. Sodium lauryl sulfate has such a bad name that some organically conscious stores refuse to stock products containing it. Parabens, widely used as preservatives, are derived from a petroleum or crude oil base and can cause rashes and may even mimic the action of the female hormone estrogen.

Charlotte Vøhtz, who began making organic beauty products after her young daughter's eczema and allergies were linked to chemicals in her environment, says it's the cocktail of chemicals that causes problems. "I would never point at one ingredient and say this is a bad one, it is a combination—we don't have enough knowledge of the interactive effect of these things."

Saving face

The most natural—and the cheapest—beauty boost you can give yourself is plenty of sound sleep, exercise, water, and a balanced diet rich in unadulterated organic fruit and vegetables. Cutting down on smoking and alcohol, and managing stress will do wonders for skin, hair, and eyes.

But we all know that real life isn't that simple—even with the best intentions, there are times when we need a little cosmetic help. More and more responsible toiletry and cosmetic makers are offering products that are "natural," with ingredients that come straight from plant or animal sources, or "organic"—free of pesticides, synthetic chemicals, or genetic modification (GM soy is used in conventional cosmetics). Mixtures of plant oils, natural preservatives such as yucca and grapefruit seed extract, and ingredients that read like an exotic dinner menu—avocado, turmeric, cinnamon—may indeed be good enough to eat.

High prices for quality natural ingredients push up the cost of natural cosmetics, although they compare favorably with many conventional brands. But expense doesn't guarantee safety—high-priced toiletries and cosmetics can be as chemical-laden as cheaper versions. The way to be sure is to read the ingredients lists. Learning to recognize the worst ingredients

HINTS AND TIPS

Don't get in a lather

Can't bear to get rid of favorite cosmetics and toiletries? Cut down the amount you use instead. Most of us overuse beauty products, ignoring instructions to use just a coin-sized amount of shampoo in favor of massive lather. Dilute shampoo by mixing with herbal infusions and essential oils. If products contain SLS, rinse them off as quickly as possible to minimize chances of skin or eye irritation.

HINTS AND TIPS

Take it easy

Combat the aging effects of stress with relaxation. That doesn't have to mean yoga—although it's great for stress-busting and boosting blood flow for healthy, vital skin. Sharing a bottle of organic wine (preferably red for its healthy antioxidant effects) with good friends once in a while might work just as well for you!

(those used in larger amounts in a product are listed earlier on the packaging) will help you separate the good from the bad, resulting in better health.

"If you don't want to eat it, you don't want to put it on your skin."

Charlotte Vøhtz, maker of organic beauty products.

However, too frequently labels are confusing. Plant ingredients are listed by their botanical name, so how do we know that glycyrrhizic acid is in fact a natural antibacterial from liquorice root? "If you don't know about chemistry you're into big problems," agrees Charlotte Vøhtz. A simple strategy is to go for products with fewer long names and warnings.

Some manufacturers helpfully list the familiar names of ingredients, or label their product "contains organic ingredients," specifically marking the ones that are organic. Don't be surprised if you can't find totally organic products—organic ingredients are often not available or are prohibitively expensive.

Health check

Trying to avoid all of these ingredients is a sure path to stress! Even excellent natural products use some of them, so use this list to reduce, not eliminate, them in your life.

• *Sodium lauryl sulfate (SLS)* Used in toothcare, hair care, bath lotions, shaving gel, makeup, skin care

• *Sodium laureth sulfate (SLES)* Used in bath lotions, shaving gel, skin care, makeup

• *Propylene glycol* Used in nail care, makeup, sun care, skin care

• *Aluminium chlorohydrate* Used in deodorant

• *Petrolatum (also called mineral oil jelly, paraffinum liquidum, baby oil)* Used in makeup, sun care, skin care

• *Talc* Used in makeup, skin care

• *Alpha hydroxy acids* Used in skin care, makeup

• *Artificial fragrances* Used in skin care, makeup, toothcare, sun care, hair care

• *Artificial colours* Used in skin care, makeup, toothcare, sun care, hair care

• *Butyl, ethyl, methyl and propyl paraben* Used in most types of cosmetics and toiletries

• *Tallow (animal fat)* Used in hair care, soap

• *Toluene* Used in nail care

• *Formaldehyde* Used mainly in nail care

A natural smile

A bright smile does wonders for anyone's appearance, and keeping this asset in top shape the healthy way is easy. Natural toothpastes take dental care back to basics with simple ingredients including natural abrasives, herbs, baking soda, and essential oil flavors such as mint, citrus, cinnamon, and fennel.

Many steer clear of SLS, which is best avoided if you're suffering from bleeding gums or mouth ulcers, and parabens. Instead they use natural preservatives, such as citric acid or grapefruit seed extract). Natural dental products also avoid antibacterial agents such as triclosan, a broad-spectrum antibiotic, and instead use the natural antibacterial properties of tea tree oil, cloves, cinnamon, or myrrh.

People new to natural toothpastes will be delighted with the range, from children's versions to formulations for sensitive teeth, but could wonder why so many are fluoride free. Their makers believe that although fluoride helps prevent tooth decay in children, adults might be getting too much of a good thing. The theory is that fluoride builds up in our bodies, crowding out other valuable nutrients including calcium, and possibly leading to brittle bones as we grow older.

Natural dental floss uses natural waxes and flavors without artificial colors and preservatives, and alternative mouthwashes avoid alcohol, artificial sweeteners, or preservatives. (If you need to use mouthwash, consider whether your flossing routine or your general health needs a shake-up.)

Safer smells

Synthetic scents can linger like a bad smell, and they can be much worse for us than we might think. Artificial musk, for example, can accumulate in our bodies contaminating fat, blood, and breast milk, according to Friends of the Earth.

Natural products that shun synthetic scents, opting for essential oils from plants, can't recreate fancy fragrances. "You can't create the same wonderful scent of Chanel No. 5 if you're using a few essential oils," says Charlotte Vøhtz. "Very often they're using up to one hundred chemical compounds to make a scent, it's a tricky business."

But essential oils smell wonderful in their own complex, subtle way, and can make their artificial counterparts seem harsh by comparison. And they have the added bonus of being therapeutic—sandalwood oil helps dry skin, while lavender relaxes and balances the entire system. It's worth consulting a professional aromatherapist to find out which oils suit you best and which to avoid (rosemary shouldn't be used by epileptics, for example, while others, including myrrh, pennyroyal, and sage should be avoided by pregnant women.)

People sensitive even to natural scents should look for "fragrance-free" and "unscented" products, although this doesn't always guarantee that scent hasn't been added—double-check by scanning the ingredients list for any mention of fragrance.

A close shave

We've been suspicious of aerosol products since we heard that they contained harmful greenhouse gases. And even though they've been free of CFC greenhouse gases for two decades, they still contain other environmentally-harmful gases such as carbon dioxide as well as flammable petrochemical solvents. Instead of aerosol-propelled foams, choose pump-action containers —and a shaving brush with a natural cream makes a perfectly good lather.

HIT OR MYTH

It says "natural" and "organic" on the label, so it must be better

Not necessarily, because there are no agreed definitions of "natural" or "organic" cosmetics. "Anyone can produce a 'natural' product and it can be 99 percent chemicals and 1 percent natural," says organic beauty product maker Charlotte Vøhtz.

While one manufacturer may go as far as picking rose petals only at sunrise when their life forces are thought to be strongest, less scrupulous companies label products as "natural" when they contain harsh detergents and synthetic preservatives. The same goes for "organic." Unless the product is certified organic, a manufacturer may have just wafted some essential oils through water and called the product organic.

Don't be taken in by the term "hypoallergenic," either—there's no guarantee that these products are less likely to cause a reaction, so test on a patch of skin before buying. Remember that natural ingredients can also cause problems, so don't automatically trust any product—check for ingredients you know you react to, or test on a patch of skin first.

For a latherless approach try a mixture of natural plant oils and essential oils for a moisturizing, fragrant shave that's as effective as foams and creams.

Hair care

Hair is a dead give-away of the state of our inner health, our environment, and what we use to clean and style it. Too frequent cleaning with harsh shampoos can strip hair of natural oils that keep it shiny, while problems with an itchy scalp could be caused by sodium lauryl sulfate. Natural shampoos and conditioners use gentler, plant-based ingredients, but beware of hair products that have hijacked plant images so they look organic—check the label for the actual list of ingredients. The following recipes guarantee natural shine with healthy ingredients.

REMEDIES

Honey rinse

Stir 1 teaspoon honey into 4 cups of warm water. After shampooing, pour mixture through hair but don't rinse out. Dry as normal.

Or: Beer combined with cider vinegar makes a good conditioner for fine hair—the smell quickly disappears!

REMEDIES

Rosemary rinse

A rosemary rinse will leave brunette hair gleaming. Make an infusion by pouring boiling water over the rosemary in a teapot, leaving to infuse for 10–15 minutes. Cool and use in the final rinse.

Or: Chamomile will put highlights into fair hair— pour over the hair several times for brighter locks.

Synthetic hair dyes derive their ingredients from petroleum sources, and studies have linked hair dye with increased risk of cancer. Less seriously, they may irritate skin, so test before using by dabbing a bit behind your ear and leaving it on for two days. The plant powder henna is a popular alternative, creating red shades ranging from dark brown to reddish blonde (although it won't lighten hair). It's messy, though—if you're not careful it'll stain your hands and bathroom as well as your hair.

HINTS AND TIPS

Hair

• *A scalp massage is deliciously relaxing and therapeutic, while improving blood flow to the scalp and making hair shine. For a quick self-treatment, pull at the scalp with rigid fingers, gently pull at hair roots, and tap over the scalp with your knuckles.*

• *Hair brushes with natural bristles draw oils from roots to ends, making hair shiny and healthy—although people with chemically-treated hair should stick to plastic brushes.*

Going about in a cloud of hairspray is no longer fashionable, and the fine chemical mists that aerosol sprays deliver have never been good for health. Look for pump-action spray bottles, or shape hair using plant-based styling gels and natural plant waxes.

Fun in the sun

Experts suspect that using sunscreen encourages us to spend more time in the sun, increasing the risk of skin cancer. Maybe so, but it's still a good practice to slather on sunscreen, particularly "broad spectrum" products that protect against both UVA and UVB rays.

HINTS AND TIPS

Solid sunscreen
Lightweight, loose-fitting, long sleeved shirts, trousers or long skirts protect the body against harsh sun. Tightly woven fabric is best—if light shows through it, UV rays can get through too. Avoid wearing wet clothes as the sun's rays pass through these more easily.

Natural sunscreens use ingredients such as shea butter and edelweiss for UV protection, and add natural antioxidants such as avocado oil (a source of vitamin E) to protect the skin against damaging free radicals. Dry, peeling skin will love moisture-rich cucumber, while aloe vera soothes sun burnt skin—but make sure products contain a high concentration of these ingredients.

Artificial bronzers contain colors that either stain the skin or interact with the protein on the surface of the skin to turn it brown (or orange!). Avoid these additives by using sesame oil, which offers some natural protection against the sun's rays and nourishes the skin at the same time—but take care to avoid over-exposure.

Alpha hydroxy acids (AHAs), used in cosmetics to reduce wrinkles and other signs of sun-damaged skin, are an old beauty trick—women in eighteenth-century high society used acidic green pineapple juice to slough off wrinkles. But they can irritate skin and increase sun sensitivity, so look for products with an AHA concentration of 10% or less, and a pH of 3.5 or more, and test on a patch of skin first. AHAs include glycolic acid, lactic acid, mixed fruit acid, sugar cane extract, and malic acid.

No sweat

We've got bacteria to thank for body odor. Sweat itself is not offensive—it only becomes a problem when the skin's bacteria begin to break it down. Natural anti-bacterials like tea tree oil, sage, rosemary, and lemongrass stop this from happening, and they're widely used in alternative deodorant sticks, creams, and sprays.

These natural antibacterials do a good job of keeping odor at bay, although you might need to reapply them during the day. What they don't do well is prevent perspiration—so compromise by saving conventional deodorants for days when it really matters. But a little sweat could be a small price to pay for health—the aluminum chlorohydrate used in conventional deodorants stops perspiration by blocking pores, effectively plugging one of the body's natural elimination points for toxins. That's why problems with excessive perspiration are best investigated, not "treated" with increasingly powerful deodorants.

Crystal sticks work by leaving a thin layer of the salts on the skin that prevents bacteria building up. They're made from naturally-formed mineral salts that contain ammonium alum, but they don't block pores. They are as effective as other alternative deodorants.

DID YOU KNOW?

Sexy smells?

Natural it may be, but do we really want something quite this organic? A London firm has developed moist tissues soaked in the scent of fifty human pheromones, the sweat molecules that create sex appeal. The facial wipes are said to make people more attractive to the opposite sex within a three foot radius and for up to twelve hours. But one scientist has suggested the pheromones, which come from clean sweat, could become as smelly as common body odor after a night's dancing—and what happens when the effects wear off?

Sanitary products

Where would women be without the convenience of disposable sanitary protection? The average woman in developed countries uses about 10,000 sanitary pads or tampons in a lifetime. So why do some women opt for washable fabric towels, and even a reusable rubber "cup" similar to a diaphragm?

They're motivated by concerns about their health and the environmental effects of tampons and pads—including possible links between dioxin residues and some cancers in women. Manufacturers have cleaned up their act—by using better bleaches, for example—but the rayon and cotton used to make tampons and pads may still contain low levels of dioxins and pesticide residues.

Tampons also have a proven association with Toxic Shock Syndrome (TSS), which is a rare but potentially fatal illness. TSS has been linked with higher absorbency products, so choose the lowest absorbency that will be effective for you, and use all-cotton tampons, because they are less likely to lead to TSS.

For most of us, the convenience of disposable products is a priority, so it's just as well that organic

HINTS AND TIPS

Dispose of disposables

Avoid products designed to be disposed of after a brief use, such as razors. Buy versions that last longer, and avoid over-packaging. Where disposability is necessary—tissues and cotton balls, for example—choose recycled or organic versions.

cotton tampons and towels are available—GM-free and nonchlorine bleached. These don't seem to be as absorbent as mainstream brands, so first-time users should initially try them on lighter days. Avoid pads with nonbiodegradable plastic liners and tampons with plastic applicators.

Makeup made over

Natural beauty therapist Claire Besent is not a fan of makeup. "Any avoidance of makeup is good," she says. "It will generally clog pores—the skin needs to breathe, and if you clog pores you just make it stagnant." The beauty-care product line she uses deliberately offers only a few basic makeup items because its makers believe that healthy skin should need no cosmetic assistance.

Makeup can be a chemical minefield, with thousands of ingredients. Mascara may contain parabens, which can not only cause allergic reactions but can have an anaesthetic effect on the eye. This can prevent wearers from realizing they've got mascara flakes in their eyes, leading to damage or infection. The average woman consumes around 4½–11½ pounds of lipstick in a lifetime—an unwelcome diet of petrochemicals and synthetic fragrances. And, as for nail products, these can harbor some of the worst chemicals around including formaldehyde and highly toxic toluene.

When nature needs a helping hand, go for kinder makeup that eschews artificial dyes and preservatives. More palatable lipsticks, for example, are made of waxes from bees and plants, plant oils, and essential oils. Try natural ranges of mascara, eye pencils and eye shadows, and foundation, and nail products free of formaldehyde and toluene. For cleaning up afterwards, plant oils and herbs make an effective makeup remover.

DID YOU KNOW?

Color me beautiful

Colored cosmetics go back centuries—European beauties used to blacken their eye brows with elderberries and redden their cheeks with a mixture of red wine, wood shavings, and rock alum. Modern colors come from coal or petroleum, plant and animal sources, and appear on labels as "FD&C" or "D&C" and a name such as "Yellow No 5." Natural colors include annatto, which comes from seeds, saffron, beetroot red, chlorophyll green, and carrot orange.

HINTS AND TIPS

Inside out

Dry skin needs to be tackled from the inside as well as the outside. Increase your intake of essential fatty acids, the beneficial fats found in cold-pressed sesame, hemp, or flax oils, as well as oily fish, such as mackerel and herring (although you shouldn't eat too much of these fish because they can contain toxins from the ocean.)

Skin deep

Stress, pollution, and aging are tough enough on our skin without using harsh skin care products. Good skin care improves and balances skin so that less of the product is needed. Some products have the opposite effect, as natural product maker Charlotte Vøhtz found. "Ordinary products, we all fall for them with their nice packaging, but they never did anything for my skin," she says. "I had to keep using more of the product because my skin was dry! I started to work with natural oils in products and my dry skin improved in two weeks."

Look for cleansers that retain the skin's natural pH and moisture levels and don't use harsh ingredients such as alcohol. Good exfoliators gently remove dead skin without taking healthy skin with them (a natural abrasive like oatmeal works well), while moisturizers based on plant oils and healing botanical ingredients nourish skin without petroleum-based oils and synthetic fragrances.

If you find yourself with dry skin and no moisturizer to hand, simply put a small amount of a cold pressed oil on your skin after a bath or shower. Olive and sunflower oils are natural and rich in polyunsaturated fatty acids which are beneficial for the skin and, as they're absorbed, for the inner person as well. Try scenting these oils with a tiny amount of an appropriate essential oil (choose oils packed in glass rather than plastic). Because you need less than a drop for one application—prepare a larger amount and keep this in the refrigerator to use as needed. Tone with witch hazel, or the water from fresh parsley soaked overnight.

For luxurious, cleansing face packs, mix clays such as kaolin or Fuller's Earth with a litle water to help draw out impurities—add essential oils and ingredients such as honey and oatmeal. The following simple recipes from the National Honey Board incorporate the healing properties of honey.

DID YOU KNOW?

Face fruit

Some natural beauty products contain ingredients—such as grape seeds, pine bark, and green tea—that act as antioxidants and may protect your body against free radicals that damage skin cells and accelerate skin aging. They also contain vitamins A, C, and E and beta carotene, said to strengthen capillaries and stop enzymes from breaking down the collagen and elastin that make skin elastic and youthful. With the possible exception of vitamin E, however, it's uncertain whether they actually work on skin; including them in your diet is a better bet. Be wary of products made to look natural with fruit images on the packaging—check the label for the real story.

Honey cleansing scrub

Mix 1 tablespoon of honey with 2 tablespoons finely ground almonds and ½ teaspoon lemon juice and rub gently onto the face. Alternatively, grind rolled oatmeal into smaller pieces and mix it with a little warm water and honey to make a smooth paste. After using, rinse off your face with warm water.

Facial toner

Blend 1 tablespoon honey with a peeled, cored apple and smooth mixture over face. Leave on for 15 minutes before rinsing off with warm water.

Honey moisturizer

Mix 1 teaspoon of vegetable oil with 1 teaspoon of honey and ¼ teaspoon lemon juice. Rub into hands, elbows, heels—anywhere that has dry skin. Leave on for ten minutes and then rinse.

DID YOU KNOW?

Natural winners

• *Honey makes a superb natural moisturizer and contains antioxidants that may protect skin from damaging UV rays. It also has a firm place in the medicine cabinet. Honey expert Professor Peter Molan's research has revealed anti-bacterial and anti-inflammatory properties; honey from New Zealand's native manuka plant has even healed serious wounds including leg ulcers and septicemia where conventional treatments proved ineffective.*

• *Tea tree oil, from a tree native to Northern Australia, was used by Aborigine tribes for healing for thousands of years—and Australian soldiers fighting in World War II were issued it as part of their first aid kit. It is a natural antiseptic for minor skin conditions such as spots and one of the few essential oils that can be applied straight to the skin. Don't put it on sensitive skin that's dry or cracked, or in your eyes or mouth.*

• *Hemp oil's centuries-old beauty secrets are being revived in soaps, shampoos and conditioners, hand creams, moisturizers, and lip balms, which incorporate the moisturizing properties of its essential fatty acids. It helps to heal minor skin problems, including acne, and adds body and shine to hair.*

In a lather

There's nothing simpler than soap, right? In fact, many soaps these days are synthetic detergent products dressed up with artificial perfumes and colors. The best natural soaps use plant-based oils from almonds, cocoa butter, olives, and hemp with essential oils, herbs, spices, and flowers. For a clean wash, straight from nature, certain plants—the aptly-named soapwort, North America's Soap Lily, and bracken, to name a few—contain saponins that lather in water to create a gentle yet effective soap.

CASE STUDY

When a 17-year-old, Canadian schoolboy ran a little gel through his hair and dabbed some deodorant under his arms, he wound up being expelled from school and arrested. The reason? He lives in the city of Halifax, Nova Scotia, which has a "no-scent encouragement policy." City representatives believe that commercially-produced scents contain toxic chemicals, so they've banned them in public places, including government buildings, most schools, and, increasingly, in private workplaces.

Casualties of the rule include an 84-year-old woman escorted from a council meeting for having a touch of perfume behind her ears and employees who have been sent home to wash off their scents.

The winners are Halifax residents who can't tolerate chemical fragrances. Between 15 percent and 30 percent of Americans are thought to be sensitive to chemicals, and some have a condition known as multiple chemical sensitivity (MCS) which means they're sensitive to everyday chemicals like those found in cosmetics. Because the symptoms (which include headaches, mental confusion, and nausea) are so general and there are no tests for the condition, critics say it's all in their minds.

Halifax's action has hit the fragrance industry where it really hurts—its pocket. Fragrance sales in the town have plummeted since the ban. The industry's response has been to run advertisements in two major Halifax newspapers rejecting claims that fragrances are harmful, but urging scent users to keep their aromas within their "personal scent circle"—an arm's length from the body.

Are the Canadians wacky—or wise? Bans on fragrances are spreading south, with workplaces and public places in several U.S. states already saying no to scent.

Better buildings

Healthy homes, like organic foods, aim to be less of a chemical "cocktail" and more about natural goodness. Crafted with respect for the environment and the health of the people who live in them, organic homes combine beauty with a low-chemical environment using natural building materials. The payoff? Homes that work in harmony with the environment, your health, and your spirit.

America is peppered with healthy homes, from a Bel Air ranch house remodelled in low polluting and energy efficient building materials, to affordable housing made from straw bales in Minnesota. But creating a healthier home doesn't have to mean swapping your existing home for designer digs. By thinking organic when something needs redecorating or replacing—using organic paints, for example, or replacing a synthetic carpet with a wooden floor—an organic home can be achieved gradually.

And with an ever increasing array of healthier building and decorating supplies, there's no reason to swap one toxic interior for another, or to sacrifice comfort and looks for health. Better products tend to cost more, but not always—it might come down to a choice, for example, between two equally-priced mattresses, one that's chemically-treated to be flame proof and one that's naturally fire retardant.

Make intelligent purchasing your ally: apply the same question you ask of organic food—How has it been made?—to choose healthier products. Eco-interior designer Victoria Schomer even swears by her powers of smell for sniffing out chemical-laden products. "My nose is one of the best tools—in my trade, I'm often down on all fours sniffing for formaldehyde or mold!"

"We are exposed in our homes to the hidden effects of gases and vapors from synthetic materials made from petro-chemicals, to heavy metals and pesticides in water and food, and to the same combustion pollutants that cause acid rain."

—David Pearson, architect and author of *The New Natural House Book*

A breath of fresh air

We've cleaned up our act since a Victorian writer observed, "Coal contributes an important element to the character of the room as it is responsible for a fine layer of ash everywhere." But while we've banished obvious pollutants like coal, modern times have brought new and often invisible health hazards to homes. Experts estimate that indoor air levels of many pollutants can be two to five times—and occasionally one hundred times—higher than outdoors.

Indoor air pollution is such an important health issue—after all, most of us spend up to 90 percent of our time indoors—that the Environmental Protection Agency ranks it among the top five environmental health risks to the public. Texas has taken the unprecedented step of creating guidelines for improving the indoor air quality of school buildings that were making students and teachers sick.

Quade Stahl, Indoor Air Quality chief at the Texas Department of Health, knows just what the culprits are: "We have stain-resistant carpeting and permanent press clothes. We have stronger cleaning solutions. We use particle or pressed board, not wood. We come up with new chemicals to manufacture these new products, but we don't know what health effects they have, especially at low concentrations and combined with all the other pollutants in the air."

Synthetic building materials and furnishings can slowly release harmful gases known as Volatile Organic Compounds (VOCs), such as formaldehyde. Gas fires and stoves emit vapors, including carbon monoxide, which can lead to allergies or even be deadly if not checked and serviced regularly. Paints release solvent gases and contain heavy metals. Add to this the chemical cleaners and pesticides used around most houses and the result is a chemical cocktail that causes "sick homes."

In summer, when we throw doors and windows open, these chemicals ventilate out. But winter sees homes closed against the cold, and in houses that have had leaks and draughts plugged to minimize heat loss and save energy, it's harder for moisture and

HINTS AND TIPS

Testing times

If you have health problems you suspect are related to chemicals in your home, tests can be done to measure formaldehyde and VOC levels in the air. Industrial hygiene consultants, environmental consultants, or environmental laboratories will carry out an individual indoor air survey. A cheaper option is a test kit costing just under $400; if that shows potential problems, then call in the experts.

chemical vapors to escape. Sealed houses steam up like plastic bags as moisture from cooking, showering, heating, and even breathing is trapped—causing mold and fungi and making insulation less effective. Condensation on windows is a tell-tale sign of this.

So just like our own skin, healthier homes "breathe" to maintain even temperature, moisture levels, and air quality even when they're closed up. Breathability means that even if there are chemicals inside the home—and let's face it, eliminating them completely is unrealistic—they'll ventilate out. Naturally porous building materials such as timber or straw and sympathetic wall coverings such as those listed below are key to a breathable home.

Organic, low-solvent paints look great used over clay plaster—use texture effects to replace wallpaper.

Traditional wall-colorings, such as lime wash, are making a comeback for their looks and environmental credentials after falling out of favor in the 1960s. Distemper is a traditional white paint for interior walls; if oil-based distemper is used, it won't rub off in water. Paint based on casein, which comes from milk, has been around for five thousand years and doesn't contain solvents or preservatives. All three are breathable, durable, and can be colored.

Wallpaper may contain plasticizers that emit toxic gas, and the glues used to stick it to the wall can be harmful. Choose the paper carefully and use pastes and primers free of formaldehyde and heavy metals to hang it.

Paint

Alan Sim was working as a builder when he discovered organic paints: "I was looking for an alternative to my getting migraine headaches every time I picked up a paintbrush—these had no white spirit." So impressed was Sim with the alternative paints that he became a partner in the company.

What Sim discovered is that paint typically contains petrochemical-based solvents that let off harmful gases, causing allergies, asthma, and skin irritations—which is why new laws now regulate the VOC content of paints. The most intense fumes "off-gas" for three to four days after applying the paint, so good ventilation is crucial, and they're still detectable for three to four years after that, albeit in extremely diluted form. Even water-based paints, with fewer toxic solvents than oil-based versions, contain other chemicals to improve the paint's consistency.

Organic paints also need solvents to keep the paint in suspension before it's applied, but instead of synthetic solvents they opt for natural versions such as citrus oil from orange peels. These can still cause allergic reactions because the oils are more highly concentrated than in nature. So, as with conventional paints, air a freshly-painted room thoroughly to allow the solvents to dissipate.

With raw materials such as plant oils and waxes, and earth and mineral pigments, these paints are porous so they'll let the organic house breathe. As Alan Sim puts it, "do you want to live in an environment surrounded by plastic, or in a natural environment that is breathing, moving, sympathetic, and living?" Healthier paint strippers, plaster, and joint fillers complete the job.

HINTS AND TIPS

Paint

• *When painting, take care to ventilate the house well, and avoid working with dangerous substances, such as lead paint often found in older houses (particularly if you are pregnant or if children are around).*

• *For cleaning hands of wet paint, grease, and grime, use nontoxic, natural heavy-duty cleaners made from nonpetrochemical ingredients including abrasive pumice, citrus solvents, and lanolin from sheep's wool.*

• *Ideally, buy just enough paint for the job, but if you have leftovers, share them with neighbors or donate them to a local charity. Don't pour paint down the drain!*

• *Throw out half-used cans and containers of paints and chemicals; removing them from the home will help make indoor air healthier because gases can leak even from closed containers.*

To use natural paints, you will need a little patience. Without as many heavy metals, they take longer to dry and might not produce as hard and durable a surface as conventional paints—and they can become shiny in high use areas like around light switches. Expect to pay more for paint that doesn't harm health or the environment— ingredients like orange peel oil don't come as cheap as conventional solvents.

The good news is that there's no need to compromise on color. Natural needn't mean dull. True, color ranges do tend to be smaller and more muted, but paint makers cater to lovers of bright paint with everything from sunflower yellow to flaming red. Natural pigments can mean that color varies between batches, so make sure you buy enough for the job from one batch.

Natural underfoot

It may pay to shun shag. Allergy specialists have discovered that carpets could cause asthma and allergies. Dust mites thrive in them, and they can absorb and store toxic substances from around the home. "Carpets can give off all kinds of things, as well as being a haven for dust mites, mold, bacteria, and they can hold a lot of pet hair," says indoor air quality expert Quade Stahl.

Designer William McDonough dismisses carpet as "little more than a heap of potentially hazardous petro-chemicals that must be toted to a landfill" when it's finished with. Carpet is often synthetic and can contain VOCs including styrene, a suspected carcinogen; 4PC, which is responsible for that "new carpet" smell, and formaldehyde.

Wood is not only easier to keep clean than carpet, it tends to harbor fewer allergens. Solid wood flooring is generally free of chemicals, whereas cheaper laminate versions involving a thin strip of wood glued to a base of plywood or chipboard can contain formaldehyde. Finishing wooden floors with natural varnishes can involve more work than conventional polyurethane coating—some benefit from a polish every six months—but they are every bit as long-lasting. Based on natural resins, they're breathable and will move with wood as it expands and contracts. "You've put down a nice wooden floor, then you cover it with a hard plastic sheet which is very hard and will last for years," says expert Alan Sim. "But you're no longer in contact with the wood, you've lost the breathability."

But there's a lot to be said for the comfort of carpet—lounging on hard

HINTS AND TIPS

Color therapy

Color adds personality and interest to an organic home and can even influence mood.

• Red will inject warmth into your home—in the ancient art of feng shui, it's associated with the fire element. It needn't be strident—an autumnal russet blends handsomely with other natural materials such as stone or fiber flooring, as do browns, creams, and taupes.

• Yellow's vibrant energies bring warmth and light to the home—perfect for a room that gets little natural light.

• Soft greens or blues are calming and cooling. Lighter colors mean less need for electric lighting.

HINTS AND TIPS

Healthy floor

For healthy flooring straight from nature, turn to
• Wood
• Natural linoleum or marmoleum
• Terracotta tiles (preferably unglazed for breathability)
• Wool or natural fiber carpet
• Slate
• Limestone
• Sandstone

wood just isn't the same. Natural fibers offer handsome, durable alternatives. Good choices include pure wool (soft, durable, and inherently flame-proof), coir (a strong fiber from coconut husks), sisal (less rough than coir but still durable), and jute. Choose from plain and patterned weaves as well as a few colors—although their natural honey and earth tones are warm and stylish. Despite being natural, some will have been treated with insecticides, mildew, and fire retardants, so make sure you check with the manufacturer.

PVC or vinyl flooring is not a healthy choice; it contains toxic substances that can contribute to asthma. It also poses disposal problems: burning PVC (or some old carpets, for that matter) releases carcinogenic dioxins into the atmosphere, so it ends up in landfills. Natural linoleum or marmoleum (made from linseed oil, wood powders, and tree resins) are healthier options and are also more breathable.

HINTS AND TIPS

On the floor

• *When buying carpet, ask the retailer about carpets with lower emissions. See if they will unroll and air the carpet before installing it, and then ventilate your home well immediately after the carpet's laid (for this reason, lay carpet in summer if possible).*

• *Most residential carpets are laid using tacks, but if adhesives are needed, use natural versions made of pure plant binders.*

• *Subflooring or underlay used to cushion floor coverings can also release toxic emissions, so look for those made from formaldehyde-free particle-board.*

• *Rugs and other wall coverings add comfort, color, and personality to a room—they're easily shaken and aired and create natural insulation. If you've got the time and the inclination, make your own rug or wall hanging by threading scraps of old fabric through loosely-woven sacking (this backing is available from craft shops).*

Soft comforts

Relaxing into a comfortable sofa or bed is all the better for knowing it hasn't been chemically treated. Curtains, upholstery, and bedding are often treated to make them crease resistant and fire-retardant. Among the various flameproofing treatments, brominated fire retardants can act as hormone disruptors and are so persistent in the environment that they've been found in the blubber of whales in the Atlantic ocean.

But organic choices needn't sacrifice safety; some natural fibers, like silk and wool, naturally resist fire. Master upholsterer Jeff Wilkes helps people sleep easier with his totally organic, chemical-free wool and cotton, handmade mattresses. "If you put a match to wool, you get a puff of smoke and that's it," says Wilkes, whose mattresses pass fire tests without needing any chemical treatment.

HINTS AND TIPS

Fabric
Organic and unbleached fabrics can be bought by the yard for making curtains, cushions, and homemade duvet covers. Mail order outlets will, for a small charge, send swatches and the cost is often recoverable when an order is placed.

Where flameproofing is necessary, less toxic treatments can be used. Electra Colios began making futons fifteen years ago, and motivated to reduce the amount of chemicals in bedding, she uses the naturally-occurring mineral borax as a low-toxicity fire retardant for her unbleached and undyed cotton mattresses.

Organic sheets, duvet covers, and pillows make the perfect complement to a healthier mattress. As natural fabrics, they soak up sweat and moisture better than synthetics, for a dryer, healthier sleep. Wool blankets are warm in winter and cool in summer, and organic versions won't have been treated with organophosphate pesticides or chemically mothproofed. In addition, many of these blankets are beautiful in their own right and would make a fine throw for an old sofa in need of a quick and easy revamp. In the bathroom, go for organic towels, bathmats, and even shower curtains.

Good wood

If you thought wood was the epitome of unadulterated naturalness, think again. Between the tree and the timberyard, wood is commonly treated with chemical preservatives, often required by authorities, to guard against woodworm and rot. Even interior timber is chemically-treated to kill fungi and insects. A healthier alternative to the commonly-used chromated copper arsenate treatment is the mineral boron. Some types of wood simply don't require treatment, and good design and building work can help avoid the need for chemicals—a warm, dry home, for example, will discourage rot.

Multi-density fiberboard (MDF) is cheap and readily available. But like other "composite" board—particleboard or chipboard, for example—it's made from wood chips bound together by chemicals and adhesives and often contains formaldehyde. Seek out formaldehyde-free board or board treated with phenol-formaldehyde—it's less toxic than urea-formaldehyde.

DID YOU KNOW?

Healthy mortgage
Regenerating old homes is good for the environment because it recycles materials and can involve fewer chemicals. Many lenders, however, refuse to mortgage certain derelict or unusual properties—for example, log cabins or earth shelters. But some offer special mortgages for green homes built or remodelled in an environmentally-conscious way.

HINTS AND TIPS

Think about it

Putting thought into your kitchen could pay dividends in better health. A well-designed kitchen with places for easy chopping, washing, and cooking means we're more likely to want to cook, with consequent benefits to our health.

When buying wood, check out its environmental credentials; deforestation and unsustainable logging practices are rife in many parts of the world. Ensuring timber comes from a sustainable source can mean relying on the integrity of the furniture maker, who in turn has to trust his suppliers. Not always a foolproof method, as that venerable institution, The British Museum in London recently found out. Despite receiving assurance the timber it was using came from sustainable sources, the museum was unwittingly using illegally-logged timber from Amazon rainforests.

Wood that bears the Forest Stewardship Council's (FSC) mark of approval is a safe bet. The council operates worldwide to ensure forests are managed in an environmentally-appropriate way, and while its timber and products—which range from chipboard to toilet seats—aren't strictly organic, the scheme does ban the use of GMOs.

Well furnished

With the exception of lovers of minimalist interiors, for most people a home isn't complete without furniture.

During the summer, furniture-maker Felicity Irons spends two months harvesting rushes from the river that runs near her home. She combines the rushes with locally-harvested oak to form beds, screens, chairs, and tables, using no chemical treatments. Other natural fibers that make attractive, long-lasting furniture include willow, or imports such as bamboo and rattan, preferably cultivated not wild. Check with manufacturers that the fibers haven't been chemically treated after harvesting, and ask about treatments such as linseed oil or natural varnish that could extend the life of the furniture.

When buying wooden furniture, make sure you know the wood has been responsibly harvested and manufactured. Try to avoid cheap wooden furniture, particularly if it's for children, because it tends to be made from a composite board like MDF and could give off formaldehyde.

Some furniture makers use wood reclaimed from old industrial and agricultural sites. Recycled wood saves trees and its weathered look is stylish. One example of this is the home of sculptor and furniture maker J.B. Blunk, nestled among Californian hills and made entirely from previously used wood. Leftovers from sculptures, old chicken coops, even old pine beams used to launch new ships—they've all been lovingly crafted into a truly organic, original home. And just to prove that organic is beautiful, design magazine *The World of Interiors* recently devoted several pages to the house.

Following Blunk's lead, add creative spirit to an organic home by giving new life to unwanted furniture. That old adage about one man's junk being another's treasure is so true—check out local yard sales, classified advertisements, and put the word out among friends that you're open to their cast-offs; you'll probably be doing them a favor. Restore finds using natural strippers for old varnish or paintwork, and polish with natural varnish or pure beeswax to protect them and to bring out the natural grain. For more exotic furnishings, check out specialist architectural salvagers who reclaim everything from old toilets to fireplaces.

HINTS AND TIPS

Harnessing nature

• *Organic homes bring nature indoors as much as possible. Next time you visit the beach, collect driftwood—already cleaned and bleached by nature, it can be fashioned into anything from a child's mobile to a picture frame or lamp base. Large logs make natural stands for bookshelves or a coffee table topped with glass or wood.*

• *To add to the seaside theme, buy smooth pebbles (available from garden centers and interiors shops—don't take them from the beach) and scatter them around candles in the bathroom or around potted plants.*

• *Using natural, chemical-free, breathing materials lifts the spirit of a home. Create even more good feelings by adding personal touches—a piece of furniture found in a junkyard and lovingly restored, or a wall hanging made by a friend. Liberate photos from the back of cupboards and frame them to enjoy a visual history of good times.*

See the light

Nothing adds life to a home like natural light. Healthy houses make the most of natural light and the sun's heat to create a cheerful atmosphere that depends less on electric lighting and heating. A good house design has most windows on the sunny side of the house and fewer on the cold side in a cooler climate, and vice versa in hot regions. Special low emissivity (Low E) glass that's coated to reflect heat back into the room will significantly reduce heat loss.

Double-glazing cuts out noise and heat-loss, but try to avoid windows made with PVC frames. The manufacturing process can create toxic dioxins, and they can leak harmful additives, according to Greenpeace. They're not easy to recycle so disposal involves either burning—which releases more dioxin and other contaminating compounds—or burying them. Wooden-framed windows and doors offer a healthier option, often using sustainable wood and natural varnishes.

To make the most of the sun, make sure curtains are drawn back to let optimum light in during the day, and use strategically-placed mirrors to reflect light. Light-colored décor will also brighten a home—but weigh these benefits against the amount of cleaning products needed to maintain a pristine look, particularly if you have children!

Where you do use artificial light, standard tungsten bulbs are best for your health. Flickering fluorescent lights cause headaches and other problems, even when the flicker is imperceptible. Ask for electronic fluorescent tubes—they don't have this problem, and they're also more energy efficient and longer lasting. As for full spectrum lights, these may give out slightly higher levels of potentially damaging UV light than normal bulbs. Unless you're suffering from depression bought on by lack of sunlight (Seasonal Affective Disorder), they're probably not worthwhile.

DID YOU KNOW?

Bright idea

Scientists have found a way of making light bulbs that last one hundred times longer than traditional bulbs and consume just 10 percent of their energy. The same technology could be used to write at least four times more information on CDs and optical disks than is currently possible.

DID YOU KNOW?

Kinder candles

The soft glow of candles can really make a room atmospheric and ambient, but their paraffin content could add unwanted toxins to the air. And, according to the Journal of the American Medical Association, some household candlewicks may contain enough lead to exceed safety guidelines for children. Candles made from the ubiquitous soybean are said to burn 30–50 percent longer than paraffin candles, and are completely biodegradable. Beeswax is natural and sweet-burning, but some candles labelled "beeswax" are in fact a blend of beeswax and paraffin. Buying tealights in glass or ceramic holders saves waste—when they're finished, refill with store-bought candles or make your own with melted beeswax and a wick.

CASE STUDY

Walls of straw

When organic peach farmer Al Courchesne decided to build a new home for his farm workers out of straw bales, they were skeptical. So, too, was one local passerby who called local fire officials, concerned the straw building was a fire hazard.

Neither had cause for concern, it turns out. The workers appreciate their new accommodation, and the firemen left convinced the straw was safe and even toying with the idea of building their new firehouse out of straw.

Frog Hollow Farm is one in a string of twenty-five or so homes that pioneering architects Skillful Means have built in the past five years for farmers, retired people, and even Silicon Valley techies. "Our feeling is they need it as an antidote to how they spend their working life," muses Skillful Means's John Swearingen. "It provides a balance to their life."

Straw bale homes are catching on for several good reasons. Farmers are only too glad to have a surfeit of unwanted straw taken off their hands—they'd only have to dispose of it themselves, and that's getting harder as the government has cracked down on how much they can burn.

More importantly, for their occupants, straw bale homes make for comfortable living. The thick walls block out noise and their sheer mass means they absorb and store heat effectively. That means a more even indoor temperature, regardless of what the weather's doing, and less money needed for heating and air conditioning. Kept reasonably dry, they don't rot—even in the humid winters of northern New York and Nova Scotia bale buildings perform well.

The nontoxic building materials have proved suitable even for people sensitive to multiple chemicals, and the thick stucco plaster that covers the straw on interior and exterior walls seals in potential allergens such as spores. Low formaldehyde composite board, sustainably harvested wood, and low emissivity paints are par for the course. Straw bale homes are good in earthquakes, absorbing the energy without breaking apart—crucial qualities in quake-prone California.

These homes are mainly custom built, so for now they don't compete with budget housing. That could slowly change as people recognize the benefits. John Swearingen notes that already people are seeing that straw homes are "not just a funky thing that people have out in the back woods." With time and money spent on researching more cost efficient construction methods, these attractive, comfortable, long-lasting, and energy-efficient homes could well be available to more Americans.

Naturally fashionable

Shirts made from flags, kimonos fashioned from old quilts, and faded jeans transformed into luxurious Hollywood dresses; fashion designers are embracing recycling to create what *Vogue* magazine has christened "salvage style."

Designers aren't always motivated solely by environmental concerns—it's often cheaper to recycle than to buy new fabric—nevertheless they are part of a growing trend towards eco-conscious clothing. Focusing on natural and organic fabrics with little or no chemical treatment, this is clothing for comfort and health. Mainly the domain of small, committed pioneers that tend to sell via mail order, these clothes aren't main street or shopping mall fare—yet. Nor could they be called glamorous, but all the basics are there and lines are growing more exciting all the time.

Healthy alternatives

Many people prefer natural fabrics because they're renewable, cheap, recyclable, biodegradable, and naturally designed to be tough, while synthetic fabrics are derived from petrochemicals and aren't nearly as biodegradable. Natural materials are often more comfortable to wear, working to keep you warm, cool, or sweat-free—unlike some synthetic fibers that one eco-clothing retailer likens to "wearing a little plastic bag with holes."

Being natural doesn't guarantee health, though. Cotton is natural, but it is also one of the most environmentally-harmful plants around, requiring massive amounts of pesticides and water. Greedy irrigation practices have robbed Uzbekistan's Aral Sea of 60 percent of its water over the past fifty years, and now pesticide and herbicide run-off from cotton fields is poisoning fish in the region's lakes. As organic clothing retailer James Doogan puts it, "If cotton was a food it would be banned, because of the high concentration of chemicals used in manufacturing it."

Nor do natural fabrics escape chemical treatments to bleach, sanitize, and brighten them, and to help them resist fire, wrinkling, and shrinking. Some of these treatments are potentially harmful (the amount of formaldehyde used on textiles has been limited already because it irritates mucous membranes and skin).

Organic clothes have no pesticide residues or chemicals, and those who wear them swear they're softer and less likely to cause allergic skin reactions. Unlike food, organic clothes are unlikely to carry a logo confirming they're organic, so until they do, you'll have to take suppliers at their word.

Not quite organic, but also strictly controlled, are eco-certified fabrics. They're made following stringent environmental guidelines that limit chemicals (including formaldehyde), effluent and air emissions, and ban harmful dyes.

HINTS AND TIPS

Soak new clothes and bedding in hot water with baking soda or vinegar to remove pesticide residues, followed by a thorough wash.

Fabric facts

Cotton Cotton meets about half of the world's fiber requirements, and such large scale, intensive production means the crop consumes an estimated one third of the world's pesticides. It is calculated that a set of queen-sized sheets made from non-organic cotton requires 1¼ pounds of agricultural chemicals. Then there are the chemicals used in processing—the waxy outer layer of the cotton has to be scoured off by chemicals before it will accept dye, and raw cotton is then bleached white using chemicals such as chlorine. Cotton crops may also be genetically engineered to resist the bollworm pest. A tiny proportion of world cotton production is "organic," meaning that it's free of pesticides and chemicals, or "green," which is cotton that's specially woven so it doesn't need chemical finishes. Some unbleached cotton is produced, but it's not necessarily grown without pesticides.

Eco-fleece This relative newcomer is made from recycled plastic drinks bottles, preventing billions of bottles going to landfills—one zip fleece pullover uses approximately twenty-five two-quart, plastic soda bottles. It's largely made into sportswear, although one Japanese underwear firm fashioned a range of soft cloth and lace underwear from chemically-processed bottles (using three-and-a-half quart bottles to make a bra and underpants). However, it won't biodegrade, and although it's eco-friendly, it's not chemical-free.

Hemp As long ago as 1938, *Popular Mechanics* magazine marvelled at the more than twenty-five thousand products, from cellophane to dynamite, that could be made from industrial hemp (*cannabis sativa*). Once vital to world commerce, it was used to make ropes, fishnets, paper, fabric, lamp oil, and sails before antidrug sentiments sealed its fate. Now hemp is making a comeback. Greenlands, a clothing store in Amsterdam, sells wall-to-wall hemp garments, from men's trousers and shirts to women's knitwear and hats. In addition, they sell hemp and organic fabrics by the yard.

Led by its environmental credentials—it is quick-growing with high yields, outruns weeds so needs no herbicides, and resists pests—hemp is destined to be a major fiber in the future. But it is still viewed with suspicion by politicians because of its association with narcotic strains of *cannabis*—even though hemp grown for fiber contains virtually none of the active substance that makes marijuana popular.

Linen The advent of synthetic fibers negatively impacted linen crops, despite a history of cultivation that stretches back to Roman times. It is making a comeback as natural fabrics regain popularity. The fiber flax plant, which grows more quickly and needs less chemical weed control than cotton, produces a very strong fiber that resists dirt and is cool in summer. Linen cloth is often woven with viscose rayon or nylon, with consequent effects on its biodegradability.

Nylon Nothing screams "synthetic" like nylon, which since its invention in 1938 has become synonymous with stockings and static. Like other synthetic fabrics, nylon is largely oil-based; its manufacture is energy-intensive and can release greenhouse gases. Landfills across the world are testament to the slow biodegradability of nylon and other synthetic—although nylon can be used as fuel to reclaim its energy. Because nylon isn't very absorbent it requires synthetic dyes.

Polyester Also based on petroleum, and more difficult to dye than nylon. DuPont recently introduced a new polyester using bioengineering, which is made from cornstarch instead of oil.

Rayon Made from purified wood pulp, with similar characteristics to cotton. Great care needs to be taken to ensure processing isn't polluting, and unscrupulous sourcing of wood pulp can be an environmental issue. Wood pulp is dissolved by chemicals and beached with chlorine, creating toxic substances such as dioxins.

Silk This luxurious fiber is natural, but formalde-hyde can be used to extract the silk from cocoons. It is highly absorbent and helps to regulate temperature—in winter it keeps you warm, in summer it's cool. Artificial compounds used in pro-cessing can destroy the cloth's breathability.

HINTS AND TIPS

Ironing out the wrinkles

Clothes labelled "easy-care" or "non-iron" have been treated with chemicals to make them easier to launder. Dr. Charles Yang of the University of Georgia's textiles department has found an alternative to using formaldehyde to produce wrinkle-free cotton—citric acid—which is less hazardous to the environment.

Tencel A relatively new fabric made from wood pulp and produced with nontoxic solvent that is 99 percent recoverable and recyclable, according to manufacturers. They say that no harmful fumes are released into the environment during its manufacture. Tencel readily accepts dyes—meaning less dye is needed—and it's a fluid fabric that resists wrinkles and shrinking.

Wool You'd think nothing could be more natural than wool: it's easily recyclable, highly absorbent so it needs less dye to color it, and it is naturally fire resistant. But the chemicals used to get the wool from the sheep's backs to ours can pollute runoff water when the wool is cleaned, and they can make the wool allergenic.

Used to control the blow flies, lice, and ticks that can plague the animals, organophosphates have been blamed for brain damage and automatic nervous system damage in people exposed to concentrated amounts. In Wagga Wagga, Australia, three sheep shearers successfully sued a wool grower when they were exposed to organophosphates during sheep dipping.

Organic wool does away with these problems. James Doogan uses wool from organically-reared Irish sheep for his hand-loomed woolen jumpers, socks, hats, and scarves. The sheep don't go through chemical dips, and only plain soap is used to clean the wool. It's all done by hand to minimize energy use, and no dyes are used, especially as the white, light gray and dark gray wool is naturally beautiful.

Better by design

Lucinda Chambers, fashion director of *Vogue* magazine, is not convinced that the limited colors and basic designs of organic and eco-friendly clothing will catch on with the average clothes-buyer. "I think people are too vain to really take on board that concept," she says. "It's not synonymous with glamor, and glamor is at the heart of the fashion industry." At the Organic Café Natural Homestore in London, England, which is pioneering organic clothing on the high street, clothes are natural-dyed with onions and indigo—but still buyer Negar Esfandiary admits "I couldn't wear 100 percent organic, I'm quite adventurous with my clothes."

But textile and clothing designers are using their artistic skills to make organic clothes attractive to more people. "You can make organic but it often looks awful—so it doesn't reach many people," points out Lykke Kjaer, one of a group of Danish textile designers producing sustainable yet attractive designs.

Textile designer Louisa Wood is aiming to transform hemp's frumpy image. "The organic movement hasn't really experimented with bright colors," she says. "Hemp dyes amazingly well since it's so absorbent, so you don't need so many chemicals as cotton to dye it." Wood has won a scholarship to travel to China, a major hemp producer, to learn just how hemp fabric is made. With this know-how under her belt, she plans to experiment with the "beautiful, deep, soft colors" of vegetable dyes.

Dye debates

Behind the preponderance of beige-colored eco-clothing lies a compelling environmental and health argument. Chemicals used to produce some dyes are harmful, even potentially carcinogenic; the process uses a lot of water and runoff can be highly polluting.

But we're used to our clothes coming in a dazzling array of colors, so designers are looking for compromises that won't harm the earth. Some swear by natural dyes, used for centuries until the first synthetic dyes were developed in the nineteenth century, arguing that they're chemical-free, non-toxic to handle, and come from renewable resources. But vegetable dyes require "mordants," such as alum and copper sulfate to "stick" the dyes to the fiber and stop them from fading.

And some designers believe synthetic dyes are the only realistic choice for large-scale clothing production because many natural dyes require a massive amount of natural resources to produce. It took twelve thousand shellfish to produce just .005 ounce of a purple dye popular in ancient times, and if indigo was used to dye all the world's cotton, as much as a third of the globe's agricultural land would have to be set aside to grow it.

Designer Lykke Kjaer uses just six synthetic dyes, carefully chosen so they don't include heavy metals and don't need a mordant. Some manufacturers use low environmental-impact dyeing processes whereby fabrics aren't bleached before being dyed, and the recycled water used is cleaned before it's put in the sewage system.

DID YOU KNOW?

Dyeing naturally
• *Arizona cotton-grower Sally Fox has pioneered a way of coloring cotton without using dye. She's specially bred (using traditional methods) wild colored cottons with commercial white varieties to create organic cotton that grows in browns and greens that intensify with washing.*
• *In Hawaii, one clothing company uses the red earth of Kauai to dye clothes, while the Japanese have used bacteria to create a natural, bluish-purple pigment to dye textiles.*

All washed out

The large amounts of water, energy, and detergents we use to clean and dry our clothes could be the most polluting stage of the life of a garment. Although this sounds depressing, it actually gives us control over the impact our clothes have on the world.

Choose energy- and water-efficient washing machines and more environmentally-friendly laundry liquids and powders.

Avoid buying clothes that need drycleaning because of the strong solvents that drycleaners use. Perchloroethylene has been shown to cause cancer in animals, and studies show that people breathe in low levels of this chemical from stored dry-cleaned clothes and from wearing them. If you get clothes back with a strong chemical smell, ask for them to be dried properly. A handful of cleaning outlets use "wetcleaning," which requires milder chemicals.

Extend the life of clothes to lessen demand for new garments. Mending may sound old-fashioned but it saves money and resources.

Resist the urge to bump up dryer temperatures, which uses more energy and can prematurely age clothes. When cotton fabrics are repeatedly machine dried at higher temperatures they tear more easily than those tumble-dried at room temperature, drip dried indoors, or dried outside in sunlight. Hot drying also produces more lint, and machine drying cotton garments when they're wet is more damaging than tumbling them when they're partially dry.

When the shoe doesn't fit

For some the lure of a new pair of shoes is impossible to resist; the Philippines' Imelda Marcos is surely just the most famous example of the footwear hoarding that goes on in some wardrobes! If you can't curb shoe-buying habits, natural shoes at least offer healthier and increasingly more fashion-conscious options, although they're still more likely to be sandals than stilettos.

Vegetarian and vegan shoes substitute breathable materials such as fake suede and microfiber for leather, but most natural shoes are made of leather. Such a durable material that leather shoes will probably outlast your interest in them.

One Oregon-based shoemaker is making leather even more environmentally friendly by sourcing it from cattle that haven't overgrazed grasslands and haven't been stoked with artificial hormones, antibiotics or pesticide-sprayed feed, and by using a more environmentally-sensitive tanning process. The soles are made from sustainably harvested wild Amazon latex, hemp canvas is used as an upper material for some styles, and water-based, nontoxic glue is used instead of the more typical solvent-based glues. The company also uses recycled materials, including rubber outer soles made from recycled car wheels.

Second time round

Gone are the days when we sat down and mended clothes, eking out their lifespan. Global trade and slicker manufacturing has put cheap, fashionable clothes well within our means, so it's little wonder that lurking in our collective wardrobes are billions of dollars worth of unused clothes.

Vogue's Lucinda Chambers is a great believer in not buying too many clothes. "There's a huge turnover in fashion, in what's in and what's out, so I think that you have to hold up things that are in fashion and really think about why you like them—for what they are, or for what they represent? I always ask myself, will I like it when I'm seventy?" she says. "If you're not sure, leave it and go back the next day when the emotion and excitement has cleared."

DID YOU KNOW?

Eat my shorts!
Russian scientists are designing a bacterial cocktail to digest astronauts' cotton and paper underpants, reports New Scientist *magazine, and the resulting methane gas could be used to power the spacecraft. The search for the right bacteria could take another decade, while the complete unit is not expected to be ready until 2017.*

Donate unwanted clothes to friends or charity shops (these also yield real bargain buys that are often retro-stylish). Some stores will resell second hand clothing, so you could profit from recycling. And unusable clothes make free cleaning cloths.

"I do buy a lot of stuff and recycle it—I make it shorter, cut pants off and transform them into capri pants, put trims on," says Chambers. "I always have three bags on the go—one for the charity shop, one for friends, and one for the second-hand shop."

CASE STUDY

A compostable choice

When designers William McDonough and Michael Braungart were asked to create a new fabric, the company they were making it for suggested using a mixture of cotton and recycled fibers from plastic drink bottles—a combination of "natural" and recycled fiber that seemed to be an ideal, environmentally-friendly product.

But the designers saw a number of environmental problems with the approach. Cotton production accounts for a significant percentage of the world's insecticide use, the plastic bottle's fibers could not safely go back to the soil, and McDonough was uneasy about putting recycled plastic bottle fabric next to human skin because of the harmful materials they may contain.

A total redesign was called for, and the result was an "edible" material that would biodegrade when no longer needed. The new design used wool from free-ranging sheep and fiber from ramie, a plant similar to nettles, that is produced without chemicals. Faced with a selection of more than eight thousand chemicals for the finishes, dyes, and other processing materials, the designers chose just thirty-eight to ensure the finished product was free of mutagens, carcinogens, heavy metals, endocrine disrupters, and other toxic substances.

When the fabric reaches the end of its useful life, it simply decomposes. Offcuts from the manufacturing process are turned into felt, which farmers use as a ground cover for crops to control weeds and insulate soil, and which eventually decomposes to feed worms and microorganisms.

Shoes, too, have come under McDonough and Braungart's scrutiny. They believe that with each step, the sole of the average shoe releases tiny particles of potentially harmful substances. The solution is to make soles that are a biological nutrient, nourishing nature instead of harming it. Other parts would be "technical nutrients," able to be used in other products when the shoe is discarded.

Waste not

Bringing the creative spirit of organic agriculture indoors could cut down your home's demand for new products. In the organic garden, little is wasted —vegetable scraps, paper, and weeds go on the compost heap, old CDs become bird-scarers—and doing the same inside will reduce the amount of energy and chemicals used to make new products and keep more waste out of landfills and incinerators.

Less is more

In our consumer society, where more is better and advertising fuels a voracious appetite for buying new products, making efforts to buy less can seem akin to jumping off a moving train. Not everyone will agree with feminist author Germaine Greer when she says "when a female shopper enters the shopping environment…she offers herself up to a process of seduction," but there's no denying that "retail therapy" has a strong attraction for most of us.

Indeed, compulsive shoppers—90 percent of them women—have been known to rack up debts of between $5000 and $100,000 for the tension release they get from shopping. Even for the mildly afflicted, there's a certain freedom—not to mention savings and environmental benefits—to be gained by resisting that one-season wonder you know you'll hate in a year's time.

We can also vote for better products with our wallets by practicing "green consumerism"—buying products designed to be kinder to the environment—or "ethical consumerism," which takes into account a product's green credentials as well as wider issues, such as whether the manufacturer invests in the arms trade or tests on animals.

Energy the smart way

All energy is not created equal. Burning fossil fuels to generate energy pollutes the air and damages the health of thousands of Americans, not to mention the effects on global climate change. By comparison, harvesting power from wind and sun—for example, as Vermont-headquartered Green Mountain Energy does—is clean and green. Until companies like Green Mountain are producing much more power this way, households can cut their contribution to global warming by making their homes more energy efficient.

Insulate. Heating a noninsulated, drafty home wastes energy and money by heating outdoor air. Loft insulation is one of the easiest and most cost-effective ways of improving energy-efficiency in the home, but some insulation products, such as foam and fiberglass, can make some people ill. Natural options include wool, cellulose (recycled paper—but this too can cause problems), cork, mineral wood, and flax or hemp fibers.

Install energy-efficient appliances. What you save in lower running costs will compensate for the higher initial cost. Look for appliances with the Energy Star label denoting energy efficiency—replacing your existing equipment with Energy Star appliances could ultimately cut your household's energy bill by 30 percent.

Lighting. Use bulbs that run on less electricity and last up to ten times longer than normal bulbs. Just one energy-efficient, compact fluorescent bulb will save the average homeowner $110 and replace sixty-two gallons of oil. Use the bulbs in areas where lights are left on for long periods. Instead of lighting a whole room, use lamps to illuminate only the areas being used.

Run your appliances correctly. Defrosting the refrigerator regularly makes it more energy efficient, while turning the hot water cylinder thermostat down to 140 °F saves energy and money and prevents scalding. When doing laundry use low water temperatures, economy

DID YOU KNOW?

Undermining consumption

"Reality for Men" is an advertisement shot in tasteful black and white. It looks for all the world like a Calvin Klein campaign—until you notice that it shows not a firm, youthful torso but that of a paunchy, hairy man. It's the work of Adbusters—the Media Foundation, a Canadian group that places "subvertisements" on American TV—spoof ads that mock expensive corporate ad campaigns.

Adbusters and groups like it are tackling companies' marketing hype and the public's overconsumption, which together see 20 percent of the world's population using more than 70 percent of its resources. More is not always better, say these groups, and consumption won't make us happy. "Do we really need electric toothbrushes?" asks Europe-based organization Enough. "14 different brands of them? Gadgets to get the bobbly bits off woolly jumpers, slice the top of boiled eggs, or massage our toes?" To drive the message home to shoppers, the busiest shopping day of the year, the day after Thanksgiving, is designated "Buy Nothing Day."

cycles, and full loads—most detergents work just as well in cool water as hot.

Finance. Take out an energy-efficiency mortgage. These are available to buyers of new homes that are energy efficient, and for existing homes where energy improvements can be made.

Second time round

Where previous generations repaired and mended, we rush out to buy replacements. And where they depended on glass and crockery, now even organic food comes cocooned in plastic and cardboard—modern packaging may prevent more food from spoiling, but it also adds significantly to the ton or so of garbage the average household throws away every year. Some manufacturers run refill programs, and may even offer a discount over buying ready-packaged goods, but such programs are rare.

A smart way to deal with overpackaging is to give it new life. It's cheaper and greener to wash and reuse glass and plastic containers than make new ones—reincarnate them as candleholders and vases.

New life

Mention the word "recycling" and people either look guilty or profoundly bored. Recycling is no substitute for reducing waste in the first place by buying fewer products and re-using them, but it does conserve resources, save energy and cut down on pollution. Industry is finding more and more ways to use recycled materials: an American designer has made tiles, countertops, and bathroom surfaces from car

HIT OR MYTH

Dishwashers are worse for the environment than washing by hand
While washing dishes by hand for a family of four uses 5–6.5 gallons of water a day, an energy-efficient dishwasher for the same family uses 4–4.5 gallons of water per cycle—less water than handwashing, if it's fully loaded each time. But, factor in the energy used to run the dishwasher, and it loses hands down against human muscle power. So, if you must have a dishwasher, choose the most energy-efficient dishwasher you can afford—the higher initial cost will easily be recouped by lower running costs and it will be kinder on the environment.

DID YOU KNOW?

Run like clockwork
Solar radios powered by the sun will run for hours without the need for electricity, while wind-up flashlights mean you'll never be at the mercy of old batteries. If you're more ambitious, fit solar panels to your home to heat 50 percent or more of your household's hot water. The $3500 or so you spend on a solar water heating system will typically be paid back in lower energy bills within seven years—followed by up to fifteen years of free hot water.

bumpers, recycled carpet fibers, and crushed CDs mixed with cement. Not all of these "new" products are compatible with a chemical-free household, though; recycled car wheels used to make rubber flooring, for example, can give off unwelcome gases.

Few of us are likely to keep recycling if it means removing the entire contents of the hall cupboard to get at the paper bin every time! Make recycling easier by setting up a simple system. In the future, homes may have built-in recycling slots in the kitchen that let you simply "send" used packaging down a hatch, but until then, try using plastic bins with easy-to-remove lids. They will contain leaks and are easy to clean. Use one for each type of material, or as many as possible if space is limited. Supermarket bags make a free receptacle for collecting paper or cardboard.

When the bins are full, empty them through a curbside collection program or at a nearby recycling depot. Not every area has collection facilities for all types of materials. Plastic is particularly difficult to recycle. Aid recycling by not buying packaging that's a mixture of several materials, as it's harder to recycle.

One of the most uplifting ways of recycling—and improving the health of your home into the bargain—is a therapeutic "spring" cleaning. Tackle cupboard and attic clutter—are you really likely to need these things again, or could somebody else make better use of them? Give useful items away to a charity shop or friends, or sell them at a garage sale and use the proceeds to buy something that you really want.

HIT OR MYTH

Plastic wine stoppers are better for the environment than corks

One argument is that plastic corks help the environment by saving cork trees from being felled. But cork farmers, backed by university specialists and conservationists, have fought back saying that such accusations are untrue. Cork trees are never cut down—the bark of the cork tree is carefully stripped by hand about every nine years, and the tree lives on. And the traditional cork farming methods give valuable food and shelter to wildlife.

DID YOU KNOW?

Green loo
You can save water in your toilet by putting a brick in the tank at the back. Or, for the really enthusiastic, composting toilets use no water, instead they employ bacteria to evaporate urine and break down organic material so it can be used by plants.

Food scraps Fruit and vegetable scraps make excellent compost, and compost bins are available for even the smallest of yards. Some homes even have the luxury of built-in chutes that deliver kitchen waste directly to a bucket under the sink. Special bags for collecting kitchen scraps are available. They can be composted

together with the waste because they're made from potato starch.

Paper and card Keep cardboard and junk mail separate from paper—they often have separate collections. Wax-coated packaging material used for packaging fruit, vegetables and fish can't be recycled, although scientists have found a way of using corn protein to make a biodegradable coating to replace wax. Milk and juice cartons can't be recycled as paper or cardboard as they have a plastic lining.

Cans Some recycling centers will only accept aluminum cans (easier to recycle and worth more), others take both aluminum and steel. Remove labels and crush cans before recycling. A quick rinse in leftover washing up water is enough to clean them. Aerosol cans made from steel or aluminum are recyclable—make sure they're empty before you deposit them, and don't crush them.

Glass Glass has the benefit of being recyclable again and again without a drop in quality. Remove metal or plastic first and rinse in left-over dishwater, and deposit at a bottle bank—these are usually sorted by color.

Plastic Plastic soda bottles and milk jugs are among the many plastics that can be recycled, but in general, recycling plastic is expensive because of the wide range of types that need to be collected, separated, and sorted—if your area has no plastic recycling facilities, that's probably why.

HIT OR MYTH

Recycling is better for the environment

In some cases, the energy needed to collect and process waste materials outstrips what would be needed to put them in a landfill. It may take more energy, for example, to send collection vehicles around for just one material than to collect all waste together and sort it at the other end. And recycling processes use energy and chemicals. But until we come up with a better solution, recycling reduces the amount of virgin material needed, cuts air and water pollutants, and keeps waste out of landfills. By 2005, recycling will reduce greenhouse gas emissions by forty-eight million tons, equivalent to the amount emitted by thirty-six million cars.
Car trips to the recycling depot with a few empty wine bottles will soon undo the benefits of recycling. Lightweight and robust bicycle trailers make easy work of biking the recycling to the depot, and the only engine involved is your legs.

TIP

Recycling Christmas

It only comes around once a year, but it makes a real mess, including millions of Christmas trees and dustbins full of packaging. Recycling or reusing bottles, paper and jars can reduce the waste; kindergartens and schools may welcome used cards. Avoid waste completely by making natural decorations—bunches of cinnamon sticks tied with ribbon, limes with designs carved in the skin, pastry shapes glazed so they're hard and long-lasting.

DID YOU KNOW?

Hazardous waste/oil/batteries Household hazardous materials make up a tiny percentage of residential waste but cause most of the pollution problems associated with landfills. Once you buy a hazardous product, you're responsible for disposing of it safely—don't put it in normal trash collection or down the drain. Take hazardous wastes to a designated site or contact the local authority for disposal guidance. Many retailers selling non-rechargeable batteries will also take them off your hands for recycling, and the same holds for lead acid car batteries.

Clothing/shoes/textiles Renewing or recycling clothes means less waste and pollution created by clothes manufacturing. Modern textile reclamation businesses sift through discarded clothes and send them to charity shops to be sold to homeless people and developing countries. Waste textiles are cut up to make industrial cloths and wipers, and even "new" yarn and wool.

Home office

Working from home is an increasingly popular choice, so it's worth considering what can be done to run the office to reduce waste:
• Buy recycled paper, files, pens, and even toner cartridges for printers. The back of used paper can be used as draft computer print-outs and notepads. Re-use envelopes by covering old addresses with stickers—many charities sell these.
• Pens from everyday ballpoints, to highlighters and markers, cost more but are biodegradable, recycled, and refillable.
• Switch computer equipment off when you're not using it, and investigate the power-saving facilities on your computer.
• Old computers are often worth something to a local school or charity, and there are business that recycle or recondition parts or whole computers.

Cool runnings

Our car culture is smothering us. Cars emit carbon dioxide, the main greenhouse gas leading to global warming; the poisonous gas carbon monoxide, which can cause tiredness, stress, and breathing problems; and nitrogen oxides and sulfur dioxides that cause smog and acid rain. Inside, they're chemical cocktails.

Spurred by legislation in California, major car manufacturers are developing electric and gas-electric cars, but meanwhile there are easy ways to cut down your contribution to pollution. Car pool, walk, or bicycle and benefit from the extra exercise—parents concerned about transporting children on their bikes can be assured by research showing that risks associated with child seats and trailers are low.

For those not on a strict timetable, taking public transportation can be more stress-free than fighting traffic yourself. Reap even more benefits by using the time to consciously relax. But when that's not an option, follow these tips for running your car so it makes less impact on the environment and public health.

• Turn off the engine if the car is stationary for two minutes or more.

• Inflate wheels to the correct pressure, to save up to 5 percent on your fuel bill.

• Park in the shade where possible—sun on a hot engine increases emissions, causing a smog that can trigger asthma and other breathing conditions.

• Buy smaller cars that use less fuel.

• Maintain the car to reduce emissions and enhance fuel economy.

• Avoid sudden acceleration, high speed driving, and revving the engine—these burn more gas and emit more pollution.

CASE STUDY

Energy from Enertia

North Carolina architect Michael Sykes has made renewable energy the keystone of his solid wood homes. At their heart is Sykes' Enertia solar heating system that maintains comfortable temperatures in both summer and winter by treating the house as a massive heat pump.

A south-facing sunroom fuels the pump, harvesting the sun's heat. It rises through ceiling vents into the attic where, in summer, much is vented out, and the rest travels down a space, called an "envelope," between the outside and inside walls on the north side of the home to the basement where it's cooled. In winter, the heated air warms the basement, sending warm air throughout the house.

Dense timber walls absorb heat or cold, depending on the season, and also insulate a home—the stud and dry walls of most American homes do not do the same. Solar collectors on the roof heat hot water, and an underfloor heating system is channelled beneath varnished pine flooring. Altogether, the big, heavy construction of Syke's home holds heat for more than twice as long as a conventional, lightweight home.

The future

Every year, an estimated fifty million Americans spend up to $230 billion on products that match their social and environmental principles. And none too soon; dedicated pioneers of organic living have toiled for years to promote the benefits of healthier products.

What's changing now is that unlike the expensive, often ineffective "green" products of past decades, the new generation of healthier home cleaners, clothing, building materials, and beauty products are just as good and as affordable as their conventional counterparts. And they're not just available to a clutch of committed customers—healthy products are becoming increasingly mainstream.

The surge of enthusiasm for organic food is leading us to wonder why our homes, too, can't be healthier. We've realized that polluted indoor air in offices can make us sick— the headaches, nausea, lethargy, and other symptoms of "sick building syndrome" are well documented—and that's prompted us to focus attention on our homes.

Architect Bill Dunster, the creative force behind a futuristic development of healthy, energy-efficient homes, believes that healthy interiors are crucial: "I think it's absolutely essential—we're very conscious of all the toxins you get with proprietary paint systems, so the walls will be breathable emulsion. We've got near zero PVC, it's just used in the wiring, we're conscious of minimal use of plastic, and minimal carpeted areas—we're using lots of tiles."

It's not just trendy specialist stores that are tapping into the rising tide of interest. U.K.-based international department store Marks and Spencer is stocking organic underwear. Meanwhile, in the U.S., sportswear retailer Patagonia switched to organically-grown cotton back in 1996 for its entire line and is very pleased with the results.

The benefits of this burgeoning interest? Better, more attractive designs for a start, as larger companies invest in exciting designs. Lower costs, too, are in the cards— although some healthier products cost more than their mass-market counterparts, this is usually because the raw materials are more expensive to produce. As greater demand leads to bigger buying power and economies of scale, this will change.

Healthier building materials are likely to come to the fore in the future and change the way homes are built. Take hemp, for example, which makes a strong, healthy building material. A pilot project in the U.K. is setting out to prove that by building test homes—more precisely, two hemp homes—among a new housing develop- ment of otherwise conventional brick homes. Their performance will be compared with the brick homes, and if the results prove favorable, hemp will no longer be a niche, novelty product.

We'll also see product design turned on its head to create a healthier world. Influential thinkers William McDonough and Michael Braungart believe the future lies not in the "reduce, reuse, and recycle" concept, which they argue simply lessens the impact of a flawed system. They propose a fundamental change in product design, arguing that products should be designed to break down biologically, or to provide material and parts for other products. Already, researchers at Bangor University predict that cars of the future will be made from molded cashew-nut oil and hemp—renewable, cheap, and naturally tough.

DID YOU KNOW?

California's water shortage crisis has forced the state to look at ways of recycling toilet water into drinking water—in a few years' time, 20 percent of the water coming out of taps in California could be water purified from toilets. And in South Burlington, Vermont, raw sewage is cleaned by bacteria, microbes, fish, and snails to produce sparkling, clear water—pure enough for irrigation, toilet flushing, or car washing.

CASE STUDY

Healthy homes for the future

An urban Toronto house that is healthy for both the people living in it and the environment is paving the way to better homes.

The three-bedroom home enjoys healthy air quality thanks to efficient ventilation, low emission paints, easy-to-clean hardwood and tile floors, and joinery made from products that don't emit vapors, such as formaldehyde.

Energy-saving measures, such as generous-sized windows to capture maximum natural light, increased insulation in walls and attic, triple-glazed windows, and energy-efficient light bulbs—coupled with solar panels generating electricity—mean the home costs under $300 a year to run. To reduce dependence on the car, the home is built in a central location with public transport services.

The home's water comes solely from rain and snow and is conserved with low-flush toilets, low-flow shower-heads, and water- and energy-efficient appliances. The home's waste-water is treated on site with micro-organisms, oxygen, UV light, and charcoal, technology so effective that it turns sewage into water that can be used to flush toilets and to water the gardens.

The Healthy House is the result of a competition run by Canada Mortgage and Housing Corporation, which wanted to show that sustainable, healthy houses could be designed for the Canadian climate. But is it just a concept that won't really figure in our future?

Its proponents say the home proves that healthy housing is a reality—now. Despite the fact that it is a specially funded demonstration home built using relatively expensive technologies (the costs of which would be recouped over 15–20 years through energy cost savings), they say future healthy homes will be affordable thanks to reduced costs because of economies of scale and increasing availability of specialized building materials. And, already, other buildings in Canada are adopting the innovative technologies used in Toronto—the water treatment system for one has been enthusiastically embraced by homes in the remote north where water has to be trucked in and sewage trucked out.

10 steps to an organic home

1. Gradually shaping an organic home is as simple as finding healthier options next time something needs replacing. Ask questions about how a product is made and what chemicals are used to track down the best products.

2. A home that breathes makes for healthier living because it lets moisture and toxins out even when doors and windows are shut.

3. Cleaning products are a major source of chemicals in the home. Consider carefully if all those cleaners are really necessary—most homes need only a few. Natural alternatives are readily available.

4. Plants and flowers freshen air and add energy and life to a home—some remove chemicals from indoor air.

5. Infusing your home with individual character is as important for health as clearing out chemicals, so look for ways to personalize it.

6. The toiletries and cosmetics we keep in our homes contain chemicals that can harm our health, so reduce the need for them by eating organic food, exercising, drinking enough water, and managing stress, and using gentler products.

7. Good sleep will do more for good looks than many beauty products can; organic mattresses and bedding make for a chemical-free sleep.

8. Choose organic and unbleached clothing (including shoes) for comfort without pesticide residues or chemical treatments.

9. Think of organic living as starting at your front door, and try not to bring anything over the threshold that won't enhance your home. Consider what goes out as well; re-use it if possible to avoid throwing it away, or recycle.

10. Make your home a low energy user—choose energy-efficient light bulbs and appliances, use appliances in ways that cut energy use, and try to walk, ride, or take public transportation instead of taking the car.

Resource material

To dig deeper into organic issues try the following contacts. I've included some websites that are outside the U.S. because they are useful and informative regardless of where you live.

Better building

Abundant Earth
For mail order healthy home products including organic cotton shower curtains, beds and bedding, indoor air filters, and more.
Tel: (888) 51-EARTH (513-2784)
http://www.abundantearth.com

Air Quality Sciences
For indoor air quality test kits.
1337 Capital Circle
Atlanta, GA 30067
Tel: (800) 789-0419
Fax: (770) 933-0641
Email: info@aqs.com
http://www.aqs.com

Architectural Record
Green architecture site with useful links to suppliers of eco-conscious building materials.
www.archrecord.com/GREEN

Candleworks
Soybean wax candles made without paraffin.
http://www.candleworks.org

EcoChoices
Internet retailer supplying natural and organic beds and bedding, and furniture.
http://www.ecochoices.com

Forest Stewardship Council
Promotes environmentally-appropriate, socially-beneficial, and economically-viable management of forests. Provide lists of retailers and manufacturers of FSC-certified products.
Tel: (877) 372-5646 (toll free)
Fax: (202) 342-6589
http://www.fscus.org

Green Builder
Internet site with excellent listings of companies providing better building materials including boron-treated timber.
http://www.greenbuilder.com/sourcebook/

Green HOME
Organization that builds green homes using volunteer labor. Access through the website a searchable database of salvaged building materials and another listing more than 600 green building materials and products.
2022 Columbia Road
NW Apt 208
Washington, DC 20009-1309
Tel: (202) 24-GREEN
Fax: (202) 562-4336
http://www.greenhome.org

Healthy Flooring Network
UK-based network of organizations and individuals concerned about asthma and allergies.
Email: info@healthyflooring.org
http://www.healthyflooring.org

Interior Concerns
Consulting services on healthier home environments. Also access to resource directories by region.
Tel: (415) 389-8049
http://www.interiorconcerns.org

Lifemaster 2000 No-VOC paint
Low odor, no VOC paint from ICI, makers of Dulux paint.
http://icipaintstores.com

Safe Home Products
Internet retailer of air purifiers, micro-fiber cleaning cloths, natural soap, soy wax candles, and more.
http://safehomeproducts.com

Treske Solid Wood Furniture
Furniture handmade in England using wood from sustainable sources—choose from a range of designs or bespoke products.
Station Works
Thirsk
North Yorkshire
YO7 4NY
Tel: +44 1845-522-770
Fax: +44 1845-522-692
www.treske.co.uk

United States Environmental Protection Agency
Excellent source of information on indoor air quality.
http://www.epa.gov/iaq

Healthy housekeeping

Country Save
Environmentally safe household products. Website contains a useful guide to removing all sorts of stains.
http://countrysave.com

Earthwise Animal
Natural flea control and other pet products.
http://www.earthwiseanimal.com

Earth Friendly Products
All natural environmentally safe household cleaners and personal care products.
44 Greenbay Road
Winnetka, Illinois 60093
Tel: (800)-ECOS (3267)
http://www.ecos.com

Ecover
Effective, natural range of cleaning products with safe ingredients and low environmental impact. Sells in local health food stores.
Tel: (323) 720-5730
http://www.ecover.com

Fleabusters
Borate powder product for ridding carpets of fleas.
http://www.fleabuster.com

Mountain Green
Biodegradable, non-toxic cleaning products available direct and from natural food stores.
Tel: (888) 878-5781
http://www.mtngreen.com

Organic Solution
Natural products for dogs, including organic shampoo, dips, and sprays based on flea-repellant citrus oils.
http://www.wingnet.net/~organicsol/

Planet
Environmentally kinder cleaning products, including an unscented spray cleaner.
Tel: (800) 858-8449
Fax: (250) 478-3238
http://www.planetinc.com

Personal care

Cosmetic, Toiletry, and Fragrance Association (CFTA)
For the other side of the fragrance issue. The website has a useful guide to common names of cosmetic ingredients listed by their botanical name.
http://www.cfta.org

eNutrition
Web retailer of natural beauty products from shaving cream to deodorant crystal sticks and organic tampons to toothpaste.
http://www.enutrition.com

Gladrags
Cotton Flannel menstrual pads, colored or undyed, unbeached organic cotton.
Tel: (800) 799-4253

Jurlique
Known as "the purest skin care on Earth," skin care and makeup from natural ingredients organically-grown in the unpolluted hills of South Australia.
Freephone: (800) 854-1110
www.jurlique.com.au

National Honey Board
For information about the healing properties of honey.
http://www.nhb.org

Natracare
Organic, non-chlorine bleached cotton sanitary protection including tampons, pads, and shields. Available from natural products stores or mail order from several natural product sites on the Internet including www.mothernature.com.
Tel: (303) 320-1510
http://www.natracare.com (*go through to the US website from here*)

Organic Essentials
For organic cotton products including sanitary care and cotton balls, wipes and buds.
Tel: (800) 765-6491
http://www.organicessentials.com

Thursday Plantation
Australian company making tea tree oil deodorants, skin care, hair care, essential oil, toothpaste and foot care.
Tel: +44 1274 488-511
Fax: +44 1274 541-121
http://www.thursdayplantation.com

Tom's of Maine
Natural products from a company with a commitment to healthier, environmentally-kinder products including shaving cream, toothpaste, dental floss, deodorants, and shampoo.
http://www.tomsofmaine.com

Waikato Honey Research Unit
Home of honey expert Peter Molan and another fascinating site on the health benefits of honey.
http://honey.bio.waikato.ac.nz

Naturally fashionable

California Organic Clothing Company
Organic clothing by mail order.
Tel: (626) 564-8266
http://www.organiccottonandhemp.com

Deep E Footwear
Footwear made with recycled and renewable materials, using processes with lower environmental, health, and safety risks.
Tel: (877) 385-2719
http://www.deepe.com

Grass Roots
Organic and natural clothing (including custom tailored pants, skirts, and tops, and hemp jeans), footwear, accessories, and body care.
Tel: (800) 226-0924
http://www.g-roots.com

Patagonia
Outdoor clothing made from recycled plastic bottles and organic cotton.
Tel: (800) 336-9090 (toll-free)
http://www.patagonia.com

Pesticides Action Network
Independent U.K. charity addressing the health and environmental problems of pesticides.
http://www.gn.apc.org/pesticidestrust

Waste not

Adbusters—the Media Foundation
Organization concerned with "the erosion of our physical and cultural environments by commercial forces." Challenges and parodies advertising.
http://adbusters.org

Alliance to Save Energy
Organization promoting energy efficiency—useful website with lots of tips for the home. National database of lenders offering energy-efficiency mortgages, plus an interactive home energy check up.
http://www.ase.org

Cellulose Insulation Manufacturers Association
For information on cellulose insulation.
Tel: (937) 222-2462
Fax: (937) 222-5794
Email: CIMA@dayton.net
http://www.cellulose.org

Clivus Multrum
Make composting toilets in various models.
15 Union Street, Lawrence,
MA 01840
Tel: (800) 962-8447
Fax: (978) 557-9658

CREST
Information on renewable energy and sustainable technology, with fact sheets for each state offering energy saving tips and local information. Excellent links, including one to a database for homeowners interested in financing resource for energy-efficiency projects.
http://solstice.crest.org/index.shtml

Eco Shop
Energy-saving home and garden accessories such as solar-powered battery chargers.
Tel: +44 870 300-111
Fax: +44 870 300-222
www.solar.org.uk/ecoshop

Energy Star Products
For information on washing machines, refrigerators, dishwashers, and room air conditioners with the Energy Star rating that denotes energy efficiency, including a store locator.
Tel: (888) STAR YES
http://www.energystar.gov

Ethical Consumer
U.K.-based magazine aimed at helping readers make informed choices by comparing brands on an ethical basis. Website has lots of interesting links.
Unit 21
41 Old Birley Street
Manchester M15 5RF
United Kingdom
Tel: +44 161-226-2929
http://www.ethicalconsumer.org

Green Mountain Energy
Supplier of energy from renewable sources. Website gives the low down on where your state's power comes from.
Tel: (888) 246-6730 (toll free)
http://www.greenmountain.com

Kohler Company
Eco-sinks that make composting kitchen waste easy—a plastic chute leads straight from the sink-top to a plastic bucket under the sink.
Kohler, WI 53044
(920) 457-4441, (800) 4-KOHLER
http://www.kohler.com

Wastewatch
A U.K.-based organization that works with community groups, local authorities, and industry to educate and raise awareness of waste reduction, reuse, and recycling. Useful information on waste reduction and recycling for houseowners.
http://www.wastewatch.org.uk

General

EcoMall
Huge online shopping center with links to retailers of all sorts of environmentally-kinder products, including natural pest control, bedding, hemp products, green office supplies, and pet products.
http://www.ecomall.com

Green Marketplace
Mail order store offering organic clothing with a business range for women, as well as beauty care, cleaning, childcare, and gardening products.
http://www.greenmarketplace.com

MotherNature.com
For natural home goods, pet products, bath and body products, and aromatherapy and candles.
Tel: 1 800 517 9020
http://www.mothernature.com

The New Natural House Book
An excellent, in-depth look at healthier houses and how to create them.
By David Pearson, Gaia Books, 1989, 1998

What Doctors Don't Tell You
Newsletter offering in-depth, critical insights into what goes into our cosmetics, toiletries, food, and more.
Satellite House
2 Salisbury Road
London
SW19 4EZ
Tel: +44 20-8944-9555
Fax: + 44 20 8944-9888
www.wddty.co.uk

Working Assets
Credit card that gives ten cents to nonprofit groups every time it's used.
Tel: (800) 877-3872
http://www.workingassets.com

organic

chapter three

garden

Thinking organic

Growing organically works, and is worth doing, whatever the size of your garden. If you live in an apartment in town and your garden is a window box, or your crops consist of a row of herb pots on a windowsill, you can start to think organic. As your garden grows you will begin to see changes in your environment and benefits to the world outside your gate.

Health and safety

People grow organic foods for a variety of reasons. These might be ethical, financial, emotional, concerned with health and safety or freedom of choice, or just for the sheer pleasure of eating organic food and being surrounded by organic flowers alive with bees and butterflies. Most often it is a combination of all these but perhaps the initial motivation is to produce healthy food in a safe environment.

If you are not using chemicals—pesticides, herbicides, fungicides, artificial fertilizers—you don't have to worry about safe storage, protective clothing, children, pets, and wildlife coming into contact with them, or water runoff into fishponds. Nor are there withdrawal periods for produce. You can walk out into the garden, pick an apple at the peak of its goodness and flavor and crunch into it there and then.

The debate continues about the difference between organic and conventionally produced food but people are increasingly reluctant to accept official reassurances about the safety of inorganic methods.

If you garden organically you not only avoid the obvious risks, but also remove the threats to the multiple layers of life in our soil, from the more noticeable worms and beetles to the thousands of microscopic organisms present in the earth. Since these are the allies in your organic campaign you will start to feel the benefits as they do.

The wider world

And of course, as soon as you opt for "cleaner" gardening you will begin to benefit the wider environment. Nature does not recognize garden boundaries. Birds, insects, wind-born pollen, and seeds make our gardens just a part of the living world. Every change you make towards a more natural way of gardening will shift the balance in favor of the vitality of that world.

It is, of course, no comfort to us if the pesticides that we ban in the West are used in the countries that our food comes from, often inappropriately and with far fewer safeguards.

The wider world is also affected by the foods we ourselves demand and where they come from. The average North American supermarket stocks apples from Argentina, Chile, South Africa, and New Zealand, red peppers from Holland, and a whole range of exotic fruit from South America. Even though much of the food consumed will have been produced within the continent, this may still mean that food has traveled long distances to your plate.

These "food miles" add a huge energy cost to our food, for transportation and refrigeration and, because they increase the distance between plant and plate, there is bound to be a loss in nutritional value. There is a school of thought that food most suited to us is grown locally. Food processing itself also adds to the environmental cost.

Buying exotic or out of season foods from abroad also encourages the growing of cash crops. The economies and agriculture of many developing countries are distorted by vast tracts of land being turned over to the production of luxury crops for export. While this brings in cash (for agribusiness, at least) it makes huge areas of land unavailable for growing food crops for local consumption.

Such a use of land is vulnerable to food fashions in the West—for example, mangetout may be right off the dinner party menu next year—and such farming is generally highly chemicalized. (This applies especially to the growing of flowers in developing countries to provide exotic blooms for the western market. Saying it with a bunch of organic home-grown flowers would be much more meaningful.)

DID YOU KNOW?

Short drift

Lawn herbicides are easily tracked indoors and can contaminate carpets for over a year. Residues on floors and surfaces can then become a source of exposure for young children. Detectable spray drift was located forty-eight feet away from sprayed areas, in large enough quantities for detectable residues to be tracked indoors.

Source: EPA and Batelle Memorial Institute research 1996

Earthing ourselves

Growing our own organic food on the other hand keeps us in touch with our own plot of earth. The Native American walking meditation, "Give your foot to the earth" recognizes that earth is the foundation of all our life and that we need to keep in contact with it.

Moreover, it is apparent that for many people gardening, and particularly the growing of food, is a great stress reliever.

Whether this is because of the physical exercise and fresh air, or the satisfaction at producing your own vegetables, fruit, flowers, or herbs, or some much more subtle process at work, doesn't matter. The average American spends nine and a half hours per day in front of a screen of some sort—television, cinema, or computer. Being in touch with the natural world and being aware of the progress of the seasons, is bound to make us just that much more whole.

Understanding where our food comes from is part of this process and this is particularly true for children. Getting children involved in gardening from an early age is one of the best ways to give them this understanding and is also one of the most useful skills you can give them.

> ### DID YOU KNOW?
>
> **What you can't see…**
> *Up to 80 percent of pesticides sprayed on Asian rice paddies (including many banned in the U.S.) are used for the wrong pests or sprayed at the wrong time.*
>
> Source: International Rice Research Institute report 1997

Supply and demand

One third of U.S. consumers buy organic food at least once or twice a month, and 85 percent strongly favor nationwide labeling standards for organic food. However by 1997 (the most recent year for which figures are available) only 0.2 percent of all U.S. cropland was certified organic. Many American farmers are keen to convert to organic methods but the organic subsidy is only a tiny fraction of the billions of dollars allocated to conventional subsidy programs. Meanwhile, each year, three hundred different chemicals are sprayed onto 95 percent of crops.

Consumer demand will gradually bring about an increase in organic produce. But, because demand still far outstrips supply, growing your own will also save you money. In fact the growing demand for organic food will also mean that you will have no trouble in selling any surpluses that you have to your friends and neighbors. Though seed is no longer cheap and costing your time might alter the balance somewhat, there is great satisfaction when the food that you are putting on the table at dinner time, is healthy produce that you have not had to buy. Just one packet of cauliflower seed could produce forty heads of cauliflower for the price of one from the store.

Variety and taste

You also get far more choice. Growing your own gives you a huge choice of varieties. The Home Garden catalog for Johnny's Selected Seeds contains ten varieties each of carrot and sweet corn, twenty-eight kinds of lettuce and thirty-one different varieties of beans (bush beans, pole beans, fava (broad) beans, dry beans, shell beans, soybeans). These variations are not just to do with taste, storage quality, or the look of the vegetable on the plate. It also gives you a choice of disease resistance, and suitability to your particular growing conditions—particularly important when you are growing organically.

For flavor, you can't beat growing your own. This is partly because the food will be that much fresher. The vitamins in a fruit or vegetable are at their peak just before they are ready for picking. Once picked a series of chemical changes occurs as the plant converts sugar to starch or closes down its outer cells to conserve its inner vitality. So the taste of freshly picked produce reflects its nutritional value.

DID YOU KNOW?

Food flight
The average food molecule consumed in Canada travels one hundred miles from source to plate.

Source: "Get A Life" Wayne Roberts & Susan Brandu, Get A Life Publishing House

In addition the varieties you can grow at home may have much more flavor than commercial varieties in the first place. Those grown on a large scale and those that have to survive mechanical harvesting, transport, storage and still have some "shelf life," may be chosen more for their thick skins, or their uniform shape, or their capacity to ripen uniformly for easy harvesting, rather than their tenderness or flavor.

And, of course, once you have been growing for more than one season you can start taking note of what varieties your family likes, selecting your regular crops, and introducing one or two new varieties each year.

Freedom to choose

Altogether you will be far more in control of what you eat. This is even more important in the age of genetically modified food. The GM debate will continue to rage for some time, but organic gardeners are concerned with the mounting evidence about the safety of GM crops. Growing your own organic food will greatly reduce the impact of GMOs on you and your family. But you will still be affected by their use in the wider world and there is great scope for getting involved in the campaigning side of the organic movement. Such campaigning is not obligatory, but supporting an organic organization such as The Rodale Research Institute will add your voice to those concerned about the wider implications of what we grow and eat.

As soon as you start to grow organically you will have begun to take control of your food, your health, and your impact upon the wider environment.

Basic principles

The organic gardener has the same attitude with their garden as the holistic therapist has with the body. The organic approach to health sees the body not as a machine with separate parts that can go wrong and are then corrected or replaced, but as a whole organism in which all parts interrelate. In the same way, the organic approach to gardening treats the garden environment as a whole and aims to boost the health of that environment rather than just feeding or curing individual plants.

Back to the soil

The basis of all good gardening is the soil. It might look unexciting, but it carries all the nutrients, minerals, and trace elements needed by your growing plants, and is home to millions of tiny organisms that make it a living, vital environment for them.

So all your garden activities should be helping to keep the soil "in good heart" and the basic rule is to feed the soil rather than the plant. Artificial fertilizers give the plant a quick boost but are then, just as quickly, leached out of the soil. They can further cause excessive, sappy growth that leaves the plant "overstretched" and more vulnerable to pests and diseases. The cell walls are softer and more of a target for insect attack.

Balance and vitality

Feeding the soil with organic matter means that the plants take up nutrients more gradually and in the proportions that they need. This does not mean that you can never offer "first aid" (diluted urine can do wonders for growing plants that show the characteristic pale yellow leaves of nitrogen deficiency) or that there is no point in foliar

DID YOU KNOW?

Pesticide pests

A report in Pesticides News *quotes research from Duke University, North Carolina, showing that when three pesticides (used at their correct levels) were combined, the toxicity was increased by a factor of several hundred.*

Source: MAFF Annual Report of Working Party on Pesticides Residues 1999

FACTS

Counting the calories

Forty calories of energy go into the production of a can of corn for every calorie of food energy in the can.

Source: The "Toronto Star" 1999

DID YOU KNOW?

Worms

U.S. Department of Agriculture tests show a huge reduction in earthworm numbers, and damage to the soil fungi, following use of fertilizers such as ammonium sulfate. Applying organic compost or manure on the other hand increases the worm population by approximately 13 percent.

Source: "The Therapeutic Garden," Donald Norfolk, Bantam Press 2000

feeding (such as a seaweed spray). However, the basis of your fertility is a healthy soil.

There is a whole range of constituents in the soil, held in balance if the soil is healthy. Our nutrition and health increasingly depends on subtle elements—from protein, to vitamins and minerals, to trace elements, and an even more indefinable "vitality" in foods. In the same way the soil is more than a combination of minerals. Artificial feeding with a dose of two or three minerals may cause a glut of one particular mineral that in turn may lock up others in the soil and make these minerals unavailable to plants.

Working with nature

Organic gardeners work alongside nature rather than in opposition to it. Rather than the negative approach of "how to get rid of weeds and kill pests" (though the organic gardener does actually do both on occasion) it is a positive policy of using natural methods to keep things in balance. So chemical pesticides, herbicides, and fungicides are abandoned in favor of preventative methods of pest and disease control.

Organic gardeners are the original "recyclers." Rather than garden "waste" being a problem to be taken down to the dump, or burned at home, almost everything is recycled within the garden. As much household waste as possible is composted or recycled and all the products of the garden itself find their way, via composting, mulching, or structural use, back into the garden.

These basic rules provide the framework for your organic gardening. The following pages explain how to start.

The groundwork includes understanding your soil, knowing how to improve it, and ways of protecting and feeding it, including the art and science of compost making. Then you can get on with planning, laying out, and planting your vegetable garden.

Once you start to think organic it becomes logical to make your whole environment healthy and safe. Fruit, herbs, and flowers all benefit from the organic approach. Growing under cover and growing in containers are also included.

Having done all this work you will want to reap the benefits. Pest, disease, and weed control will make sure that you, and not the bugs, get the rewards, and there is a whole battery of resources at the disposal of the organic gardener.

Finally you can harvest, store, and even save seeds for next year, and settle down to the thoroughly satisfying job of planning the next season's gardening.

Starting with the soil

There are five ways to keep your soil happy and healthy: composting, mulching, green manuring, crop rotation, and not walking on it. In other words—keep the soil fed and protected, give it variety and avoid rough treatment.

Each of these techniques is covered in detail below but the first step is to discover what sort of soil you are starting with and how to correct the initial imbalances. The more you understand about what's going on in your garden the more successful and satisfying your gardening will be—but don't feel that you need to get buried in the complexities of it all! Just understanding and applying one basic rule—to feed the soil with organic matter—will get your garden moving and growing in the right direction. So don't get intimidated by all the technical stuff. Just get out there and make a compost bin.

Soil has a structure. This can be either compressed with airless "clods of earth," or it can be a delicate structure of soil particles interspersed with air and water. What we put onto and in the soil, how much pressure we apply with our boots or heavy watering, how much we expose it to heat or cold, rain, or drying, and even what we grow in it, will all affect the structure.

The soil that you start off with in your garden will be the result of what naturally occurs in the area where you live and also how the previous owner has treated it. You will be able to see how compressed and generally poor (or rich!) it looks but it will help if you can discover the texture of the soil and find out whether it is acid or alkaline.

What sort of texture?

Soils are composed of sand, silt, clay, chalk, peat, or a combination of these. The difference is in the size of the particles and the amount of nutrients that they carry. The texture can be analyzed by a simple hand test. Hold a teaspoon of soil in the palm of the hand and gradually add a little water, molding the soil until it is as close to plasticene as you can get. The feel of the soil between finger and thumb—whether it is gritty, smooth, or sticky—and how easily it can be rolled out or formed, shows what kind of soil it is.

Sandy Soils contain large particles, have a gritty feel, and can't be formed into rolls or rings. They contain little plant foods and, because they drain very quickly, what nutrients they have can be lost. But these soils have good aeration, are easily worked, and warm up quickly.

Silty Soils feel very silky to the touch. They have small particles, so they can pack down when wet but are moderately fertile.

Clay Soils are very sticky to the touch and can easily be molded in the hand. They contain the smallest particles, and therefore can be heavy and cold when wet, but hard and cracked when dry. Thus, they have poor drainage and a low air content and are slow to warm up in spring. Their advantage is that they can be quite high in nutrients.

Chalky Soils often contain a lot of large particles so they drain easily. They are very alkaline, which limits the range of plants that can be grown in them.

Peaty Soils do not drain well and can be very acidic. They have high organic matter content but usually a low nutrient content.

Loamy Soils are a mixture of sand, clay, and silt, so they provide many advantages.

You cannot change the texture of your soil (short of excavating and replacing it, which is possible for small, raised beds,) but you can change the structure. Soil structure depends upon the way the individual particles hold together. An ideal structure contains "crumbs" of soil, through which water and air can move freely but which retains nutrients. Heavy rain or watering, or pressure from walking or machinery, will break down the crumbs. Long-term chemical farming also has this result.

Adding organic matter helps the particles to form into crumbs, improving aeration and drainage but also helping the soil to hold moisture. So adding compost, manure, or other bulk organic materials can be helpful, whatever the soil you start with. It will lighten clay soil, improve the drainage, and allow more air in. On the other hand, it will give more substance to sandy soils, improve their water-holding capacity, and of course, raise their nutrient levels.

Acid or alkaline?

The acidity or alkalinity of soil is measured as a pH level: 7 is neutral, above 7 is alkaline, and below 7 is acid.

The level can be measured with a simple test kit, available from garden stores or catalogs. The analysis is useful because it affects what you can grow well and tells you when you need to correct the balance for a particular crop. Certain vegetables will be more vulnerable to pest and disease attack if the level is wrong for them. For example, potatoes will be more susceptible to scab if the soil is too alkaline, whereas brassicas (the cabbage family) would be much more likely to get clubroot in acid conditions.

Making the soil too acid or too alkaline will also affect the amount of nutrients available to plants. Most vegetables and fruit grow well in a soil with a pH of about 6.5.

The best policy is to treat just the area of ground that the particular crop will be occupying. That way, if you are practicing crop rotation each section of the garden will be limed, for example, every four or five years.

Rich or poor?

Soil can also be tested for the level of nutrients it contains. Simple home test kits will give you the levels for at least the three major elements—nitrogen, phosphorus, and potassium. These three are important for, respectively, shoots, roots, and fruits, and the test results will show you what you need to supplement.

	Important for:	Deficiency causes:	Use:
Nitrogen	foliage growth and health	pale, yellow-green leaves, and stunted growth	animal manures, urine, comfrey and nettle manures, horn meal
Phosphorous	root development	poor root development, and blue tinging of leaves.	natural rock phosphate, or bone meal
Potassium	fruit formation	stunted plants and fruit, and brown scorching along the leaf edges	comfrey, seaweed meal, or rock potash. Use wood ash in the compost heap

Most importantly—for the long term creation of a balance of all the essential nutrients—there is nothing to beat feeding the soil with good compost.

Other minerals and various trace elements are also important to healthy growth of plants. In general, although obvious deficiencies can be corrected by specific first aid applications, overfeeding with any one element will also cause problems. The answer, once again, is to add organic matter in the form of a good compost.

To dig or not to dig

In the long-term, you are aiming to create a stable environment that is not putting the soil structure, and the life within it, under stress. Traditionally gardens have been dug each year, to remove weeds and break up the clods to produce a fine structure. On heavy soil, in particular, this would be done in the autumn to allow winter frosts to break up the soil. In the spring the soil would be raked to a fine tilth, and then systematically compressed by walking to and fro on it. Don't Do It!

We are now increasingly realizing that soil is best left undisturbed. In natural conditions the soil remains unturned but is gradually built up as leaves fall and vegetation dies down. Worms and other soil creatures process this decaying matter and pull it down. Seeds fall, germinate, and grow in the rich compost on the surface and the cycle starts again.

In our gardens we should aim to reproduce this natural process. The only difference being that we can control what we want to germinate and grow. So, the only time that beds really need to be dug are those that are first being brought into cultivation, in order to remove perennial weeds and break up hard-panned soil. The most thorough way to do this is by double digging, that is, cultivating the soil to two spade depths—explained below.

Double Digging

Mark out a trench across the width of the bed and dig out the soil to one spade depth. Barrow this soil to the other end of the bed. The next spade depth is thoroughly forked over and compost or manure mixed in with it. The next trench is marked out and the soil from this one is turned into the first trench. And so on down the bed, filling the last trench with the first batch of soil that you dug out.

After this, all that is needed is shallow surface cultivation to incorporate more compost. Remove weeds by hoeing or shallow forking. And the only time that you should need to do pre-Christmas digging is if your soil is very heavy and you want to produce a seedbed ready for the spring.

Cutting and covering

Double digging is hard work. If you have the time to wait, ground can be prepared by "cutting and covering." Cut down all the surface vegetation and cover with polyethylene or carpet. The polyethylene should be opaque black. The heavier the gauge, the better because it will exclude the most light and will last longer.

Cutting and covering

Black poly will need to be weighted down or pushed into the ground. Push the spade in and pull it back towards you. Push about six inches of the poly in, using a thin piece of board (the spade would split it), and push the soil back with your foot. If you do this along each side it will prevent the wind from lifting it up.

Carpet will need to be weighted down with wood or soil. Use hessian-backed carpet rather than foam-backed because the latter will disintegrate into the soil.

Or Use a thick layer of hay or straw. Once it has been damped down by the first shower of rain it will not blow away. Though using hay risks introducing grass and weed seeds, if the layer is thick enough they will not germinate under the hay. When it is first removed the ground can be left for the first flush of weed seeds to germinate and be hoed off.

Or To combine the best of both systems, first cover the soil with thick cardboard. This can be collected free from stores if you check what morning they put out their packaging for the garbage collection. Add a thick layer of hay or straw. Then you can make planting holes through all the layers and the whole covering can be left in place around the growing plants to rot down gradually.

Some gardeners keep a permanent covering of straw on their soil, only drawing it aside for seed sowing, and never dig at all. Others apply a regular layer of compost, simply spread upon the surface and left for the worms to incorporate.

Mulching

It is a good general rule never to leave the soil uncovered. Wind, rain, and extremes of temperature can all affect its structure, and bare soil will, in any case, be rapidly covered with weeds. If the ground is not producing a crop it can be sown with a green manure (see below) or mulched.

A mulch is basically a cover for the soil. It can be inert, such as carpet or polyethylene, or "live" such as a layer of compost or

FACTS

Superweed

Transgenic organisms found in GM crops can introduce new allergens into our food and can crosspollinate with wild plants to create superweeds.

Source: Botanical Society of America symposium 1997

manure, hay, or straw. The advantage of live mulches is that they will feed the soil. Even hay and straw will gradually rot down. Unless they are applied very thickly they will not be completely light-excluding and the most vigorous of the perennial weeds, such as docks, may come through. However, these individuals are easily removed.

Mulches can insulate the ground from heat and cold, or from excessive rain, and it is important to put them on when the soil is in the condition that you want to maintain. So the soil must be reasonably moist to start off with, and must not be cold. Add them once the soil has warmed up in spring.

Inert Mulches

If black poly is to be left on and planted through, then watering will have to be directed through the planting slits or by means of a seep-hose underneath. Woven polyethylene mulches are also available, and these suppress weeds but are permeable to rain. Carpet is also suitable for permanent ground cover on paths, for example, and can be covered with bark or chippings for appearance.

Cardboard and newspaper are the cheapest of the inert mulches and will eventually rot in, but don't use glossy papers because of the chemical print. A thick layer of paper will be needed and can be covered with bark or straw to keep it down and to improve the appearance.

Live Mulches

Of the live mulches the best would be compost or manure. Leaf mold is low in nutrients but is good for suppressing weeds and increasing the moisture retentiveness of the soil. Live mulches that have not been composted will cause nitrogen robbery if dug in—nitrogen is needed for the breakdown process—so hay, straw, and bark need to be left as a surface mulch. However they will gradually rot down on their own and the worms will pull in the composted material.

The compost heap–every garden should have one

The compost bin is at the heart of the organic garden. Every garden should have one, no matter how small the area. You could even have a worm bin in the kitchen.

There is great mystique attached to the making of compost and the composting process is complex and amazing; however, what you actually have to do is very

---

HINTS AND TIPS

Mulches

• *suppress weeds*

• *keep in the moisture*

• *protect the soil from heavy rain*

• *insulate the soil from heat and cold*

• *provide shelter for worms to get on with their good work*

• *"live" mulches also feed the soil*

simple. A pile of natural materials left on the ground will gradually, but inevitably, return to the earth. A pile of logs would take a long time; a heap of grass clippings and apple peelings would go down very quickly, and neither "compost" would be of very good quality. But the process would happen without any help from you.

When you make compost you are just improving on the process: perhaps speeding it up, so that your compost is ready sooner; heating it up so that more weed seeds and disease spores are killed off; or improving the structure and nutrient level of the finished compost, so that you can use it for different purposes.

There are various "recipes" for making compost but the basic ingredients are:
- **Warmth**, some sort of shelter and insulation
- **Air**, via some sort of ventilation
- **Moisture**, but not too much
- **A good mixture of compostable materials**, see below
- **An activator**, to get the process started

Given these conditions the most varied and unlikely materials will compost down into the right stuff—dark brown, crumbly, and sweet-smelling.

Keep it together

A composter of some sort not only keeps it all tidy, but helps the heap to heat up by keeping it together and insulating it from the wind and rain. The warmth encourages the activity of the organisms that break down the compost. The higher the temperature you can reach in a "hot" compost, the greater the sterilizing effect on weed seeds and disease spores.

The size of your bin will depend on how much material you've got to fill it (it's hard to make too much compost), but a bin much smaller than a meter square is unlikely to heat up sufficiently.

Air is needed to aid this process, just as fires need air to burn. Rather than having slatted sides to the bin, start the heap with a layer of coarse material so that air can get in at the base, and create mini-chimneys in the heap by inserting vertical rods as it is built up, which can be removed at the end.

Two or more bins in a row will enable one heap to be composting down as the next is constructed. You can buy a standard wooden bin or you can build your own if you have basic carpentry skills.

The ideal bin is a wooden one, made of planks butted together. This can be made with three fixed sides and a removable front, for easy removal of the finished compost.

Alternatively you can make a series of frames which can be placed one on top of the other as the heap is built up and removed once it has composted.

Another, cheaper way of providing an insulated bin is to use a double wall of chicken wire, stapled round four posts, with straw or hay packed down between the walls. This will obviously need rebuilding each season.

If you have a large area, another temporary bin can be made with straw bales. These give excellent insulation and can be made to any size. The bales will eventually rot and can then be composted themselves.

There are also commercial plastic composters available. A very large heap can be made free standing, as long as the sides are firmed and as near the vertical as possible, and can be covered with old carpet or weighted down with bricks. These heaps need to be made all in one go (see Hot Or Cold on page 142.)

Cover it up

Some sort of covering to the bin will help keep the warmth in and the rain out. Without any moisture the composting process would not happen—but too much rain will cool it down and produce a soggy collection of half-composted material. The ideal texture is that of a squeezed sponge. If the compost is too dry you may notice the white threads of "firefang" in it, or that ants may be nesting in it. So moisture needs to be introduced as the heap is built up, by watering from the tap or water butt, or by applications of HLA ("Household Liquid Activator" or urine). Once the heap is completed it should be covered with a wooden lid (sloping to aid runoff), heavy carpet, or thick poly, fixed and weighted down to prevent it from blowing away. A thick hay mulch would also provide good insulation and protect from excessive rain.

Site the bin for ease of use. If it is close at hand rather than at the very bottom of the garden you are more likely to use it—though a small collecting bin can be kept in the kitchen and emptied daily into an intermediate bin outside the door. Since it is

easier to move the ingredients than the finished compost, site it on the highest point of the garden, if possible. That way you can barrow finished compost down to the beds. Set it on bare soil, so that worms colonize the heap and excess liquid drains off.

The ingredients

The key to good compost making is a variety of ingredients that bring different nutrients to the heap and also support different kinds of fungi and bacteria. When all these work together, they break down the heap. A mixed heap will work more effectively and faster.

Anything that has once lived can go into the heap, the greater variety the better, but there are a few cautions to heed, so check the boxes and the notes below.

Do use	And for your activator	Don't use
kitchen vegetable waste	animal manures (*but see right*)	cat and dog feces
tea leaves, coffee grounds	comfrey	metal
egg shells	nettles	glass
garden vegetable waste	seaweed	plastic
weeds	(from unpolluted beaches)	disposable diapers
dead flowers	grass clippings	coal ash
cardboard and paper	compost accelerator powder	meat and fish scraps
wood ash	urine	
old wool or cotton clothing		
mushroom compost*		
straw and hay*		
wool or feathers*		

* Check that mushroom composts, straw, and hay are from organic sources, that wool waste does not contain residues from chemical dips, and that feathers come from acceptable production systems. If you are concerned about organic gardening you will almost certainly be concerned about animal welfare also. Manure should be stable manure, from horses or cows. Pig manure is too cold and wet.

Grass clippings should be well mixed in, because if they are in a thick layer they will become slimy. Card and paper, on the other hand, are very dry materials. Some organic gardeners make compost simply with a mixture of paper (not "glossy" paper), and clippings well mixed together.

Leaves are best composted separately. They take longer to break down and produce a compost that is low in nutrients, but excellent for improving soil structure and moisture retention. Normally leaf mold needs to be stacked for two years, enclosed in a simple wire bin, but the process can be speeded up by turning, adding lawn clippings, chopping up (run the mower over a layer of leaves on the lawn), or watering with urine.

Hot or cold

There are two methods of making compost, depending upon the time and energy that you have to spare.

The cold and slow compost is built up gradually, ingredients added onto the top of the heap as they come to hand. When the heap is finished, it is covered and left to get on with things. According to the time of year, it will take six months to a year to compost down. The resulting compost will provide the same amount of nutrients (depending on the ingredients) and benefits to soil structure but will not have heated enough to destroy weeds and pathogens.

The hot and quick compost is made all in one go. It will be ready much sooner, and will have heated enough to destroy the undesirables. For this method the ingredients are collected separately—kitchen waste, weeds, nettles, manure, grass clippings, etc.—and the heap is then layered up rather like a giant sandwich, watered between layers and covered. Over the next few weeks it will collapse down to an alarming (or encouraging) extent. It is then turned out, mixed up so that the cool outer layers are turned inwards and more air is introduced, and turned back into the bin. If you are really keen, or desperate for quick compost, you can repeat the process again several weeks later. Made this way over the summer, compost will be ready in a few months.

A worm bin in the kitchen

Worms make very high quality compost. Because it is basically worm casts there will be no weeds in it and its nutrient levels are high. The method is suitable for small scale composting and the container is hygienic enough to keep indoors. In fact, since the worms work best at a temperature between 36°F and 51°F, the house or an insulated

HINTS AND TIPS

Collecting "bits"

It is not always easy to gather, or store, enough material to make compost all in one go. You could combine the two methods by spreading all the compostable material in the chicken run. The hens enjoy scratching through it all (and supplement their feed in the process). Start the breakdown of the materials, mix it up efficiently, and at the same time add the activator in the form of their manure. When there is sufficient material it is gathered up into the bin, watered if necessary, and left to complete composting.

The bin will need

• *air holes at the top*

• *a thick layer of wet newspaper to cover the vegetable waste, added little and often, on top of the bedding, made of well-rotted compost*

• *leafmold or shredded paper on slatted boards over sand or gravel to give good drainage*

• *some drainage holes at the base*

shed is ideal. For indoors, using one of the commercial bins, with a tap for the runoff, is best, but for a shed or outdoors you could make your own from an old garbage can.

Follow the do's and don'ts listed on page 141 for compost ingredients, but avoid grass in any quantity.

To extract the compost you can encourage the worms to the top with a fresh layer of something tempting, leave it for a couple of weeks and then scrape it off with most of the worms in it. Tip out the digested compost and start again. See small classifieds in the back of *Organic Gardening* magazine for supplies of worms or hunt through your existing compost for the little red "brandling" worms.

Strong stuff

Manure can be used on its own but should be from animals bedded on straw rather than on shavings. Goat manure is good because of their varied diet. Fresh manure should be stacked and covered and used well-rotted. Stacking for nine months is recommended if the manure is from a nonorganic farm. If you keep hens, wood ash scattered on the droppings board will not only keep the hen house dry and sweet but will produce a concentrated fertilizer with a combination of nitrogen and potash. Sawdust could also be used. The decaying sawdust uses up the excessive nitrogen in the manure, producing a milder mixture.

Comfrey, mentioned already as a compost activator, is one of the most important plants for the organic gardener. Though there is still some caution about its use internally, it is invaluable for garden use. It has more nitrogen than farmyard manure, equivalent phosphate, and much more potassium. So, it is worth planting even a small patch of it, which can be cut two or three times per year and used in the compost heap, in potato trenches, made into a liquid manure, or mixed with equal quantities of leafmold.

HINTS AND TIPS

Make liquid manures from

• *a hessian sack of animal manure suspended in water*

• *comfrey leaves filling a barrel and covered with water*

• *nettles prepared as for comfrey*

All of these can be left for several weeks and then strained and used undiluted or diluted five to one on seedlings. They can get very smelly so it helps to cover the bin.

HINTS AND TIPS

Concentrated Comfrey Manure

This manure is made by packing leaves into a barrel without water but with a tap for the runoff at the bottom. A "comfrey column" can be made from a length of plastic drainpipe stuffed with leaves, with a bottle of water resting on the top of the leaves to gradually push them down. They will disintegrate and the resulting liquid will emerge at the base of the column. This manure will be much richer and should be diluted ten or twenty to one.

Spreading the benefits

Compost or leafmold should be applied at the rate of about one barrelful per five square yards of ground; use manure at half this rate. They are best applied in the growing season, that is, where crops are about to be grown or are already growing. If applied in the autumn or winter, much of the goodness will leach out with winter rains, though the composts will benefit the structure of the soil at whatever time. Chapter 3 will tell you which groups of crops benefit most from composts and manure. Worm compost—because it is produced in smaller quantities and is of high quality—should be used for special applications, for example, in planting holes or seed rows, or as an ingredient in seed or potting mixtures.

Green manures

You can grow crops especially for composting. Sunflowers or Jerusalem artichokes produce a bulk of coarse material that would make a good base for a compost. You can also grow green manures for incorporating directly.

Green manures or cover crops are plants selected for the bulk of organic matter they provide or the goodness they can give to the soil. They are, in fact, a form of live mulching with all the benefits of mulches and the addition of extra nutrients when they are dug in. They can be sown wherever a bed is free of crops—and allowed to die down or be dug in—to benefit the soil directly. Thus, they make use of spare ground, keep it covered and weed free, and make extra nutrients available for the following crops. Some, such as Winter Tares or Grazing Rye, have the extra benefit of inhibiting seed germination and so are suitable for beds to be planted with young vegetables, potatoes, or onion sets rather than for seed beds.

Which green manure you sow will depend on the time of year, how long the bed will be free for, and what section of the garden it is in. For example, some belong to the brassica family (B) and are susceptible to the same diseases. Others are legumes

(L), in the same family as beans and peas, and can fix nitrogen in the ground.

Below are just a few examples of green manure. They are generally broadcast rather than sown in rows, although you should check the packets for spacing and quantities. Composting, mulching, and green manuring will all help produce the optimum conditions for growing. Now you can get on with planning and planting.

Green manures: Legume/Brassica		Sow:	Duration months:
Alfalfa/Lucerne (L)	Very deep rooting and rich in minerals, but to get the full benefit you need to have spare ground for a whole season.	Apr-Jul	1 year plus
Red Clover (L)	High nitrogen and very good for improving soil structure.	Apr-Aug	3 months or more
Mustard (B)	A fast grower and good weed suppresser. Brassica family. See crop rotation.	Mar-Sep	1-2 months
Grazing Rye	Very bulky crop and can be sown late but can be tough to dig in.	early spring to late summer	overwinter
Hairy Vetch (L)	Early sowing for weed suppressing but will overwinter. Very good for both fertility and structure of soil.	Mar-May	2-3 months
		Jul-Sep	overwinter

The vegetable garden

Planning your layout can be one of the most enjoyable parts of gardening. Writing "carrots" and "onions" in neat lines feels like you are half way to growing them. But, first work out what you actually like eating, and look at the seed catalogs to get some idea of how much you can expect to harvest from, say, a four-yard row of seed bed. You will avoid ending up with pounds of beets that nobody actually likes, and it will make best use of your valuable space.

If you have a small garden you may decide to leave out fall- and winter-eating potatoes. In a very small space, the most productive use of your vegetable plot may be a variety of salads. These can be sown in succession and can be cut-and-come-again mixtures like mesclun mixes, including lettuces, endive, or various oriental salads.

Scale

Even if you only have room for a bed one yard by one yard you could grow a variety of vegetables by the "Square Foot Gardening" method. The bed is divided into nine equal squares, using strings stretched across, with one "crop" planted in each square. One square could hold five lettuces, nine beets, a thinly sown group of carrots, a patch of mesclun mix, or four mini-cabbages. Because the area is so small, it is never trodden on, and needs no space between the crops for access, it can all be top quality, nutrient-rich soil. As crops finish, the soil can be replenished and replanted, and the yields can be surprisingly high over the year.

On a larger plot a system of narrow beds has a lot of advantages. Some sort of design is useful whatever the size of the garden as it will help you to keep it organized and enable you to create the style you want in your plot. You may want a formal vegetable garden with the crops lined out in orderly beds. Or you might prefer the cottage garden style with vegetables, fruit, and herbs interspersed with flowers. However, even the most apparently casual style needs to have an underlying plan.

Draw an outline of your plot to scale, and mark out the beds. Add in any permanent plantings such as fruit trees. Keep copies of this outline plan and then each year you can fill in the cropping plan for that year. This is essential for planning your crop rotation (see page 148) and will serve as the basic record of previous years.

Keeping records

Keeping a record of what you actually did is even more important than the original plan. Noting down what you have sown, where, and when, prevents you from hoeing it up, resowing before it has emerged, or forgetting to sow it altogether.

The record can be a simple layout of the garden, large enough to provide three or four lines within each bed to write in the crops you have sown or planted out, with the date. You could also add an abbreviation for the origin of the seed, that is, the seed company that you used, or if you used your own saved seed. This is useful for checking on the quality of the seed, for example, how well it germinated.

You could also keep a more complete record that would include the harvest and any other comments.

The list below is quite detailed, (you could even add the weight of each crop harvested), or you might keep much simpler records. Any information is useful in helping you choose next year's varieties, plan your sowing dates, or alter the way you manage a crop.

HINTS AND TIPS

Garden diary

A sample garden diary entry from April 15th:
"Worked in the garden all afternoon. Planted the early potatoes, parallel rows in beds 3 (manured) and 4 (green manure, grazing rye, dug in). Then I planted out bed 10 with brassicas—cauliflowers and summer cabbages—while Graham cleared paths with the new turfing spade and the wheeled hoe. One of the wild drakes returned to the pond but the duck had taken her ducklings off somewhere so he was gone by suppertime. Netted the new brassicas against the birds. Frost at night."

Vegetable	Carrot	Broad Bean	Eggplant
Variety	Ithaca	Windsor	Black Beauty
Source	Johnny's	Saved	Shepherd's
Amount sown	3 x 6 yd rows	6 yd bed; 6" each way	2 seeds in 10 pots
Where	Bed 7 (roots)	Bed 5 (pulses)	Greenhouse
When	3.20.00	9.13.99	4.11.00
Germination	Medium, took a long time (sown too early?)	Good, up very quickly	9 out of 10
Thinned/planted out	5.19.00	no	planted tunnel 6.10.00
Harvested	during July	during June	August/September
Crop	good quantity of medium size roots	heavy crop	4+ per plant
Comment	some carrot fly damage, crop might have been heavier if thinned earlier	escaped blackfly damage but needed support against winter winds	smallish fruit but good flavor

A more informal way of recording your activities is with a garden diary. It will include some of the information in the record detailed, but might also record the weather, troubles with slugs and groundhogs, different recipes for seed and potting composts, a new compost heap built and covered, and so on. If you keep animals, then notes on animal care can be included, and the whole diary makes very interesting, and useful, reading in subsequent years.

Crop rotation

Crop rotation is one of the most important ways in which organic gardeners maintain the health of their land and plants and is therefore an essential part of annual planning. It simply means growing the same group of crops in a different bed each year.

Vegetables can be divided into four or five main groups. Similar vegetables have similar growing requirements and are likely to suffer from the same pests and diseases. So, it makes sense both to grow them in the same area of the garden and to move the whole group regularly to avoid the build up of problems. In addition, the different crops can leave particular benefits behind them for the next crop. The order in which the groups follow each other is also important.

Crop rotation works because:

Each crop has its own pests and diseases. Moving them around prevents buildup.

Each crop has its own feeding requirements Moving them means each bed receives the correct treatment in turn.

Different crops have different effects on the soil. Moving them maximizes the benefits to the soil and following crops.

You could have a three-course rotation

The exact grouping and order of rotations may vary from garden to garden. You may wish to grow more of one group than another, and this will affect the space you allocate. However, there are several miscellaneous vegetables that do not fit in with the main groups and can be used to fill the spaces. If you do not grow all the groups you may have only a three-fold rotation. On the other hand, if you grow a good range of vegetables, including potatoes, you may have a five-course rotation.

Because the vegetables within a group are in the same botanical family they will attract the same pest. For example, all the brassicas will attract cabbage worms; or they may suffer from the same diseases, for example, blight on potatoes and tomatoes or white rot on onions and garlic. Often the spores of a disease can remain dormant in the soil for years, and are woken up into activity when their host crop is planted. The longer the rotation the better.

Some vegetables need a richer soil than others. Some positively dislike a rich soil. For example, root crops such as carrots would be more likely to fork if planted in rich soil. Other vegetables like good feeding but prefer to be on ground that was manured for a previous crop. And they may prefer different levels of acidity or alkalinity. Because potatoes will be more liable to scab if the soil is too alkaline, and they are also greedy feeders, preparing the ground with manure and putting grass clippings in the trenches will create the right conditions for them. Brassicas, on the other hand, will suffer if the soil is too acid, so the brassica bed will benefit from liming before planting. Like everything else, brassicas will move along one section each year, and so this means that the whole garden will get limed once every four or five years.

Vegetable Families
The broad groupings are:

Solanums including potatoes, tomatoes, and eggplants. This group benefits from manure. Feed tomatoes with comfrey.

Onions including leeks, garlic, bunching onions, and shallots. They like a rich soil but not freshly manured soil.

Legumes sometimes called Pulses, including pole beans, broad beans, bush beans, peas, and several of the green manures. They would benefit from compost, and will leave nitrogen for brassicas: including cabbages, kale, brussels sprouts, green sprouting, broccoli, cauliflower, turnips, rutabagas, radishes, and mustard. They like lots of compost, or well-rotted manure applied the previous winter, but they also like lime.
Legumes would also leave nitrogen for roots: including carrots, parsnips, beets, celery, celeriac, and fennel. These vegetables do not like a rich soil, so they require no special feeding.

A crop may have a particular need for one nutrient and would leave the soil depleted if it was grown there for a number of years. On the other hand, some crops benefit the soil because they are deep rooting, bringing up nutrients from lower down in the soil, or helping to break up the soil. The legumes have the ability to "fix" nitrogen from the air, storing it in nodules on their roots. This nitrogen is of particular benefit to the brassicas. It makes sense to follow the legumes with brassicas.

You could have a four- or five-course rotation

In year two the potato bed will move down to where the roots were. The roots will move up to the brassica bed and so on up the garden. There are certain diseases that last in the soil for a lot longer than five years, which is why prevention is better than cure. If you get a case of white rot in onions, for example, you will need to record where it occurred and avoid planting the onion family there for eight years or more. However, you could use that section of the bed, when the onions come round in the five year rotation, for salad crops or another unrelated crop.

Crops of perennials—such as asparagus or globe artichokes—or crops that always regrow in the same place, such as Jerusalem artichokes, can have permanent beds. Salads can be tucked in to spaces in other beds. They are usually quick growing and can be used as "crops," filling in a space in your sowing timetable. Remember that radishes and some of the oriental salad plants are brassicas and should go in the brassica bed. The cucurbits—such as summer and winter squash, and zucchini—all like good feeding and could go in the potato section (or in whatever area you have a large gap) with special extra feeding.

The rotation may be complicated further if you wish to try some companion planting (see page 178). For example, some gardeners grow onions and carrots together to deter the carrot fly by scent confusion. Or you may interplant brassicas with beans to create a visual confusion for the cabbage butterfly. Everyone has their own rotation. The basic rule is not to grow the same crop in the same place before you need to, and to give each crop the conditions it prefers.

Making your crops comfortable

The conventional vegetable garden was laid out in rows, with no permanent paths but enough space to walk between each row to harvest the crops. At the end of the year the whole garden would be dug over. However, many gardeners, particularly organic gardeners, use a narrow bed system because of its advantages.

Narrow beds work well because compost and manure can be concentrated where it is needed, crops can be closely spaced, and weeds shaded out, so soil structure is

never compacted, and weeding is easier. In addition, the ground can be worked even in wet conditions, the raising of beds improves drainage, and the separation and rotation of crops becomes much easier.

The beds are approximately four feet wide with paths perhaps one foot wide. Once the initial ground preparation has been done the topsoil is spaded up from the paths onto beds. Being raised above the path level, excessive rain will drain off and the ground will be workable even in wet weather. The beds can be edged with boards that look tidy and retain the soil, but can harbor slugs and might be expensive over a large area. Or the beds can be given a curved profile by spading up the soil. This is good for drainage, and makes it easier to keep the edges weed free, though the birds can more easily drag compost off and, in heavy rain, soil can be washed off.

Managing your beds

Once made, the beds themselves should never be stepped on. Because they are only four feet wide they can be worked from both sides, so all weeding, sowing, and planting is done from the paths. Because the paths are permanent it does not matter that they get steadily compressed, and you can safely walk on them in snowy and wet conditions knowing you are not damaging the soil structure.

Each year, as you add compost or manure, or dig in green manure, the level of the bed will rise slightly, and you will find that weeding becomes steadily easier. Even long-rooted weeds like docks will lift out without digging. You get the best value out of your compost or manure because you are treating only the beds and not the paths. Composts can be added as a surface mulch or just lightly forked in and left for the worms and soil organisms to work with.

Because the fertility of the actual growing space is higher, and there are no paths between the individual rows, you can space the plants much more closely. In fact, plants are often grown in a grid pattern rather than in rows. For example, bush beans are sown, or onion sets planted, six inches apart each way. Or you can sow short rows of seeds across the bed, which is just the right width for the small, but frequent, summer sowings of lettuce or radish.

Separation of crops, or groups of crops, is also made much easier, so a narrow bed system makes very good sense for crop rotation, for mulching areas, or growing bands of green manure. Having divided your ground up into beds, you simply divide the number of beds by the number of different groups you are growing. If you have ten narrow beds and you have a five-course crop rotation, you will allocate two to potatoes, two to brassicas, and so on.

It is important not to make the beds too long, as there will be a great temptation to step across them rather than walk up to the end, and inevitably the edges will get compressed. Instead, divide them with cross paths which will make an attractive formal pattern in the garden. Use a line to mark out the beds, and be careful not to let the paths "wander" once there are crops growing and hanging over them.

Paths

Keeping the paths clear is the major task with this layout. Because they are not growing crops there is a tendency to leave them till last and they soon get covered with weeds which spread up onto the beds. The best solution is to hoe them regularly. Or you could cover them with carpet, heavy card, or a hay mulch. All of these harbor slugs but you could use this as a convenient slug trap if you regularly lift and search under the covering. Alternatively, you could have grassed paths, mown, and edged regularly. Grassed paths would need to be wider than normal, depending on the width of your mower.

HINTS AND TIPS

Paths to success

A smaller garden could have permanent brick or concrete paths and you could create a very attractive formal effect with brick paths, and beds edged with boards. An important point to remember, however, is that if you are using painted or treated boards in your organic garden—use non-toxic products.

Narrow beds combine well with a no-dig system, but since the beds are going to be permanent it is important to do a thorough preparation of the ground beforehand. Double dig if it is necessary, or use one of the heavy mulching systems described above. Get out all perennial weeds.

Staying in control

Dividing a large garden into beds is a good way of tackling the daunting task of clearing it. You could bring one or two beds into cultivation in the first year, while marking out and covering a couple more with a long-term, light-excluding mulch so that these will be ready the following year. Then gradually extend the number of beds, stopping at the point where you are not keeping on top of the regular maintenance.

With this system the vegetable garden never gets out of hand or becomes a burden. This is an important point. All gardening—and perhaps especially organic gardening—requires patience and taking a long-term view. It also needs your time and a certain amount of hard work.

If the garden becomes only a series of tasks waiting to be done, it has defeated a lot of the good reasons listed at the beginning of this chapter. So, take your gardening lightly. Adopt all the time and energy-saving methods available to organic gardeners, and remember to take time to sit back every so often and enjoy it all. Include a seat in your garden design.

Indoors or out

The decision to sow indoors or outdoors will depend on the crop, the time of year, and the condition of your soil. For example, root crops such as carrots and parsnips, do not transplant well, and are best sown directly into the prepared bed. Other crops that dislike the disturbance of transplanting, but really benefit from a protected sowing, such as sweet corn, can be sown in newspaper pots indoors with the whole pot being planted outdoors later.

Crops such as bush beans that are frost tender, need to wait until after your last frost for outdoor sowing (though they could be started indoors earlier). Other crops which would be happy to be sown outdoors—such as most of the brassicas—may still benefit from an indoor sowing. This is not just to get an earlier crop, but is also beneficial because well-grown plants will have more resistance to pests and diseases when they are planted outdoors. Flea beetle is a common pest on brassica seedlings, and although plants can "grow through it" it sets them back. More seriously, if you have had clubroot in previous crops of brassicas, the new crop will have much more chance of resisting attack if the plants are sturdy and advanced before they go out.

HINTS AND TIPS

Make your own newspaper pot

You can buy a newspaper pot maker (a simple wooden device) that will make small "starter pots" from your old newspapers.

Fold a sheet of newspaper to the required height of your pot plus two inches. Roll it into a tube three inches in diameter and fix with a staple top and bottom, and fold in the bottom two inches to make a base. Once these are stacked in a seed tray, and filled with soil, they will keep their strength and shape long enough for you to be able to plant out a good strong seedling without disturbance. The pot will then dissolve into the ground.

Sowing outdoors means:	Sowing indoors means:
• less worry about watering	• an earlier start
• no need to harden off	• controlled conditions—soil, spacing, temperature
• some crops cannot be transplanted	
• thinning is quicker than planting out	• you can select the best plants
• no special equipment is needed	• established plants have more resistance

Warming up the soil

Having selected the seeds to be sown outdoors, the major mistakes to be avoided are sowing too early, too deep, and too thickly. Trying to steal time from nature may only result in the waste of precious seed as it rots in the cold, damp ground. Nature usually catches up with herself. Sowing a month later may even overtake the plants that did germinate from an earlier sowing. Observe, look at what else is germinating, feel the soil with your hand, and note what happened in previous years.

You could speed things up a bit by prewarming the soil, with polyethylene laid on the beds. Clear poly is better than black because it will bring up the first flush of weeds which can then be hoed off before sowing. Keeping down weed competition is very important, and sowing in rows—either along or across the beds—will enable you to hoe as soon as the seedlings emerge. Protection from pests is also important.

Careful sowing

Some seeds are very fine and are easily lost in rough soil. Getting your soil down to a fine tilth will help prevent sowing too deep which often prevents emergence altogether. While a large seed like a broad bean can be two inches deep, others like the tiny seeds of carrots need only a quarter-inch of soil over them. Follow the instructions on the packets and, if necessary, prepare a special seed bed (for brassica seeds, for example) from which the seedlings can be transplanted.

Sowing thickly not only uses up expensive seed but necessitates a lot more thinning. This is time consuming, and in the case of carrots this could actually attract pests—so sow as thinly as possible. Or try station-sowing: use a small pinch of seed sowed at the final spacings, which can be thinned down to just one, or left to grow as a clump of smaller vegetables.

If conditions are dry when you are sowing, water the drill beforehand. Watering it afterwards risks washing away the seeds. Then, unless it is very dry, avoid watering until emergence. Finally don't forget to mark the drill and record it in your diary!

Sowing indoors

With sowing indoors you are in control of the growing conditions, but that means the seedlings are much more dependent on you.

Hygiene is important, so make sure the flats are clean. Ideally they should be cleaned before putting them away the previous year, and then washed before use with a citrus-based disinfectant. As soon as the seeds have germinated they will need light. This should be all around light as much as possible to avoid the seedlings being drawn up and getting leggy and thin. If you are starting them on the windowsill remember to turn them regularly. Alternatively, sit the flat in a box with a high back covered with reflective foil.

The temperature required for germination varies with the seed, but a cold indoor situation is actually worse than the same temperature outdoors. Indoors there is less air movement and seedlings are more likely to dampen off. Remember, if they are on a windowsill, take them off at night or at least put the curtains behind them, rather than shutting them into the cold space between window and curtain.

Avoid watering the flat after sowing. This will wash the tiny seeds all over the tray. Either moisten the compost before sowing or, after sowing, lower the whole flat gently into water and allow it to soak up until the surface is just moist. You should then need no extra watering until the seedlings emerge unless they are in very warm and dry conditions. A pane of glass can be put over individual flats.

Flats may need some sort of protective framework. Cats love to sit on them. Slugs will climb up and into them. A seedling frame would solve these and the other problems above. Even small commercial ones are expensive but would be useful for starting one or two flats of seedlings at a time. A larger one could be made from a slatted bench with a wire framework above. The whole bench is encased in bubble

HINTS AND TIPS

Your seedlings need:

- *light*
- *warmth*
- *moisture*
- *protection*
- *clean seed flats*
- *the right compost*

HINTS AND TIPS

A recipe for seed compost

2 buckets loam or molehill
2 buckets leafmold or coir
half a bucket coarse sand
a handful of calcified seaweed.
Mix well and put through a coarse sieve. Fill seed flats, pressing gently down.

plastic that will provide an even light but diffuse scorching sunlight. If you are using an electric heater, make absolutely sure water cannot drip onto the heater.

The right seed compost is essential to give plants a good start. In general, a seed compost is less rich in nutrients than a potting compost, but if the seedlings are not going to be potted on quickly then a combined "seed and potting compost" would be best. It is possible to buy ready-mixed organic composts, but if you have the materials it is not only satisfying, but also cheaper, to make your own.

Garden soil on its own, even if sieved, will not do. It will not have a light enough structure, and may be low in nutrients and will probably contain lots of weed seeds. Instead, use a base of loam (from stacked turf), or the lovely fine crumbly soil turned up by moles, if you are lucky (or unlucky) enough to have them! This base is then combined with leafmold or coir (coconut) fiber. Add coarse sand for drainage and calcified seaweed to sweeten it.

A potting compost will need to be richer in nutrients as it will have to support the growing seedlings until they are planted out. Garden compost, worm compost, or comfrey leafmold could be added to the base, together with seaweed meal.

When you are picking seedlings out into potting compost handle them very carefully, holding them by the leaves rather then the stem. If they have got at all leggy plant them lower in the potting compost. Again, soak the flats from below but also mist-spray the foliage to minimize the shock of transplanting.

HINTS AND TIPS

A recipe for potting compost
2 buckets loam or molehill
2 buckets leafmold or coir
2 buckets garden compost
OR
1 bucket worm compost
half a bucket coarse sand
a handful calcified seaweed
8 ounces seaweed meal

Once the transplanted seedlings are growing strongly, and it is warm enough outside for them to be planted out, they can be hardened off. This should be a gradual process to avoid a check in their growth. From the seedling frame or windowsill, they can be moved to an unheated greenhouse or polytunnel where they should be given an extra cover at night.

After a week of this they can be moved outside during the day but should either be brought back in at night, or covered with a piece of row cover on a wire framework. Set them on slats to raise them up off the ground and do a slug check last thing at night. At the end of this second week they will be ready for planting out.

Water thoroughly before planting out. In general—plant slightly lower than they were, firm down around the plant, water well until they are established, and keep down weed competition.

At all times handle the plant with care and give it the best conditions you can. Organic pest and disease control depends above all on having well grown, sturdy plants that have not been stressed and are growing in the conditions that suit them.

Aftercare

If you need to water plants growing outdoors it is better to give them a good soak every so often rather than a more frequent, light watering. The latter will bring the roots up to the surface and the plant will then be more vulnerable to drying out. Occasional, thorough watering will encourage the plant to put down deep roots, bringing up moisture and nutrients.

Otherwise, aftercare consists of keeping down the weeds, staking plants if necessary against the wind, and keeping an eye out for pest and disease attacks. A regular look around the garden will prevent small problems from becoming bigger ones and, of course, this is part of the enjoyment of having a garden! Quite often it is easy to forget to stop for a minute, take a look at your "patch," and give yourself a pat on the back for all the work that you've done.

HINTS AND TIPS

Watering seedlings

Water for watering and spraying is better at room temperature, but if it is left standing warm it could encourage fungal growth. Horsetail and calendula both seem to have an anti-fungal effect and seedlings sprayed with water in which they are infused suffer less from damping off.

Organic all over the garden

Organic gardening is not restricted to those growing their own vegetables—it also includes fruit, flowers, and herbs. Whether you have a garden, a window box, or patio with pot plants, you can still choose to cut down the chemicals in your environment.

The fruit garden

All the reasons for growing vegetables organically apply to fruit as well. In fact, avoiding chemical sprays is even more vital in the fruit garden where you are most likely to eat the produce straight from the bush. Picking a ripe strawberry, warm from the sun, and popping it straight into your mouth, releases an explosion of taste and vitamins. Berries, apples, and plums can all be eaten straight from the plant with no fear of chemical residues.

Long-term planning

Because fruit trees will be in the ground for years, perhaps even decades, organic preparation of the ground is essential. The gradual release of organic nutrients this provides will be preferable to the quick release of artificial fertilizers. Creating a healthy environment is also vital to helping the plants resist disease. In fact, a chemical free environment will encourage the full range of beneficial insects, and these will include the predators that keep several of the worst fruit pests under control. You can't use the technique of yearly crop rotation to reduce the likelihood of disease but there are several other preventive measures you can take.

Select the planting site to provide as much sunshine and shelter as possible, but beware of creating a frost pocket. (Windbreaks on the lowest side of a fruit bed should be staggered to allow frost to escape.) Make sure that there is a good depth of soil for the extensive roots needed to support fruit trees and bushes. Incorporate compost in all soils, with the addition of sand to improve the drainage of heavy soils. Choose your plants carefully for disease resistance and hardiness. Look at what grows well in your neighbors' gardens. Selecting the right plant for your conditions and climate will avoid a lot of wasted time and effort.

Cleaning up

Hygiene is really important:

• Clear up dead and diseased leaves and prune off and burn infected branches

• Avoid planting bushes too close—overcrowding encourages diseases

• Prune bushes to let light and air into their centers

• Unless you have hens in the orchard to clean up fallen fruit, remove it before it encourages wasps.

All fruit benefits from weed control—because they will not be competing for water—and mulching is the best way of combining this with any necessary feeding. Blackberries welcome an annual mulch of well-rotted manure or compost, whereas raspberries and gooseberries are probably happier with hay or straw. Apples benefit from a more nutrient-rich mulch every third year.

Like all gardening, it is a question of using your common sense and observing how your plants are doing. The organic orchard may take longer to bear fruit than the vegetable garden, but from day one it will be adding to the organic environment, making a friendly place for bees, birds, and your family.

HINTS AND TIPS

If you are short of space then fruit can be grown against walls, as cordons, or even in containers. It can be combined with vegetables—like a permanent bed of strawberries along with the other long-term beds. Or it can be used to give structure to the flower garden.

The herb garden

Growing chemical free food is usually the motivation to start organic gardening, but it soon becomes obvious that the whole garden should be an organic environment. This includes the flower beds—even though most of the plants won't make it to the dinner table (though some of them will). And it certainly includes the herb garden.

Essentially organic

Most of the herbs used in cooking, and almost all the herbs used medicinally, are the original "unimproved" varieties. Where new varieties have been developed, with new colors or variations of foliage, they tend to lose some of their original properties. On the whole, they have not been bred like many of our vegetables into larger or blander specimens, and they have much lower feeding requirements.

This makes artificial feeding both unnecessary and undesirable, as the lush growth it produces would dilute the essential oils that give the herbs their aroma and flavor. These essential oils also increase their immunity to pests and diseases.

Herbs suffer from few diseases, and there are organic or preventive remedies for these, making chemical pesticides unnecessary. In addition, they would counteract the health-giving properties of the herbs both directly, by leaving chemical residues on the leaves (not even as easy to clean off as vegetables), and more subtly, by altering the makeup of the plant constituents. We are just starting to understand the complex properties of herbs and to realize how likely these are to be disrupted by chemical inputs.

Making a place for herbs

You may decide to grow a few herbs in the flower garden. This is very suitable if you want them mainly for their edible flowers, such as violas, bergamot, calendula, or nasturtium. The shrubby, aromatic herbs like sage, rosemary, thyme, savory, and lavender also fit in well, particularly if kept clipped back. Or you could make up an entire bed of different varieties of lavenders, pinks and roses; a brighter mix of poppies, marigolds, and nasturtiums; or even an all-white bed of white clary, yarrow, and lemon balm.

Alternatively, you can incorporate herbs into the vegetable garden: as rows or beds of bulk herbs for drying—chamomile, dill, and calendula; as companion herbs for companion planting (see below); as permanent perennial herbs along the ends of the rows; or clipped to form a low hedge around the vegetable plot.

Herbs lend themselves very well to container growing. Indeed, some herbs are best container grown to keep them under control, particularly mints. A large tub or a half-barrel could be divided into segments containing the more compact herbs—thyme, marjoram, oregano, or savory.

At the other extreme, many of the larger native herbs like golden rod, Joe pye weed, giant hyssop, and yarrow will flourish in the "wild" part of your garden (every garden has one!) and are worth encouraging for the number of birds and insects they support.

HINTS AND TIPS

The bees and the butterflies

Planting a specialist herb garden for the bees and butterflies will not only make a contribution to conservation, but will aid the pollination of your fruit and vegetables. Herbs are even more attractive to insects than ordinary flowers because they are generally more aromatic, rich in nectar, and closer to the wild forms.

A herb garden for the cook

The serious organic cook is going to want a dedicated culinary herb garden. Having fresh, delicious, aromatic herbs in hand will encourage frequent use, and benefit our health and diet. Because many of our basic culinary herbs are Mediterranean in origin, they will need appropriate conditions—sun, shelter from cold winds, good drainage, low humidity, and soil that is not particularly fertile. These conditions will concentrate their volatile oils, hence their flavor and medicinal qualities.

Since many of them are perennials it is worth doing some thorough ground preparation, removing all perennial weeds and improving the drainage if necessary. If the soil is heavy clay then you need to incorporate compost and sand or gravel. This will improve the structure of the soil and provide enough nutrients to get things established. However, in the following years only a light mulch of compost will be needed.

Herbs with long tap roots such as fennel, lovage, and angelica will continue this process of breaking up the subsoil, and after the initial digging, a no-dig system with yearly mulching will leave the soil undisturbed for the worms to work.

A good solution for unsuitable ground in the herb garden is to make raised beds. This means that you can build them up with the right soil, and they will drain well. They also raise the herbs up for you to work on more easily.

Sowing and aftercare

As with vegetables, some herbs are best sown indoors and direct. The umbellifers—fennel, dill, caraway, and cilantro—are difficult to transplant because of their tap root, although you could sow them in newspaper pots. Some herbs—such as basil or sweet marjoram—need warmth and protection to germinate. Some have tiny seeds that would be lost in garden soil conditions.

Annuals often reseed themselves. In the case of biennials, which seed in their second year, it is a good idea to start two lots of herbs in two subsequent years so that you are never without parsley, caraway, or angelica. Growing perennials from seeds takes time, and since a

HINTS AND TIPS

Cutting back

If you are growing the salad herbs such as chives for their leaves, then cut back the flowering heads. Shrubby herbs can be cut back after flowering and lush leafy herbs such as lemon balm, catnip, or mint can be cut back several times in the year to encourage new growth.

few plants will be sufficient it may be best to buy a plant and take cuttings to propagate them.

With a yearly mulch to suppress weeds and conserve moisture, the main work in the herb garden will consist of keeping them under control—staking the taller herbs and pruning the shrubby herbs. This cutting back encourages new growth and prevents plants from getting leggy and woody, with the risk of splitting.

Harvesting healthy herbs

All herbs are best used fresh and some, such as basil and lemon balm, are not worth drying as their taste is so altered. Fortunately, most can be preserved in some way, and for medicinal use there are simple preparations that will capture their therapeutic benefits.

For fresh use pick them just before you need them, taking the top sprigs from shrubby herbs to encourage bushy growth or cutting a few stems down to ground level from each leafy plant. If you want to store your herbs, aim to harvest the herb at its peak—when flavor and therapeutic properties are highest.

Capturing the essential oils

The beneficial effects in some of our most useful herbs—such as thyme or sage or lavender—come from the essential oils in their leaves and flowers. These aromatic oils are released when you crush and sniff a leaf, or even when you brush past them in the garden—another good reason for growing them near the kitchen door. Even a warm sunny day will be enough to release the oils. The best time to harvest them is on a sunny morning, after the sun has had a chance to dry off the dew, but before it has become hot enough to start releasing the volatile oils.

Cut the herbs without crushing them and bring them in to dry, out of the sun but in a warm, airy place. The aim is to dry them as quickly as possible without overheating them—air circulation is important to carry the moisture away. When you are drying flowers—such as calendula or chamomile—you can tell if you've been successful because the flowers will have kept their color. If you

HINTS AND TIPS

Harvest
The right time to harvest depends on what you want.

Leaves *Pick them before flowering, when the maximum oil content is in the leaves.*
Flowers *Pick when just properly open but before they have "gone over."*
Seed *Pick when ripe and brown—when they fall readily if tapped.*
Roots *Pick in late autumn when the leaves have died down and the goodness is stored in the roots for the winter.*

are drying roots you will need to clean them well, chop the larger ones, and spread them out on racks. These can be dried in the sun and then finished off in the "plate warming" drawer of the oven.

When they are thoroughly dry put them into jars, but don't crush them until you are going to use them. Although they look pretty in fancy glass jars on the kitchen wall, they are actually best kept in a cool dark place. And don't forget to label them! You may think you'll remember which is what, but when you're deciding whether you need some tea for your stomach ache or your headache, two lots of dried leaves can look much the same.

Medicinal wisdom

If you are using herbs for any sort of medicinal purpose then you need to get a good book, written by someone who is an authority on the subject, and who can tell you the contra-indications or cautions about particular herbs.

Herbs may be nature's medicine chest but they don't come in measured doses and labeled pills. Our ancestors learned by trial and error what was good for us and what wasn't. We have them to thank for the knowledge that you definitely wouldn't dose yourself with foxglove, or that certain herbs, while good in small doses, would make you feel very sick if taken in quantity.

You need to know what you are doing and to follow some basic rules in order to get the benefits of your own free, organic remedies. It is also wise to check with your doctor if you are not sure what condition you are dealing with.

Simple preparations

Having said all that, there are many herbs that you can use safely, and the preparation of most of them is as simple as making a cup of tea!

Herbal tea

RECIPE

Put a teaspoon of the dried herb in a pot,
pour on boiling water, cover and leave to brew,
then strain off and sweeten with honey if you wish.

The strength of flavor in a herb is a useful rule of thumb about how much to use. The most strongly aromatic herbs—such as thyme and sage—contain powerful medicinal oils, and you would use them in smaller quantities and for particular needs. For example, when you have a bad head cold. On the other hand, you could start every day with a cup of chamomile that is also mild enough for children—even to soothe teething babies.

The glorious calendula

One herb you should never be without is Calendula officinalis. Just bringing in their glorious color from the garden, spreading the heads to dry on racks, and storing jarfulls of the bright orange flowers in the pantry, is enough to cheer you up.

Calendula tea

A tea for digestive problems can be made by pouring boiling water onto one or two flowerheads of calendula. Made twice as strong it is an excellent lotion for skin problems, being both soothing and antiseptic.

Calendula can also be made up into an ointment and a tincture, and can be used by both people and animals. The tincture can also be used as an antifungal preventive when damping off seedlings—add ten drops to a mist sprayer of water.

Calendula ointment

The simplest ointment is made by gently melting together 2 ounces of beeswax and 12 fluid ounces/1½ cups of olive oil in a heavy-based pan and adding a handful of calendula flowers. Use a double boiler for safety if you are cooking on gas. Simmer for 10 minutes and strain off through muslin. You will need to pour it into the jars straight away as it will start to set, but allow it to cool before sealing. The ointment can be used on sores and to soothe and heal minor burns and cuts.

Calendula tincture

To make an alcoholic tincture of calendula add fresh or dried herbs to alcohol that is at least 30 percent proof (cheap gin will do). Use 4 ounces of dried, or 8 ounces of fresh, herb to a pint of alcohol and put the tightly sealed jar in a warm place. Set it somewhere that you will pass by frequently, because you need to shake it twice daily. Strain through muslin and store in a dark-glass, tightly stoppered bottle.

Marigold tincture is excellent for putting directly onto cuts, (it will sting but is very antiseptic and healing), or for adding a teaspoon to a cupful of warm water as a mouthwash or for washing wounds.

Wild (and respectable) medicine

Elderflower (Sambucus niger) and meadowsweet (Filipendula officinalis) are both wild herbs that are worth drying in bulk (but be prepared for a slightly unpleasant smell of cats from the elderflower as it dries).

Elderflower is a good winter herb to drink if you feel a cold coming on. Meadowsweet leaves and flowers, gathered in June and July, are very useful for all digestive problems, particularly acid stomach. Tea made with the soft furry leaves of mullein (Verbascum thapsis) is a good remedy for catarrh and all respiratory problems.

Peppermint (Mentha piperita) is effective for indigestion and can be added to elderflower and yarrow to counter a feverish cold.

Doctors are now accepting the role of herbal remedies. St. John's Wort (Hypericum perforatum) is used to treat depression, and the purple cone-flower (Echinacea purpurea) gives a powerful boost to the immune system. These, and others, are being given serious attention by the previously skeptical medical profession.

Growing your own herbal remedies means that you know they are organic, and you can harvest and use them at the peak of their goodness. Clover and cornsilk, dandelion and fennel, lady's mantle, lemon balm, and lime blossom are all worth a place in your organic garden.

The flower garden

Whether you grow flowers alongside or mixed in with your vegetables and herbs, or have no room for anything but flowers, they should be grown organically. First because they are part of the whole garden environment (and your neighbor's as well), and second because the flowers themselves will prefer it.

The bees, butterflies, and other insects that constantly fly to and fro will benefit from a chemical-free environment. We also know that chemicals can influence the scent and color of flowers. In addition, as with herbs, artificial feeding can make the plants more susceptible to disease, and encourage leafy growth at the expense of flowers.

Perennial preparation

As with your herb beds, the flowers you choose may be long-term perennials, perhaps interplanted with different annuals each year. So, they will repay a thorough initial preparation. Since you are not going to be using weedkillers, it is important to extract the perennial weeds, and to break up the soil so that it will drain well. You can then incorporate well rotted compost to give the plants a good start.

Like herbs, most flowers will not need very high fertility and an annual mulch of compost should be sufficient. Leafmold would also make a good soil conditioner, though because it is low in nutrients, plants may also benefit from calcified seaweed and perhaps phosphates, in the form of fish fertilizer.

Flower therapy

Your flower garden could, of course, be purely ornamental and this in itself can be therapeutic, particularly if you choose scented flowers.

The aromatherapists have shown us the specific benefits of particular scents, from

calming lavender to stimulating rosemary. Even just sitting in the garden on a warm evening will allow you to experience these effects and, of course, growing your own flowers will provide you with the raw materials for your own preparations.

However, you could also choose your flowers with a view to other uses. A surprising number of flowers are edible. We are used to crystallized violets or rose petals, but a more healthy way of adding flowers to our diets would be in their raw state.

For you and the bees

You could also create a flower garden specifically for wildlife. This will attract the bees and beneficial insects that will help the rest of your garden, and will also look attractive in its own right. There are many nurseries selling seeds of wildflower, that would encourage bees, butterflies, or beneficial insects, as well as flowers whose seedheads will be popular with birds.

Insects prefer the simple daisy flowers as the nectar is more accessible. The original forms of flowers are often better than the more highly bred doubles. Bees like color, particularly blues and yellows. Moths and butterflies prefer scent and paler colors, coming in the dusk to flowers such as evening primrose.

From corncockle, convolvulus, and coreopsis to salvias, sunflowers, and swan river daisies—there are enough to choose from to make color-themed beds, or simply to create a riot of hues that will be your colorful contribution to the organic movement.

Growing under cover

Greenhouses, polytunnels, frames, and cloches will all extend your gardening potential. In a small town garden you may have only a conservatory or sunroom attached to the house, but with proper management you can grow a surprising number of salads and vegetables along with your flowers. In fact you could even grow food at work!

DID YOU KNOW?

Edible flowers

Violas, pansies, pelargoniums, and hollyhocks can all be added to salads. Borage and sweet woodruff can be added to summer drinks. Pelargonium leaves can be used in sponge cakes, and rose petals can be used in sweet sandwiches.

DID YOU KNOW?

Greenhouses everywhere!

"The vast blind windowed sides of ferro-concrete office blocks are essentially unused glasshouses. If only one firm encouraged employees to use these advantages, there could be a new interest in work, and the essential lessons we all need to learn. The foyers of most buildings would grow some of the coffee needed for the morning break, and in so doing, would free land in the third world for more essential local agriculture."

Source: "Permaculture One" Mollison & Holmgren, Tagari 1990

The permaculture approach is an all-embracing vision and has much to inspire the organic gardener, but anyone can start with making their own living space productive. Even a windowsill can be used to grow herbs, and a glassed-in lobby could house tomatoes in pots or a climbing cucumber plant. And, of course, in these protected conditions you could grow a jungle of frost-tender flowers.

You're in charge

The critical point about any growing under cover is that you are in complete control of the growing environment and therefore have complete responsibility for the conditions that your plants have to put up with. You can regulate temperature, soil quality, moisture, and light levels, but also less obvious things like how clean the environment is, what pests are allowed to gain a foothold, humidity levels, and air movement.

If your covered area is of any size it is useful to keep a diary just as with the vegetable garden. Because things grow faster under cover there is more scope for a succession of crops, and if you have the space it is even useful to practice some sort of crop rotation. The confined soil in a greenhouse or polytunnel bed would be even more likely to get "tomato sick" or build up soil fungi from a succession of the same family of plants.

Even a minimal three-year rotation, perhaps moving plants between two side beds and a center bed, or replacing soil altogether every third year, would help prevent this build up. Keeping notes of these changes, a planting plan, and notes of previous crops—particularly how long they occupied space and what return there was—will help you make best use of the space.

Polytunnels and greenhouses are generally thought of as the site for the vegetable fruits such as tomatoes, eggplants, peppers, and all the squashes, perhaps with a few salads filling in the gaps. In fact, you can grow many more vegetables, particularly early in the year before the more tender plants are ready.

• A row of early potatoes can be planted in February

• Carrots can be sown then too for harvesting in May

• Summer cabbage can be planted in March

• Radish, spinach, and bunching onions for early salads can all be sown in February

• In the autumn, when the summer bulk crops are finishing off, a range of salads can be sown that will go through the winter, including hardy lettuces, land cress ,and some of the oriental salads.

Extra care

However, if you are to get such a good return from the space it is vital to keep the soil well fed, and adequately watered, and to pay attention to hygiene. Every time you take a crop off a patch of earth you are taking nutrients out of it and if you are to follow on with another crop you will need to give the soil a boost. The same applies out in the garden of course. But under cover, the crops are likely to be more intensive, possibly more greedy feeders, like the vegetable fruits. There is also less opporunity for the soil to renew itself through incoming earthworms, natural mulching, and the action of air and rainfall.

Thus, you must feed the soil well, with compost or well-rotted manure, but avoid concentrated liquid feeds. Ensure adequate watering if there is any risk of plants getting an excess of nutrients without the normal garden control of rain washing them out. Leafmold is good for mulching and to improve the structure of the soil without putting in a lot of extra nutrients.

Air and water

Watering is also largely a matter of common sense. Plants will need more water when they are growing strongly and producing a lot of fruit, and when conditions are hot and sunny. Plants in pots are particularly vulnerable and will need daily attention. Avoid watering in cold conditions or last thing in the evening. The slugs will run rampant during the night and fungal diseases will be encouraged.

Pest and disease control in the greenhouse and polytunnel is included in pest, disease, and weed control, but the most important general preventive, once you have given your plants a strong start with the correct soil conditions, is to ensure good hygiene to prevent the build up of problems.

• Keep an eye on your plants, removing any suspect leaves or plants.

• Keep the area generally tidy, clearing up old plant material and old pots.

• Clean the glass or plastic once a year, preferably at the end of the main growing season.

Some of the worst garden pests, such as carrot rust fly, and larger predators such as birds are, fortunately, excluded from the tunnel or greenhouse unless you are very unlucky. There are, however, specific indoor pests that you will need to look out for, or better still, take preventive action against. Correct ventilation and watering are important here. Good ventilation will prevent the build up of fungal diseases, and correct watering is necessary because plants need moisture fed to their roots and a degree of humidity in the air.

Red spider mite, one of the worst pests of protected cultivation, thrives in dry conditions, so keeping the humidity up will discourage it. Mulching the beds is an excellent way of keeping down weeds and keeping the soil moist. If it is a dry mulch, such as hay or straw, you need to be sure that you don't just direct water under the mulch to the roots, but that you also spray the foliage and the floor of the house. To avoid scorching don't spray young leaves in full sunlight.

Even a small cold frame will be useful for extending your growing season by getting seedlings started or providing you with salads through the winter. The same advice applies to hygiene and soil conditions. Because it is a much smaller area, pay particular attention to ventilation, propping the top up on hot days, and shading in bright sun.

Cloches are basically mini-greenhouses that are small enough to move around as you need them. They are most useful in the spring, to prewarm the soil for crops or protect young seedlings and, in the autumn and winter, to extend the cropping period of vegetables. They provide a convenient way of hardening off plants, and also protect them from birds, cats, and rabbits. There are several different designs available and some of them could be adapted for use later in the year using insect netting instead of plastic.

Growing in containers

In a town garden you may be restricted to growing in containers, and in any garden these can add interest to the hard-paved areas, provide height and structure, and enable you to grow plants against the house walls. Except for large, permanently sited containers they also have extra benefits—you can move them around, turn them to take advantage of the sun, and take them in under cover in the winter.

There is a huge range of containers available, from conventional pots to elaborate ceramic planters, wooden tubs, old troughs, and chimney pots, or anything that will contain earth.

They depend on you

Plants in containers—even more so than those in a polytunnel or greenhouse—are completely dependent on you. They are confined to the soil you provide and reliant on you for moisture. It is not just a question of watering them regularly, even if they are outside and being rained on they will still need a regular check.

Correct drainage is critical. Plants die from overwatering as much as from underwatering. Whatever the container, you must create drainage holes if they don't already exist, and put in a layer of gravel at the base. The potting compost should also include sand to ensure it is free-draining.

The potting compost has got to provide the plant with its nutrients for life, with the possible addition of some liquid feeding or a mulch. The potting mixture recommended in *The Vegetable Garden*, would be suitable for most plants, but for the vegetable fruits an extra bucket of manure could be added to the recipe.

The care and management of plants in containers is very similar to those grown under cover. It is important to check regularly for any signs of pest and disease attack, to practice good hygiene— for example, clearing dead leaves off the surface of the pot—and to give plants space between the pots. If you are replacing a plant in a pot then replace all or part of the soil, depending on the size of the pot and the size and condition of the original plant.

Fruitful plantings

Container growing is very suitable for herbs and, of course, flowers, but larger containers can also be used for fruit. The largest tubs can even hold a fruit tree, as long as it is on a dwarf rootstock, and bush fruit would also be suitable. For strawberry towers or barrels, ensure that water gets to all the layers of plants.

You could also grow a range of vegetables in addition to the usual tomatoes, eggplants, and peppers. A bucket-sized tub could hold cut-and-come-again salads, or could be thinly sprinkled with carrot seed. A larger tub with a wigwam-type support in it could hold climbing beans or peas. Beets, spinach, radishes, nasturtiums, and arugula for salads, or oriental greens could all flourish in tubs, and their cropping season could be extended by carrying the tubs indoors at the end of the season.

Once you are confident about the gardening basics the only limit to your gardening is your imagination! Plants can be trained up the side of and over structures and sheds, potted up in all sorts of containers at all levels, and mixed together in beautiful combinations. For example: white-flowered pole beans can be mingled with Painted Lady sweet pea on a climbing frame, a screen of Verbena bonariensis behind a row of standard tomatoes, or flowerbeds edged with green or red frilly cut-and-come-again lettuces. Hanging baskets can be filled with tiny tomatoes and deep blue lobelia, or strawberries can combine with a red trailing nasturtium. Colorful kale and cabbages, or the splendid yellow flowers and extravagant leaves of a zucchini, provide structure in a border. Mounds of golden marjoram with purple alliums coming up through them in the spring, or the startling scarlet and yellow stems of Bright Lights Swiss chard in a bed of foliage plants, will break down the barriers in a garden.

Pests, disease, and weed control

After all your preparation, care, and attention, you'll want to make sure that you, rather than the pests, get the benefit. Tackling pest and disease problems is always assumed to be the great bugbear of organic gardening but, if your garden is properly managed, you should have fewer problems than in the nonorganic garden.

A major problem with chemical pesticides, apart from the toxic residues, is that pests are building up resistance to them, so that even the most powerful chemicals are failing to tackle the new generations of "superbugs" that have evolved in response to heavy pesticide use in the past. Obviously a new approach is needed to the problem.

GMO or OGM?

The new approach that the chemical companies are following is that of genetic modification. One aim is to breed resistant varieties. But, there are concerns as to what is then passed on to whoever or whatever eats that plant, particularly if the resistance takes the form of the plant containing the pesticide itself. Another aim is to breed plants that can cope with the ever increasing quantities of pesticide needed to kill the superbugs, or even plants without their own resistance so that pesticides are essential. The company can then sell the package of GM seed and the necessary pesticide.

The approach in organic gardening management is radical in a different way. Chemical solutions respond to each problem individually with a corrective measure—a herbicide to cope with the weed problem, a fungicide to cope with fungal diseases, a pesticide to cope with insect attack, or a chemical nutrient to cope with an obvious deficiency. The organic gardener treats the garden as a whole organism.

Since everything interrelates in this garden environment, the health of all the individual parts depends upon its overall health. The soil is the basis of this, interacting with air and water and all the myriad creatures in and around it. The two basic principles of organic pest and disease control are to boost the health of the soil and to work with the natural allies in the environment.

Don't get discouraged

Before we look at all the things that you can do to tackle all the problems you might come across, you must remember that your garden will not be constantly bombarded by pests and diseases! Reading gardening books can be a bit like reading medical dictionaries, and you might end up thinking it is all too fraught to attempt. Actually, most things just get on with growing without keeling over as soon as your back is turned. What you are aiming to do is to maximize their health, vitality, and productiveness by the extra help you give them.

Soil support

The methods for boosting the health of the soil have been covered earlier in this chapter:

Creating a good soil structure by incorporating organic matter in the form of compost, leafmold, manures, and green manures.

Protecting that structure from the damaging effects of wind, rain, and sun by means of mulching, and avoiding rough treatment.

Feeding the soil with organic nutrients in the form of compost, manure, green manures, and other organic fertilizers.

Correcting the balance of acidity and alkalinity in the soil.

DID YOU KNOW?

European corn borer moths lay eighteen times more eggs on sweet corn plants grown on chemically farmed soils than on corn grown in organically managed soils. Differences in the plants' mineral ratios are probably the cause—organic soils are more likely to contain the full range in the right balance and plants can absorb what they need.

Source: Research conducted at Ohio State University by Larry Phelan, from "Agriculture, Ecosystems and Environment," Vol. 56, 1995.

Having established a healthy soil, the practice of crop rotation is one of the most important means of maintaining it. Then the next requirement is to plant out only healthy plants, suited to that site. Ideally, rear your own plants, following the sowing and growing instructions in our *Groundwork* section, planting out strong seedlings in soil that is appropriate to them. The seedlings need to be sturdy rather than tall. Remember that feeding with artificial fertilizers can sometimes leave plants more vulnerable to attack.

Planting into the right conditions will mean that the seedlings can get away quickly without being stressed and will find what they want in the soil. For example, if you are planting brassicas then you may need to check that there is sufficient lime; or the soil needs more, or less, plant foods depending upon whether it will be supporting onions or carrots. If you are buying plants or have been given them by a friend, check very carefully for pests and diseases before you plant out. You don't want to be bringing in root rots on a gift of cabbages. If you are planting potatoes make sure you are putting in healthy seed potatoes from a good supplier.

Give your plants the best possible start. They need to maintain health by your good management. The emphasis is on prevention of problems.

Undermine the competition

Competition from weeds will shade out, smother, or starve your young plants. Your most useful tool is the hoe. Hoe in dry conditions, as you will be more likely to kill the weeds and will create a thin dust mulch on the surface that, paradoxically, will prevent the soil from drying out. Hoe the weeds before you can actually see them, that is, just before emergence. Use a collinear hoe or a stirrup hoe with a blade that pivots back and forth. A small winged hoe can be used between closely spaced plants.

Close spacing is actually a useful way of shading out weeds. Growing on narrow, high fertility beds makes this more possible, and if plants are in a staggered grid they will achieve maximum cover of the bed. One or two initial weedings will be sufficient, and by then the plants will have spread to shade out the weeds. You could also underplant your vegetables with a crop such as white Dutch clover which will not mind the shade but will itself put some goodness into the soil.

There are, of course, weeds and "Weeds." Not only are some of them useful in their own right—such as wild herbs or insect attractants—but a shallow rooting, spreading weed such as chickweed can act as an underplanting. Left under bush beans or cabbages, chickweed can actually conserve surface moisture in dry conditions without competing with the crop. The "proper" plants need to be established first, but once they are up and growing you can remove the more aggressive weeds and leave the chickweed to spread.

Tagetes minuta, a marigold which is actually very tall, but has very small flowers, is reputed to suppress ground elder when planted up against it, by means of its root secretions.

Several of the green manures—such as alfalfa, buckwheat, or clover—form effective weed-excluding mulches. Hairy vetch planted early in the season will have the same effect and both vetch and grazing rye grass, when turned in, have an inhibiting effect on seed

DID YOU KNOW?

Pesticide pests

A report in Pesticides News *quotes research from Duke University, North Carolina, showing that when three pesticides (used at their correct levels) were combined, the toxicity was increased by a factor of several hundred.*

Source: Pesticides News 47, quoted in The Organic Way, issue 160 2000

DID YOU KNOW?

Even at "safe" levels, the frequency with which chemicals are used in the house and the backyard is thought to be responsible for Multiple Chemical Sensitivity—a condition that sensitizes sufferers to even low levels of other substances, such as tobacco and car exhaust fumes. "We now understand more about the mechanism of chemical effects on human health. It is not a question of a single substance poisoning an organism... but rather a multi-stage process which interferes with the whole system."

Source: Professor Nicholas Ashford of Massachusetts Institute of Technology, from Chemical Exposures: low levels and high stakes. Nicholas Ashford and Claudia S. Miller Wiley, New York, 1998

germination, so weed seeds will be held in check to some extent while young plants are getting established.

Then there are the inert mulches mentioned previously—various grades of polyethylene, permeable sheets such as weed-barrier landscape fabric, or commercial or do-it-yourself paper mulches that can be covered with grass clippings and will gradually break down into the soil.

Finally, if you really can't live with your weeds, you could get a flame thrower. These are expensive, but there is a small model for small gardens and they are a very efficient way of killing weeds.

Confuse the enemy

Interplanting or underplanting also serves to confuse the pests. Some pests find their target crop by sight.

A cabbage butterfly apparently recognizes the shape of a cabbage against the dark brown background of the earth. Interplanting late brassicas with a bush bean would break up this visual pattern. The brassicas may also benefit from the nitrogen left behind on the bean roots when the beans have finished cropping.

Other pests find their host crop by scent, and an adjacent crop with a strong contrasting scent would confuse this message. A common combination is carrots interplanted with onions, though to be effective there needs to be about three times as many onions as carrots. This sort of association is known as companion planting, and some gardeners organize their vegetable plantings around this system.

Companion planting can work in several ways: confusing pests, as above, deterring them by using a plant with an unpleasant scent, or attracting pests away from the vegetable toward the companion plant. The strong smell of French marigold, planted in the greenhouse between tomatoes, is said to keep away whitefly using its strong smell. Chives planted around roses are not only reputed to protect them from disease but also, surprisingly, to enhance their perfume. Sage and tansy deter the coddling moth from fruit trees because of their high camphor oil content.

There has been some research into the more subtle effects of these associations, which suggest that plants have a "fingerprint"—observable in the laboratory as a pattern on paper—and that plants with a similar pattern make good companions, boosting the growth and vigor of each other. For the same reason other plants may be bad companions for each other.

Much more research needs to be done to verify these plant combinations but you may find it useful to observe what is happening in your own garden.

If you have a herb garden you can also make use of the dried herbs in your vegetable and flower gardens. The strongly aromatic herbs, powdered and dried, and mixed with the seeds that you are sowing can repel mice and, possibly, slugs.

A tea made with chamomile—"the plant physician"—is said to strengthen sickly plants. All herbal debris is useful, containing minerals and other constituents that make a good general tonic for pot plants. Dried leaves sprinkled around the stems of plants, or an infusion watered onto them also helps. A good herb gardening book will give you specific uses.

DID YOU KNOW?

Plant food

One of the worst effects of chemical pesticides is that they destroy the beneficial insects that help produce a good crop. "One of every three mouthfuls that we eat, and one of every three beverages that we drink, come from plants that are dependent on pollination by bees and other insects."

Source: The Forgotten Pollinators, Stephen Buchmann & Gary Nabhan, Island Press

Maximum resistance

Several vegetable varieties have a degree of resistance to pests or diseases. If you suffer from a particular problem in your garden it is worth selecting a suitable variety for this as well as for taste or keeping qualities. Look for blight resistance in potatoes. The variety "Kennebec," for example, is reported to "tolerate drought and resist late blight, black leg, potato viruses A and Y, and wart, but not scab." Other resistant varieties include:

• Big beef tomatoes that are resistant to fusarium rot
• parsnip lancer is less susceptible to canker
• Nevis carrots resist alternaria blight
• Plant breeders have even developed a carrot, "Fly away," with some resistance to carrot rust fly

It is worth reading the small print in the seed catalogs for levels of resistance.

Critical timing

You can avoid some problems by good timing. If you sow carrots in March or early June you will avoid the worst of the carrot rust fly attacks. April and May sowings are more susceptible.

Onions grown from sets (the small immature bulb) will be less susceptible to onion fly than those grown from seed. (This is partly because they are planted out later, but also because they don't need thinning.) Sowing broad beans in September (you need an early variety like Windsor) will avoid aphid problems as the shoot tips will be past their vulnerable soft stage before the aphids appear in May. Radish, rutabaga, and turnip sown in July avoid the worst attacks of the fleabeetle. Above all, don't sow in cold, wet soils as you will just waste seed.

A regular watering regime will also help by keeping seedlings growing strongly without a check and by helping fruit to swell evenly. Irregular watering results in tomatoes splitting which will let in disease spores. Keep the humidity up by regularly spraying—it is important to discourage red spider mite in the greenhouse and polytunnel.

Avoidance tactics

You can break the cycle of soil-borne diseases by avoiding replanting in the same area. Bush fruit will need to be renewed after a period of years (decided chiefly by observing how your bushes are looking, and how much fruit they are still producing.) Plant your new bushes in a new bed in a different part of the garden. In the vegetable garden you can rest a bed by planting it with a green manure, (sweet clover would be a good choice for a year's gap). On shrubs where the eggs of pests are laid on the new shoots you could break their cycle by cutting out the new growth two years running.

Keep it clean

Garden hygiene is super important in a confined space like a greenhouse or polytunnel, but much of the same advice applies outside as well. Destroy or burn infected plants, or damaged parts of plants, and clean the tools that have been used to cut out diseased material.

Don't leave crops in longer than necessary. This is particularly important with brassicas where crops left in over the next season encourage root and stem diseases.

As soon as you see the brown marks of blight appearing on potato foliage, cut the foliage down to the ground, cover the soil with a mulch, and leave an interval before lifting the crop. This prevents the blight spores from being washed into the soil. Check carefully any plants from friends and neighbors, especially the onion and brassica families.

Encourage your allies

The natural world around you, unravaged by chemicals, will provide several allies in your fight against pests and diseases. You can encourage them by providing the conditions they like. Plant host flowers to encourage beneficial insects. Convolvulus, verbena, scabious, and echinacea all host hoverflies, whose larvae eat large numbers of aphids (fifty a day or one thousand in a lifetime)! Dig a pond to encourage frogs and toads. Be careful not to disturb overwintering groups of ladybugs. They will repay you by eating hundreds of aphids each (5000 in a lifetime!), as well as mealy bugs and even mildews. Leave groups of stones or logs, or piles of leaves in corners. They will provide a home not only for toads, but also for the ground beetles which eat slugs, caterpillars, cabbage, carrot fly eggs, and larvae.

Learn to recognize "good" and "bad" insects. Earwigs and centipedes all eat quantities of "baddies." Spiders trap large numbers of insects. Provide winter chambers for lacewings whose larvae eat hundreds of aphids. Encourage the birds. They may eat some of your fruit, but will repay you in the number of insects and larger pests they account for. Help them through the winter by leaving seedheads on your plants, and by winter feeding.

Space control

The space between your plants will affect how well they crop and also their susceptibility to disease. Close spacing is not always a bad thing. It can shade out weeds and give you a greater crop overall. Wide spacing gives you larger individual vegetables, but closer spacing often gives a heavier crop and the smaller vegetables may be more suitable for a small household.

On the other hand, it is a good idea to sow seeds thinly. This allows the young seedlings to grow away strongly, and reduces your need to thin. Thinning disturbs the remaining seedlings and, particularly with carrots and onions, can attract the pests by the scent released. Thin carefully and ideally when rain is likely to follow afterwards and damp down the smell. Prune fruit trees and bushes to open up the branches to the air and reduce the spread of disease.

Intelligence gathering

You need to know what you are dealing with, not just in terms of insect friends and foes, but for diseases as well. Don't assume plants have a virus when it may be an easily corrected mineral deficiency, or an excess of feeding—for example, magnesium deficiency in tomatoes is from too much potassium. If your neighbor uses chemical sprays, foliage may have been damaged by spray-drift.

Keep up your defenses

You can use barriers against pest attack. Floating row cover will give frost protection, and will give early protection against pests. Later in the season, when the heavy grade cover would be too hot, a slitted row cover would be more suitable.

Cabbage mats—little squares of felt or card, or old carpet slipped round the stem—prevent the cabbage fly from laying its eggs. Heavy paper cylinders, 1–2 inches in diameter, can prevent cutworms from getting to the stalks.

You could also use mulches of grass clippings against carrot or cabbage root fly. Slugs can be kept at bay with coarse dry materials such as egg shells, wood ash, or calcified seaweed. You could make a moat around a bed of precious seedlings, use slug and snail tape around individual containers, or bottle cloches around plants (cut a plastic bottle in half and push the top half, without the lid on, into the ground).

Deterrents

Bird scare flash tape makes continuous dazzling light flashes. You could also use a homemade version with aluminum or polyethylene strips, but remove them in winter so that the birds come back to eat your pests.

Diversions

Nasturtiums attract aphids away from your precious plants; comfrey diverts slugs on their way to your potatoes.

Setting traps

Slugs and snails can be tempted into beer traps. These can be homemade, with a plastic yogurt pot sunk into the ground and filled with beer or a mixture of milk and water. Leave the lip slightly raised to stop friendly ground beetles from falling in. There are also commercial "Slug Pits" available. The yellow color of sticky traps attracts

whitefly. Light blue traps attract flower thrips, and red balls attract apple maggot flies. If you are going to introduce biological controls (see below), the sticky traps can also be used to predict when they are needed, but they should be removed before the predators are introduced or they themselves will get stuck.

Greasebands on fruit trees and sticky glue on greenhouse staging will trap climbing insects.

HIT OR MYTH

Smaller yields

It is a myth that organic yields will be lower than those from inorganic crops. Yields of organic corn were shown to equal those of corn grown with artificial fertilizers and chemical pesticides, with soil quality much improved in the organic fields.

Source: Report of research published in Nature 1998

Pheromone traps will attract and trap a variety of pest moths, (including diamond-back moths, European corn borer moths, and cabbage looper moths) by giving off the appropriate female hormones.

Go on the offensive

Small colonies of pests can be dealt with if caught early.
• Wash pests off with a fierce hose or soapy water
• Shake the plants and vacuum up the flying insects
• Pick off caterpillars or rub off groups of eggs
• Do a nightly slug check when you have just planted out vulnerable plants such as squashes

Chemical insecticides are particularly disastrous where slugs are concerned because they eat many other small creatures killed by the chemicals, have a high resistance to the chemical themselves, and survive to provide a concentrated dose to the birds and hedgehogs that eat them. Chemical slug-baits allow many slugs to recover in wet summers, and cats and dogs can get hooked on the bait, suffering paralysis of their hind quarters or even death.

Biological warfare

Biological control involves introducing a predator that will feed on the pest. This may be a hungry insect or almost invisible mites, parasites, or microscopic nematodes. They are specific to the pests and harmless to other insects and anyone else. They can be ordered by post, and you need to ensure conditions are right for the predator and that you are ready to use them on delivery.

Examples of biological controls are:

Bacillus Thuringiensis—There are several strains of this, specific to different groups of pests. They are particularly effective against caterpillars, though one strain is also effective against Colorado beetle.

Parasitic nematodes—Against armyworms, root maggots, cutworms, and many other pest borers.

Nosema locustae—Against several species of grasshopper.

Please note that if biological warfare does not appeal to you, it might be reassuring to know that the author uses none of these controls except the encouragement of naturally occurring hungry insects. With these, together with control measures, such as keeping humidity up to discourage red spider mite, and the choice of all the many other preventive techniques listed previously, any serious attacks have been avoided.

Combined efforts

The most effective strategy is to combine one or more of all the available tactics. Many of them will become built into your normal garden routine. When you come across a particular problem you can select the appropriate extra response from the methods above.

How to tackle aphids.

Rear strong, healthy plants with no artificial fertilizer

Time sowings—for example, sow broad beans early or remove the vulnerable tips on late sowings

Encourage predators—ladybugs, earwigs, lacewing, hoverfly larvae, and birds

Use diverting plants like nasturtiums

Use fine barriers such as a floating row cover

Keep an eye for early infestations, and remove leaves or rub off

Clean up in the garden—remove and burn lower leaves of brassicas

Use rotenone, pyrethrum, or insecticidal soap

The last resort

If all else fails then there are organic sprays available. Use them as the last resort as even organic sprays may kill some beneficial insects. Organic sprays are useful for specific and appropriate applications. Don't spray in windy weather. Always spray in the evening after the bees have stopped work.

Organic spray	Use to treat against
Rotenone	aphids, caterpillars, thrips, and sawfly (but note it is very harmful to fish)
Pyrethrum	aphids
Insecticidal soaps	aphids, whitefly, and red spider mite
Liquid Copper Fungicide	blight on potatoes and tomatoes
Diatomaceous Earth	ants, aphids, and slugs
Hot Pepper Wax	aphids, mites, thrips, and codling moth

And finally

There is one other possible response—give in gracefully. On a garden scale, and where you have created a balanced and healthy environment, most problems shake down—predators and pests find a balance. Each year some crops will do well and others not fare so well. You will learn what methods work best. Above all, don't get too hyped up about your garden. It is meant to be a place of earthly delight.

The harvest

Harvesting organic fruit and vegetables, chemical-free flowers, and herbs with all their natural goodness is your reward for changing the way you garden. Maximize the benefits in the way that you gather and store your produce.

The harvesting and drying of herbs was covered in *Organic All Over the Garden* and flowers would be treated in the same way. For harvesting and storing fruits and vegetables there are some good general rules.

The very best produce is what you eat straight from the garden, picked just before you need it and cooked with minimum preparation. Vegetables are best grown and then eaten in the right season. However, you may be lucky enough to have a glut, even after you've given some away. It makes sense to store some vegetables that we want to eat all year round, such as onions and potatoes.

Making the most of your crop

Gather the crop when it is at its peak of maturity, but before it has gone over. Select the best to store, avoiding any that are damaged as they will rot, and the rot will spread to your healthy crop; handle gently to avoid bruising; store in dark, cool, frost-free conditions with some ventilation and slight humidity. An insulated shed or garage, pantry or cellar is ideal. The temperature should be between 40° and 50°F.

Special conditions

Apples and pears should be handled very gently. A small crop can be wrapped individually in tissue paper and stored in boxes. The fruit can be stored in poly bags, but these should not be completely sealed—make a few small holes or just fold the top and tuck it under. Check fruit in store regularly and remove suspect fruits.

Beans Bush dry beans for drying are one of the exceptions to the rule where "peak" harvesting is concerned. They should be left to dry in the ground as long as possible.

Carrots These can be protected by drawing the earth up around them, in ridges along the rows, or in the worst weather by mulching them with straw. If the crop has been attacked by carrot fly then they are best lifted and eaten as the damage will continue. If you have severe winters both carrots and beets can be stored in barrels in sand, sawdust (not made from treated wood), or sieved leafmold, as long as it is not too damp. Lift them gently, twist the tops off, and arrange them in layers in the sand, without touching each other.

Onions and garlic Leave in the ground until the tops bend right over (do not bend them down prematurely, however neat it makes the onion bed look). Then gently lift them to release the roots and leave to dry on the surface. Lift them with a hand fork rather than pulling them. If the weather is wet, bring them in and spread them out to dry. When the stalks are "rustle" dry they can be plaited together to make an onion rope.

Onions don't need such a low temperature, but will sprout if it is too warm. Don't bother storing onions that have gone "thick-necked."

Parsnips Need to be frosted to bring out the best of their flavor, and they will survive in the ground all winter, though mulching with straw in the worst of the weather may keep the ground soft enough to lift them easily.

Potatoes Lift them carefully, working from the outside of the bed with a fork. Leave them on the surface to dry for half a day, but not much longer as they will green up. Rub any excess soil off and store in paper sacks, ideally raised up on slats.

Squash If these can dry in the sun they will develop a hard skin and will keep longer. Leave about one inch of stalk to reduce the chance of rotting. Winter squash need to be stored warmer than other vegetables, and were traditionally stored above the stables where they had a bit of warmth and humidity.

Tomatoes A polytunnel or greenhouse will give protection against early frosts. If you still have lots of tomatoes on the vine it is worth cutting the whole plant and hanging it to ripen the fruit in a shed or indoors. Alternatively, the fruit can be picked off and

HINTS AND TIPS

Onion rope
Start with three bulbs laid on the table with their stalks towards you and plait them just as you would plait hair, laying other bulbs on as you work down the plait.

Alternatively you could suspend a loop of string from a hook or chair back, pass an onion stalk through the loop and back around on itself. Each onion will be held in place by the one above, pushed firmly down the string.

stored in a drawer to ripen, with a ripe apple or banana to give off the ethylene gas that encourages this. If you have a bulk of vegetable fruits, including zucchini, peppers, and eggplants, they can be made up into ratatouille and frozen, but tomatoes on their own could be ovendried. (Most sundried tomatoes are not organic.)

Almost all other vegetables are best eaten fresh and in season, and even a small vegetable garden can provide a succession of seasonal produce. Nothing can reproduce the taste of new peas, or the first strawberries in their proper season.

Saving seeds

You can also harvest for next year's crop, and seed-saving can become a fascinating and satisfying part of your gardening. It saves money and the number of seeds you save from just one plant will probably be enough for your neighbors as well. Seeds saved from plants that have grown well in your garden are likely to grow well again as they are obviously the right ones for your conditions. It is also a way of reclaiming control of seed production. Many heirloom and heritage varieties are being lost and the increase in hybrid seed production (seeds labeled "F1" in the seed catalogs will not produce true-to-type seed) means that growers have to keep going back to the seed breeder.

Hence, the gardener is maintaining a diversity of varieties, all with their unknown qualities and benefits. The greater this diversity the safer that crop is from long-term decline, and the greater our chances of discovering pest and disease resistance in it.

Selecting the best

The best seeds will be those you decided to save rather than just the ones you found on the plant at the end of the season (though they might be better than nothing). Select the plant that you are going to save from fairly early in the season. This won't be the first in the row to go to seed as then you might be selecting for the tendency to go to seed too early! Mark the plant, or the individual pods, to make sure that you don't pick them.

If they are biennials—like carrot or parsnip—that set seed in their second year, then they will occupy that piece of ground for longer. When the seed heads are mature and dry they can be brought in and hung to dry completely, with a paper bag tied around the head to catch the seeds. Sieve the seeds to remove bits of dust and chaff, and

DID YOU KNOW?

Terminator
GM "Terminator" seeds are designed to be totally sterile thus removing the farmer's ability to save seed for the following year, a vital part of the economics of farming for the peasant farmer in developing countries.

store in cool, dark and, above all, dry conditions. And don't forget to label them!

Some seeds will cross with other varieties of the same species. Bush beans, peas, and most tomatoes do not cross, but squashes, for example, are very promiscuous, and the resulting cross from two good varieties may not even be edible itself. To save a specific variety the female flower needs to be isolated (a perforated cellophane bag will allow the flower to breath but keep out any insects), and then hand pollinated from a male flower of the same variety.

Tomato and squash seeds are best separated from the pulp and processed by the wet method. They are put in water and left to ferment. When a scum forms on the surface they are ready to be rinsed off and dried.

There are now Seed Savers networks all over the continent as people wake up to the need to preserve genetic diversity. You can play a part in that from your own patch, and benefit yourself and your garden at the same time.

Saving seeds reminds you that gardening is a continuing process and this is the joy of it. Next year we will try something different, learn from this year's mistakes, improve the soil even more, and grow an even better sunflower. All gardening is forward-looking. Organic gardening takes the longest view, never seizing the quick reward at the expense of the soil, but instead, building up its strength and health for the long term vitality of us all.

10 steps to growing organic

1. Throw away your chemicals (carefully).

2. Build a compost heap.

3. Encourage wildlife with a pond or a mini-meadow.

4. Plant flowers and herbs that will host bees, butterflies, and other beneficial insects.

5. Choose disease resistant varieties, and give seedlings a good start.

6. Practice crop rotation.

7. Mulch the soil to conserve moisture and suppress weeds.

8. Plant green manures on any unoccupied ground.

9. Use preventive rather than reactive pest and disease control.

10. Harvest at the peak of perfection, sit back, and enjoy it.

Resource material

This has been just an introduction to organic gardening. Below is a selection of books to read, organizations to join, and sources of seeds and other garden products. The organic movement is growing fast (in response to public demand!) and everyone who goes organic is adding to the patchwork.

Good books

Chicken Tractor by Lee & Forman
How chickens can help you to a productive garden and healthy soil—tilling, weeding, and manuring, as well as producing eggs.

The Edible Flower Garden by Rosalind Creasey
How to choose, grow, and eat a surprisingly large range of flowers.

Encyclopedia of Organic Gardening edited by Rodale Press
All-new edition of classic reference book. Easily accessible, practical info about gardening techniques, vegetables, fruit, and flowers.

The Herb Society of America's Encyclopedia of Herbs and Their Uses
by Deni Bown
Big reference book for background information, identification, planting advice, and uses.

Heirloom Vegetable Gardening by W. W. Weaver
Lots of relevant and interesting information about the history and cultivation of dozens of America's heirloom varieties.

101 Medicinal Herbs by Steven Foster
Historical and current uses of herbs, including dosages and contra-indications.

The Mulch Book by Stu Campbell
The labor-saving, soil-enriching techniques of mulching—what, when, and how.

The New Organic Grower by Eliot Coleman
A modern classic. A practical manual for the small market garden or large home garden, full of techniques for every stage of vegetable production.

Seed to Seed by Suzanne Ashworth
Describing the work of the Seed Savers Exchange in North America, including seed saving techniques.

Square Foot Gardening by M. Bartholomew
The techniques of a small-scale method that enables you to grow twice as much in half the space.

Worms Eat My Garbage by Mary Applehof
The complete info about redworm composting to produce one of the most valuable garden resources.

Organizations

Canadian Organic Growers
25 Sandbar, Willoway, Willowdale, Ont. M2J 2B1, Canada
Web: www.gks.com/cog/

Organic Farming Research Foundation is the only grower-directed organic farming research organization in the US, relying on donations and grants for funding their projects. Their newsletter is sent free to a mailing list of 11,000 people across the country.
P.O.Box 440, Santa Cruz, CA 95061.
Tel : 831 426–6606
Fax : 831 426–6670
Email: research@ofrf.org
Web:www.ofrf.org

The Organic Trade Association is the leading business association representing the organic industry throughout North America. The OTA aims to encourage global sustainability through promoting the growth of diverse organic trade, and its members include growers, processors, retailers, and others involved in producing and selling certified organic products. Publishes guidelines for the organic industry, "American Organic Standards."
P.O.Box 547, 74 Fairview St., Greenfield, MA 01302

Tel: 413 774-7511
Email: info@ota.com
Web:www.ota.com

Rodale Research Institute is the leading organic research group, currently led by Anthony Rodale, but started in the 1940s by J.I.Rodale. It conducts research into organic farming and gardening techniques. Rodale Press publishes books and Organic Gardening magazine.
Email: info@rodale.com
Web: www.rodaleinstitute.org

See also, some of the seed savers networks below.

Sources of seeds and sundries

Johnny's Selected Seeds
More than 900 varieties. A member of the Safe Seed Initiative that excludes any GE seeds or plants. Very informative catalog including cultural notes, garden supplies, and books.
1 Foss Hill Rd, RR 1 Box 2580, Albion,
ME 04910-9731
Tel: 207) 437-9294
Fax: 207) 437-2759
Web: www.johnnyseeds.com

Richters Herbs
Hundreds of herb seeds, plants, and dried herbs, plus large book selection.
Goodwood, Ont., L0C 1A0, Canada
Tel: 905 640-6677
Fax: 905 640-6641
Web: www.richters.com

Seeds Of Change
Certified organically grown seeds, bulbs, and perennials, specializing in heirloom varieties. No GE.
P.O.Box 15700, Santa Fe, NM 87506
Tel: 800 957-3337
Web: www.seedsofchange.com

Shepherd's Garden Seeds
Seeds and plants for vegetables, herbs, fruit, and flowers. Including heirloom varieties. No GE products.
30 Irene St., Torrington, CT 06790
Tel: 860 482-3638
Fax: 860 482-0532
Web:www.shepherdseeds.com

West Coast Seeds Ltd.
90 page catalog and organic gardening guide, including heirloom seeds for vegetables, herbs, and flowers, selected for cooler summers and mild winters.
Box 600, 8475 Ontario St. Unit 206, Vancouver, BC
V5X 3E8, Canada
Tel: 604 482-8800
Fax: 877 482-8822
Web: www.westcoastseeds.com

Organic Gardening Magazine publishes a very extensive suppliers list, updated yearly, with over 300 seed companies or nurseries, many of them offering untreated and organic seed.
Available from Organic Gardening, 2000 Rodale, Inc., Emmaus, PA 18098

Seed exchange networks

Seeds Of Diversity Canada
Seed exchange with more than 1,400 members, listing hundreds of heirloom, rare and non-hybrid vegetables. Members receive magazine three times a year plus annual seed listing.
Box 36, Station Q, Toronto, Ont., M4T 2L7
Tel: 905 623-0353
Web: www.seeds.ca

Seed Savers Exchange
The largest non-governmental organization working to save heirloom varieties, maintaining thousands of vegetable varieties.
3076 North Winn Rd, Decorah, IA 52101
Tel: 319 382-5990
Fax: 319 382-5872
Web: www.seedsavers.org

Go and see for yourself

Many organic gardens are open to the public, and if you ask around you may find neighbors who are gardening organically. There is nothing like seeing all these ideas put into practice in "ordinary" people's gardens. Actually, there is no such thing as an "ordinary organic gardener." They are all doing their bit for the world to whatever degree they can and whatever degree it is, it's worth doing.

organic

family

Pregnancy – making a good start

Most parents know that the greatest gift that they can give their children is good health. Once upon a time, this may have seemed like a simple matter of putting a roof over their heads, making sure that they had a good winter coat, and giving them decent food. The rest, parents may have reasoned, was up to chance, genetics, or divine intervention.

Today, life is more complex. We live in a polluted world surrounded daily by hundreds of man-made toxins that we can't see, taste, or even smel, but which nevertheless have the potential to damage human health. While it may appear that in spite of all this our children are being born alive and well, a closer look at infant health trends says otherwise.

Ecologists were among the first to sound the alarm alerting us to the fact that pollution doesn't just produce frogs with three eyes and birds with no beaks. The health of human babies is also at risk. Reports from the U.S. show that rates of many of the most common birth defects are on the rise. In the West, some problems, such as undescended testicles, have become so common that they are no longer recorded as malformations.

More subtle trends have also emerged. Among children, rates of allergies and respiratory problems are on the rise, as are learning and behavioral difficulties and Attention Deficit Hyperactivity Disorder (ADHD). Childhood cancers are now more common than they once were.

In a polluted world, women and children are the ones who will feel the burden more. Both are smaller and may accumulate more toxins per pound of body-weight than men. Women also have a greater amount of natural body fat than men, which means that they will be more affected because pollutants become stored in this fat. These toxins can then be released during pregnancy and breast feeding when the body is using up its stores of energy more rapidly. Babies and young children also have a less mature immune system that cannot cope with toxins.

Where do I begin?

Medical studies show that many of the chronic diseases that we accept as a "natural" part of aging—heart disease, diabetes, arthritis, and even cancer—can be "programmed" into a baby while still in the womb. What determines the programming is maternal nutrition and exposure to environmental toxins.

Today, raising a healthy baby means more than just eating well during pregnancy. It also means doing what you can to reduce your exposure to environmental toxins. Once in the body, many everyday toxins and pollutants can have a kind of "domino effect," causing damage in several different but inter-related ways. Lead, for example, can deplete the body of calcium and zinc—both crucial for mental and physical development. In turn, low levels of zinc are associated with many different types of congenital abnormalities, especially urogenital abnormalities in boys.

Not surprisingly, there has been a renewed interest in good preconceptual care and in natural methods of creating a healthy baby. For most prospective parents, making the switch to an organic, toxic-free lifestyle is a substantial and effective way forward.

DID YOU KNOW?

Fetus damage

The World Wildlife Fund has stated, in a report titled "Chemical Trespass: A Toxic Legacy," that: "It is now recognized that the fetus can be damaged by relatively low levels of contaminants which do not affect the adult...Exposure in the womb can cause birth defects and can affect our children's future ability to reproduce and their susceptibility to diseases such as cancer. Functional deficits may also be caused, such that some children may not reach their full potential. Put simply, the integrity of the next generation is at stake."

Thinking about changing

Pregnancy can be a consciousness-raising experience in several ways and many prospective parents become more aware of the presence of everyday toxins—for example, in our food and drink, and in medicines and drugs that we take—at this time.

While you may not be able to do anything about pollution from factories or cars, what you eat and drink and your home environment are largely within your control. To limit your developing child's exposure to toxins, there are all sorts of simple steps that you can take.

Change your lifestyle before becoming pregnant. As little as six months of effort can make all the difference and, many parents might reason, such an effort is worthwhile if it increases the chance that they will produce a robust, healthy child.

Fitness

Get fit, but be careful about dieting. Nutrients are the building blocks for your baby's good health. Stringent dieting accompanied by fast weight loss immediately before or during pregnancy can substantially deplete your body's store of essential nutrients. This may impact your baby's health in both the long and short term. In addition, when you lose weight quickly, toxins that are stored in fat are released into your system in large amounts.

While there is some merit in the idea of losing "toxic" fat before you conceive and replacing this with "clean" fat gained from an organic diet, this should not be attempted on your own. If you intend to diet before conceiving, make it part of a long-term health regime. Enlist the help of a qualified nutritionist who can work with you to strengthen your body, replace lost nutrients, and help aid the detoxification process. Leave six months between major weight loss and conceiving to make sure that your body is completely clear of toxins.

Don't forget dad

While the mother's health plays a major role in the health of her child, fathers are influential too! Children of men who smoke tend to be smaller at birth. Those who work in jobs that bring them into contact with pesticides and toxic chemicals are more likely to father children with birth defects. Such men often bring residues from their work home with them, raising their partners' exposure to toxins.

Some twenty different toxic chemicals with the potential to harm sperm quality and production have been found in random samples of men. Evidence has been found to show that men who eat organic foods have sperm counts that are twice as high as those who don't.

DID YOU KNOW?

Limited exposure

Seven percent of children born in the U.S. are born with birth defects that are either immediately apparent or become apparent later in life. According to the National Network to Prevent Birth Defects in the U.S., this figure could be cut in half if parents simply improved their diets and limited their exposure to toxic substances.

Food

Eat organic foods that are free from pesticide residues and GM (Genetically Modified) additives. Organic foods are also significantly higher in nutrients. On an organic diet, you and your baby will be getting more health promoting nutrients, such as calcium, iron, potassium, magnesium, manganese, and copper, in every bite.

Cut out caffeine. You probably don't think of caffeine as a toxin but, in large quantities, and especially when you are pregnant, it can be. Caffeine—found in coffee, tea, sodas, and chocolate—leeches essential nutrients out of your system, impacting on you, and your baby's health.

The most recent medical evidence suggests that consuming large amounts of coffee daily—five to six cups—can encourage miscarriage. What isn't known is whether this risk is higher in some women than in others. Caffeine also dehydrates the body. This means that the relative concentration of toxins in the blood will be higher than in a woman who limits caffeine. Instead of caffeinated beverages, try drinking organic herbal teas or grain coffees such as dandelion and chicory.

Watch out for food additives. There are nearly four thousand different types of additives used in our foods today. Many of these have been associated with developmental, behavioral, and other health problems in children. They are not very good for adults, either—often causing allergic reactions and headaches. Avoiding or limiting processed foods in your diet is the easiest way to ensure that you do not expose yourself, or your developing baby, to these substances.

Limit or avoid cured meats such as hot dogs, salami, bacon, and smoked fish. These are treated with known carcinogens (cancer causing substances) called nitrites. Prenatal exposure to nitrites raises the risk of childhood cancer. For example, it has been found that American men who regularly consume hot dogs run the risk of fathering children with an increased chance of leukemia. Likewise, women who eat cured meats during pregnancy appear to increase their child's risk of developing brain cancer. Read labels for organic cured meats carefully; organic standards have recently been changed to allow the use of nitrites in cured meats.

Drink

Limit alcohol. If you are trying to conceive or are newly pregnant, this is a good time to experiment with fruit juice-based, non-alcoholic drinks or make the switch to low-alcohol alternatives.

There is also evidence to show that consuming alcohol can interfere with normal hormonal function, making it more difficult to conceive. Once pregnant, it can prevent your baby from developing properly. Binge drinking and chronic alcoholism can

HINTS AND TIPS

Health program
A preconceptual care group has published figures that show how a pre-pregnancy health program, that includes dietary correction and reduction of toxins, can lead to an overall birth defect rate of less than 1 percent.

deplete your body of nutrients such as B6, iron, and zinc. There are no official rules for preconceptual and prenatal drinking, but official guidelines suggest that pregnant women should not drink more than one or two units of alcohol, (one unit equals one small glass of wine,) once or twice a week. Nevertheless, many women still prefer to avoid alcohol while trying to conceive and also during the first trimester, when the baby is developing.

Rethink soft drinks. Instead, for an occasional fizzy treat, try organic squashes or cordials mixed with sparkling water. Colas and other sodas are only empty calories. They contain not only caffeine but also sugar, which depresses immune function and depletes nutrients from the body. Sodas can also contain artificial sweeteners, such as aspartame, and other harmful ingredients including phosphoric acid.

Artificial sweeteners have been shown to harm the developing brain of young animals, and scientists now believe that it can do the same to human babies. They have also been shown to promote a sweet tooth, so ultimately these calorie-sparing drinks may defeat their purpose.

Recently, American researchers have made the link between soft drink consumption and brittle bones in teenagers. They are now turning their attention to what happens when mothers consume large quantities of phosphoric acid during the developmentally sensitive time in the womb. Phosphoric acid blocks the absorption of calcium and magnesium by your intestines, which means that less is available for your developing baby's bones.

Hygeine

Use non-fluoride toothpaste and check with your local water authority to see if your water is fluoridated. If it is, switch to filtered water, or a mixture of tap and filtered water, to cut down your exposure. Not many people know that fluoride is a toxic substance—a byproduct of metal refining and a widely used pesticide. It is also naturally present in foods and an average healthy diet contains all the fluoride you need. In minuscule amounts it may protect teeth. However, in high amounts it can cause brittle bones and stained, mottled teeth. Most adults and children get at least four times the fluoride that they need.

DID YOU KNOW?

Hormone disrupters

One class of chemicals causing concern at the moment is hormone disrupters. These estrogen-like chemicals are found in large amounts in pesticide residues, but also in everyday household detergents and even in disposable diapers. Scientists are concerned that exposure to these chemicals may alter our children's thyroid function and sexual characteristics. They have already been implicated in low sperm counts and there is fear that high exposure to these synthetic estrogens may predispose young girls to estrogen dependent cancers of the breast, ovary, and endometrium (lining of the womb) later in life.

Smoking

Quit smoking. There is no nice way to say it and there's too much evidence to pretend it's not true. Smoking poisons your body with carcinogenic nicotine and the toxic metal cadmium. Once pregnant, it decreases the flow of blood and oxygen to the placenta and reduces the availability of essential amino acids necessary for proper growth. Smokers are also twice as likely as non-smokers to miscarry and have ectopic pregnancy and, according to recent data, heavy smokers have as much as a 78 percent higher risk of giving birth to a baby with cleft palate or lip.

Babies of smokers are also more likely to have chronic breathing problems. Studies have shown that the lungs of babies whose parents smoke are 10 percent smaller than those of non-smokers, and that their risk of cancer is 50 percent greater. Babies of smokers are born with fewer natural reserves to fight off infection and have a 43 percent higher risk of blood disorders, nervous system and sense disorders, bladder and kidney problems, and skin disorders than children of non-smokers. Now is the time to get in touch with counselors or support groups who can help you kick the habit.

HIT OR MYTH

The placenta

Many parents-to-be are confused about the function of the placenta. Often they assume that it acts like a filter—only letting the best nutrients into their baby's system. In reality, the placenta is like a sponge. Absolutely everything that enters the mother's system also enters the baby's system via the placenta. So along with all those vitamins, minerals, and amino acids come heavy metals, car fumes, pesticides, cigarette smoke, chemicals, and drugs.

The placenta is a baby's life support system. It consists of a complex mass of blood vessels (enough to completely cover more than half a tennis court) that carry nutrients and oxygen to the baby and remove waste products and carbon dioxide. While the placenta can protect your baby to some degree, it is not a total barrier and studies show that today more than three hundred and fifty man-made toxic chemicals are being passed on to babies in increasing amounts through pathways such as the placenta.

Unlike adults, a developing baby is very sensitive to changes in the supply of nutrients and the presence of poisons. So much so that, even if the mother feels well, her child may be struggling to get what it needs to grow.

Follow a stress relief program

Stress depletes the body of essential nutrients—especially B vitamins. Mothers who are under lots of stress tend to have babies who are smaller and less active in the womb. Stress also depresses your immune system—this means that your body is less efficient at coping with the effects of inhaled and ingested toxins.

In a recent U.S. study, pregnant women who had strenuous jobs—such as those that require repetitive tasks—had a higher rate of problems, including pre-eclampsia, premature delivery, and low birthweight babies. Not all stresses can be dealt with easily, but do what you can. A large study in Sweden has recently found that the kinds of stress most likely to affect a baby's growth are lack of emotional and practical support, social isolation, and an unstable home life.

Anything that relaxes you—whether it is yoga, swimming, or "vegging out" in front of the television—should be a regular part of your routine.

Cleaning up your environment

Ironically, many of the things that we associate with making our world, and ourselves, more "civilized" are the things that pose the biggest threats to our health. For instance, air fresheners, bug sprays, household disinfectants, hair dyes, and fluoride toothpaste all contribute to a growing toxic load on our bodies.

Prospective parents can't hope to avoid all forms of pollution, but it makes sense to try and reduce the total toxic load whenever possible. Simply being aware of some of the sources of indoor and outdoor pollution can provide you with the knowledge to begin to make subtle changes in your environment.

Among the most potentially harmful substances to a developing baby are toxic metals like lead, cadmium, aluminum, copper, and mercury. These are environmental pollutants that can enter the body through inhalation or the food we eat. The greater the mother's exposure, the greater the risk is to her child. While these pollutants build up slowly in your body over time, they are slow to clear from your system. Some, like mercury, never leave the body.

Aluminum is toxic in high quantities. It attacks the kidneys and brain and can interfere with placental function. It is used as an anti-caking or bleaching agent in everyday foods such as salt, milk substitute, processed cheese, and flour. It may also be present in high levels in your drinking water. Antiperspirants and toothpastes contain aluminum and so do some antacids. Compounds containing aluminum are also used to treat public water supplies.

What you can do

• Check your cookware and kitchen utensils—a major source of aluminum exposure. Every time you use an aluminum saucepan you expose yourself to this toxic metal. If the food that you are cooking is acidic (such as apples, spinach, or rhubarb) it can release even more metal into your meal. Many pressure cookers are made with aluminum and the cooking method itself can concentrate the metal in your food.

• Avoid sodas in aluminum cans and soft drinks packed in other containers—that may be lined with aluminum.

• Avoid heating foods in foil or those served up in freezer-to-oven foil trays. Make sure foil coverings are not touching fatty foods during cooking.

• Watch out for bleached white flour products and foods containing the additive 556 (aluminum calcium silicate), E173 (aluminum—CI77000), and 554 (aluminum sodium silicate).

• Food rich in manganese will help counteract the harmful effects of aluminum.

Cadmium has been linked with both stillbirth and low birth weight. It has also been linked to pre-eclampsia. The most common source is cigarette smoke—yours and others. It is also present in drinking water, certain plastics and paints (especially with a red or orange color), enameled cookware, and some insecticides. There can also be cadmium in refined cereal products such as white flour and bread, evaporated milk, oysters, gelatin, some canned foods, pigs' kidneys from animals treated with a worm killer containing cadmium, and caffeinated drinks such as cola, tea, and coffee.

What you can do

• Avoid cigarette smoke, even the passive kind.

• Consider changing your enameled pans because cadmium can be released during cooking.

• Keep your diet low in refined foods and be aware that alcoholic drinks may contain cadmium as a preservative—another good reason to cut down or quit during pregnancy.

Copper is an essential nutrient, but in very high levels it can become toxic to the body. Mothers with high levels of copper have a greater risk of producing low birth weight babies and children with birth defects. Women get copper overload from several

DID YOU KNOW?

The effects of copper

According to Foresight, the preconceptual care group, one of the most common nutritional problems in female infertility is high levels of copper and low levels of zinc and magnesium. This view is supported by research into their program which found that high copper/low zinc affected the healthy function of the fallopian tubes, making them more vulnerable to adhesions and infection. Foresight also advises men to maintain adequate levels of zinc, manganese, and vitamins E and B12, all of which are important to healthy sperm. They also encourage couples to avoid food allergens and pollutants such as pesticides and other chemicals which can reduce fertility.

If it all sounds too easy to be true, consider the odds: only 12–20 percent of IVF treatments result in a live birth. In contrast, published research into Foresight's program showed an 80 percent success rate.

sources. Taking the birth control pill can alter the copper to zinc ratio in your body; using a copper IUD can raise levels of copper, as can drinking water that comes into the house from copper pipes. Copper is also in swimming pools that have been treated with an algicide containing copper. Cooking with copper pans or heating water in a copper kettle can also put this metal into your system because copper is more soluble in hot water.

What you can do

• Allow yourself six months from having an IUD removed, or stopping the birth control pill, before conceiving.

• Consider installing a water filter under the sink.

• Choose foods that are rich in vitamin C, calcium, and zinc, that will reduce the body's absorption of copper.

HINTS AND TIPS

Foods that prevent toxic damage

Pregnant women should not go on comprehensive detox programs. To do this risks their own health and energy and that of their baby. Instead, consider simple kitchen cupboard solutions to combat every day toxins:

• *The pectin found in apple and pear seeds can protect your body from damage by toxic metals. They work by blocking the absorption of toxins while aiding detoxification. Try making apples or pears—stewed with their seeds—a regular feature of your pregnancy diet.*

• *Garlic and onions contain powerful antioxidants that aid the body's natural day-to-day efforts to detox. Use these liberally in cooking.*

• *Peas, beans, and lentils also contain special antioxidants. They are also high in fiber that can bind to toxins and aid their excretion from the body. Pulses are a good alternative source of protein, so substitute a couple of meat meals each week for ones based on (organic) pulses.*

• *Bananas have been shown to have antioxidant qualities.*

• *Eggs protect against lead and mercury contamination.*

• *All leafy dark green vegetables—and especially those cruciferous vegetables (belonging to the cabbage family)—can inhibit the carcinogenic effects of chemicals. Include plenty of kale, spinach, broccoli, and brussel sprouts in your diet (see Organic Food and Drink for excellent recipes!).*

Lead is found in most water supplies as well as in the emissions from car engines and factories. It can also be in the food you eat because plants and animals may also have been exposed to these pollutants during their growth. Some cosmetics, such as mascara and hair darkening products, also contain lead. Lead gets into your system through your lungs but can also be absorbed through the skin. Lead contamination has been associated with deformed and dead sperm, infertility, repeated miscarriage, and stillbirth. It may also be linked with low birth weight. High levels of lead in pregnant women can predispose their children to tooth decay.

Women must be aware that if their partners work in jobs where they are exposed to high levels of lead (for example, plumbers, painters, and motor mechanics), then they can become contaminated with lead through their partners' semen.

What you can do

• Consider having a reverse osmosis water filter installed. If this proves too expensive, make sure that you run the tap a minute or two before you use the water from it for cooking or drinking.

• If your partner's job brings him into contact with lead, consider using a condom even after you are pregnant, to avoid lead being absorbed into your body from his seminal fluid.

• Tobacco is high in lead. Smokers ingest 25 percent more lead than non-smokers. Passive smoke is also a risk, so avoid it if possible.

• Avoid canned foods.

• Leave house repairs and renovations such as paint stripping to someone else.

• A healthy diet will help combat the effects of lead. Make sure that your diet is rich in foods with vitamins A, C (including bioflavonoids,) D, and E, and minerals including iron, calcium, magnesium, manganese, selenium, chromium, and zinc. Include protein and fiber in your diet, too. Eating lots of fresh garlic can also help combat the effects of excessive lead.

DID YOU KNOW?

What's in the water?

A recent study in the Journal Epidemiology *showed that toxins in water can raise a woman's risk of miscarriage. The study involved more than five hundred women and researchers found that those whose water was high in trihalomethanes were 80 percent more likely to miscarry than those whose water was low in these chemicals.*

Trihalomethanes, including chloroform and bromoform, are a byproduct of the chlorine used in water purification, and are present in virtually all water supplies.

Water can be contaminated with a number of other poisons that can harm a developing baby, including heavy metals, pesticides, and fluoride. Using a water filter—either a simple jug or a more complex device that can be installed under the sink—can substantially limit your exposure to the toxins in the water supply.

Mercury also interferes with placental function and has been linked with a higher rate of birth defects. It affects the central nervous system and brain development, and children with high levels of mercury may also be more prone to allergies. There is mercury in our drinking water and you may also ingest it by eating certain types of fish, such as canned tuna. Weedkillers and fungicides also contain mercury. But perhaps the biggest source of mercury is the fillings in your teeth. It is now widely accepted that dental amalgam leaks over time, leeching toxic metal into your body.

What you can do

• Have your metal fillings replaced by composite ones. This can prove to be expensive—although there is no rule which says that you have to do it all at one time! It is best to have fillings removed before conception. Don't attempt to have them removed during pregnancy because drilling mercury produces easily inhaled airborne dust that can get back into your system through your lungs. Instead, do what you can to reduce your mercury intake.

• Avoid canned fish, such as tuna, and also those large fish that swim in warmer waters, such as swordfish and shark. Opt instead for white fish such as cod and haddock.

• There is some evidence that eating plenty of garlic will help limit mercury absorption.

• Let someone else spray pests in the garden—or better yet, follow the advice in Chapter 4 for non-toxic gardening.

DID YOU KNOW?

Workplace awareness

Toxins that you may be exposed to at work include:

Metals for example lead, mercury, and copper

Gases such as carbon monoxide but also the off-gassing of formaldehyde from carpets, furniture, and plastics

Passive smoking

Insecticides

Herbicides

Solvents for example carbon tetrachloride, but also those used in cleaning fluids and solutions

Drugs during their manufacture

Disinfecting agents such as ethylene oxide

Fragrances such as are used in air fresheners and cleaning fluids

Cleaning up at work

Over twenty-five thousand individual chemicals are used in industry with a further two thousand compounds being added each year. If you are worried about exposure to chemicals in the workplace, consulting your general practioner may not be very helpful. This is a specialist area that may be best discussed with your company's health and safety officer or union official. There are special codes of practice which apply to pregnant women and if you think you are working with toxic chemicals then you should be entitled to arrange alternative work with your employer with no loss of pay or benefits. Because toxic chemicals can enter the mother's body after pregnancy and birth, and be excreted in breastmilk, these arrangements should continue as long as you are breastfeeding.

Even if you don't work in a job that brings you directly into contact with noxious and toxic chemicals, you may be exposed to more poisons than you might realize at your work place. A recent study, published in the *Journal of the American Medical Association*, showed that women who work with organic solvents—for instance artists, graphic designers, laboratory technicians, veterinary technicians, cleaners, factory workers and office workers, and chemists—have a greatly increased risk of both miscarriage and of giving birth to premature, low birth weight, or damaged babies.

Of course, these kinds of solvents are not restricted to the workplace. They are also common in the home—for example in cleaning products, toiletries, and paints. Information in the preceding chapters—especially Chapter 3 on the "home" that covers choosing the best paints, varnishes, and cleaning products—can help you choose alternatives that are safer for you and your child.

DID YOU KNOW?

Your options at work

If you work in a job which brings you into contact with hazardous substances or chemicals, you have a good case for asking your employer to find you alternative work while you are pregnant and while you are breastfeeding.

Employers are required to protect the health and safety of their employees and this remit includes recognizing the special needs of pregnant and breastfeeding women.

If your profession involves exposure to radioactive substances, biological hazards (such as are found in laboratory work), chemical agents, or heavy metals, then you may wish to speak to you health and safety officer to find out more about the risks of exposure and what your alternatives are.

Cool, comfortable organic maternity clothes

When you are pregnant, you're carrying extra weight and the fact that your blood volume doubles means that you can feel boiling hot even in the dead of winter. This is a good time to discover the pleasures of clothes made from natural fabrics. Unlike synthetics, clothes made from cotton, linen, silk, and wool allow the body to breathe, keeping it cool on warm days, and warm on cool days!

Most modern clothing is treated with chemicals to help it keep its appearance and to make it fire retardant. These invisible chemicals—which include pesticide residues, dyes, and fabric treatments—can be highly toxic. For example, the flame retardant used in modern clothing is a known carcinogen that can be absorbed into the system through the skin. Once this happens, it is also absorbed into your baby's system.

DID YOU KNOW?

Cutting down on toxic toiletries

In one of the largest studies ever published on toxins, a 1999 study of fourteen thousand women—published in New Scientist *magazine—revealed that pregnant women who constantly use aerosol products, such as air fresheners, deodorants, furniture polishes, and hair sprays, have significantly higher rates of headaches and post-natal depression than those who use these products less than once a week. The babies of frequent users had higher rates of ear infections and diarrhea.*

Certain everyday toiletries may also pose a threat to your unborn child's health. There is a substantial body of evidence to show that hairdressers are at greater risk of having babies with malformations than other women, and that they are more prone to miscarriage as well. This is because they are exposed daily to the poisonous chemicals in hair preparations, such as shampoo, conditioners, hair sprays, gels, mousses, and hair dyes. The average woman is not exposed to these chemicals in the same concentration, but a quick look at your bathroom cupboard might give pause for thought. If it is filled with lots of different types of hair care products, you might consider limiting your use of these products to the ones that are really necessary.

Cutting down on unnecessary toiletries is good for your budget and is a healthy habit to get into—it may help you to resist the temptation to smother your baby with the unnecessary and harsh chemicals contained in many baby products.

A non-toxic labor

If you've spent the last nine months or more avoiding toxins, eating well, and avoiding drugs, you might consider carrying on your good work during labor.

Many women work hard to protect their unborn children for nine months (or more!) and then unknowingly use some of the most powerful and toxic drugs in existence to "help" them during labor. All of these pain-relieving drugs go directly into the baby's system. And although your baby may look fully formed at birth, its insides—immune system, kidneys, liver, and lungs—are still immature. Unlike an adult's internal organs, these are not able to clear drugs from the body so easily. This means that for the first few days of life, your baby's body will be using precious energy struggling to detoxify itself. This may make your baby cranky, ill, and unable to sleep—not a very nice welcome into the world.

No one is suggesting that a laboring woman should be denied pain relief if she really needs it. But the overwhelming evidence is that birth is often more painful than it has to be because of the way it is "managed" in hospitals. For example, a woman who is on her back, or semi-reclined during labor will be working against gravity. Her

DID YOU KNOW?

Drugs in Labor

Studies on the long-term effects for babies whose mothers used drugs such as pethidine and Entenox during labor make for disturbing reading. These show a link between drug use in labor and drug addiction in later life due to what is known as "imprinting"—a memory etched into the mind during a short, sensitive period leading to specific behaviors in adult life.

Labor can involve stress for a baby. If, during this important time, drugs that relieve that stress are entering the baby's bloodstream, then the baby has received the message that this is the appropriate response to stress. While addiction itself is not the result of imprinting, it is believed to effect the tendency to use and abuse drugs at a later stage. The fact that drugs of all kinds are more available today and are more socially acceptable means that increasingly, more young adults may respond to this unconscious imprint.

Although such findings represent the extreme end of the spectrum of potential side effects of pain relieving drugs, they bring up uncomfortable possibilities which parents should consider before deciding about the use of drugs in labor.

muscles will be doing twice the work that they might have to in order to get the baby out. Her body will become fatigued much more quickly this way. Tiredness, lack of support, and a feeling as if you can't go on are the most common reasons why women ask to be completely anesthetized during labor.

In comparison, women who remain upright, mobile, and working with gravity tend to be less exhausted over the course of labor. A great deal of good information exists on more natural approaches to birth and prospective parents are encouraged to seek this out for a more comprehensive look at non-toxic labors.

DID YOU KNOW?

Aromatherapy in Labor

The largest study ever done into the use of aromatherapy in labor showed that the use of essential oils can promote relaxation and, in so doing, shorten the length of labor and substantially ease labor pain. A research team studied eight thousand women for a period of eight years. They found that among those who used aromatherapy during labor (either as an inhalation, with a massage, or in the bath), there were fewer inductions and fewer caesareans, and an almost 30 percent drop in the use of pain relieving drugs.

Newborn health

Good health may begin before birth, but the effort doesn't stop after the baby arrives. Caring for a newborn is a demanding and sometimes difficult task. While the responsibility may sometimes seem overwhelming, there is enormous satisfaction in knowing that the efforts you make now will be starting your child on the road to good, lifelong health.

Human babies are unlike any other young animals in that they are born completely helpless and with many of their bodily functions still not working optimally. This is why extra care is needed in, for example, choices of feeding and exposure to toxic chemicals and fumes.

Babies indulge in lots of hand-to-mouth activity, easily transferring more foreign substances into their bodies. Young children are also more likely to have close encounters with the pesticides on lawns and toxins in carpets because they spend a lot of time playing or crawling on the ground.

This is why a non-toxic lifestyle is essential for children. If you have been cleaning up your own act before and during pregnancy, it is not so hard to continue in this vein after the baby is born. Once again, there are no complicated solutions to protecting your child. Much of this book is devoted to supplying information so that you can make sensible, individual choices about lowering your toxic exposure. However, there are some aspects of newborn health that deserve closer attention.

The benefits of breast-feeding

Just as your baby relied upon you for protection in the womb, then it will rely upon you for some time to come for protection outside the womb. The first and most important step in providing this protection is to breastfeed for as long as possible.

No matter what formula manufacturers claim, no matter how healthy the baby in the magazine advertisement looks, and no matter how much some would like to believe it, artificial milk cannot provide anywhere near the full range of short- and long-term advantages that breast milk does.

Breast milk is economical, always the right temperature and always "on tap" and, while you are breastfeeding your baby, you are providing all sorts of other good things.

DID YOU KNOW?

Why is breast milk good?

Good bacteria—Bifidus growth factor is a helpful organism that guards against intestinal infection by discouraging the growth of yeast, bacteria, and parasites in the intestinal tract. Bifidus cannot grow in the intestines of formula fed babies.

Essential fatty acids—Necessary for proper brain development and useful for killing off parasites such as Giardia lamblia, a common cause of diarrhea in infants.

Antioxidants—Breast milk contains the full range to help your baby fight off infection and the effects of pollution. Breast milk is also high in nutrients such as zinc, selenium, and taurine, as well as immune boosting chemicals such as immunoglobulins and interferon.

Immunity to several diseases that babies are routinely vaccinated against can be passed on through the milk.

A better chance of survival for low birth weight and premature babies.

Reduced risk of gastrointestinal infections such as diarrhea, and as protection against other illnesses such as intestinal tract infections, ear infections, and colic food allergies.

The building blocks for better intelligence. By the age of three months the IQ of babies who are breast fed is three points higher than formula fed babies. By six months, the IQ of breast-fed babies can be anywhere from six to ten points higher. Breast-fed babies also show better hand-eye coordination, visual development, language, and social skills.

Natural birth control—If you are feeding in an unrestricted way you should not get pregnant during the six months after birth.

Toxic breast milk?

There has been a great deal of press recently about toxins in breast milk. Women who are considering breast-feeding their children have expressed concern that the benefits of breast milk may be negated by the presence of harmful chemicals such as pesticides.

The World Health Organization (WHO) say the "safe" daily intake of dioxins and PCBs (polychlorinated biphenyls) is around 10pg (picogram, or one-trillionth of a gram) per pound of bodyweight. Among breastfed infants the daily estimated intake of these chemicals is around 170pg per pound of bodyweight at two months and 39pg at ten months.

So how can we know that breast milk is safe? Thankfully, this is an area which has

HINTS AND TIPS

Making bottle-feeding safer

Use an organic formula. This will reduce your baby's exposure to contaminants present in conventional formulas.

Avoid formulas that contain added sugars or glucose.

Make formula as you need it, rather than storing large quantities in the fridge. This helps to avoid food borne bacteria as well as the slow leeching of plasticizers into the formula.

Use filtered water to make up formulas.

Do not heat plastic bottles in boiling water to heat the formula. When heated, the plastic in baby bottles can give off bisphenol-A, a hormone-disrupting chemical that can contaminate the formula. Sterilizing plastic bottles in this way also releases harmful phthalates.

Consider switching to tempered glass bottles that are unbreakable and completely free from harmful plasticizers and other toxins.

HIT OR MYTH

Insufficient milk syndrome

There is no such thing as Insufficient Milk Syndrome. Formula manufacturers dreamed up this advertising concept more than twenty years ago to boost sales. The vast majority of mothers (more than 90 percent) can breast feed without problems.

A woman's body makes milk according to the baby's demand. If you give your baby fluids and other foods, this will decrease the baby's demands on you and thus your milk supply.

If you follow traditional advice and feed as, and when, your baby demands, then you can't go wrong. A baby will naturally feed until it has taken all that it needs.

been studied. It was concluded that, while prenatal exposure to these levels of toxins has a definite negative effect on a baby's health and development, exposure through breast milk does not.

This does not mean that the issue of contaminated breast milk is not serious—it is. But along with contaminants, breast milk has constituents that help to fight toxic overload. The overwhelming opinion of pediatricians and child health experts is that the benefits of breast-feeding still far outweigh the potential risk of ingesting chemicals.

Remember, also, that formula made with conventional tap water is likely to contain a significant number of chemicals and heavy metals without conferring even a minute proportion of the benefits contained in breast milk.

However, if you are still worried then here are some things you can do to keep toxins out of your breast milk.

Adopt an organic lifestyle. If you don't have pesticides in your body they cannot be transferred to your baby through your breast milk.

Reduce your exposure to common household pollutants such as cleaners, disinfectants, and toiletries. The chemicals in these goods can be inhaled and absorbed through your skin. When you can't avoid using conventional household cleaners, always wear rubber gloves and open a window to minimize exposure.

Don't try to diet or fast while breast-feeding. Mostly, toxic chemicals are stored in fat. These poisons are released in great numbers when you begin to lose fat, and they can accumulate in your bloodstream and breast milk. Full time breast-feeding burns about two hundred and fifty calories per day—the equivalent of a three-mile run. Furthermore, according to child health experts like Dr Michel Odent of the Primal Research Center, the longer that a woman breast-feeds, the less contaminated her milk will become. Breast-feeding uses up calories (that is, burns up fat), and as toxic fat is burned up, this is replaced by non-toxic fat. Following an organic diet will help this process enormously.

Work some regular physical activity into your schedule. Some form of aerobic exercise can aid the release of toxins (in sweat) from your system. Another good way to rid your body of toxins is through regular deep breathing used in yoga and some forms of meditation.

HIT OR MYTH

If you choose to bottle-feed

There are several companies that now produce organic infant formulas based on cows' milk, as well as those based on soy or almonds. These are very good as follow-on milks after you have stopped breast-feeding, or for mixed feeding after a few months of exclusive breast-feeding. They can also be useful for women who elect not to breast-feed.

Bottle-feeding mothers need to be aware, however, that none of these supplies complete nutrition in itself and may also cause unexpected health problems. Some pediatricians have noted higher rates of childhood eczema associated with cow's milk formula, higher rates of asthma with soy, and diarrhea related to almond milk formulas.

If you are using these types of formulas you might try rotating them so that your child is not exposed to any one type for too long. This will reduce the risk of an allergic or intolerance reaction.

BETTER FOR THE ENVIRONMENT · 100% NON CHLORINE BLEACHED FLUFF PULP ·

A SHADE MORE NATURAL COLOUR

Treat yourself to a soak in a bath with epsom salts. This time honored remedy for aches and pains is also good for gently encouraging the release of toxins through the skin.

Remember, everything that you put in your body will get into your breast milk. So limit or avoid casual use of medicines, caffeine, alcohol, and foods with additives such as colorings, aromas, flavorings, monosodium glutomate (MSG), and aspartame. Each of these has the potential to interfere with your baby's development.

Diapers are changing

When disposable diapers first came out they seemed like a godsend to many parents. Mothers in their thousands said goodbye to washing soiled clothes and, instead, just dumped the new style diapers in the garbage with all the other household waste. Years later, the bad news about disposable diapers began to emerge.

Scientists and ecologists informed us that "disposables" weren't really disposable after all. Instead, they take thousands of years to biodegrade, which means that every soiled diaper that was ever thrown away is still festering somewhere under the earth.

The alternative to this is the reusable diaper. Several companies now produce cotton, or cotton and polyester mix diapers—usually with Velcro fasteners. Some also produce plastic or woolen outer pants, silk liners, and super absorbent cotton boosters for nighttime use.

Initially, many women might groan at the idea of using cotton diapers. They recoil at the thought of having to shake solids into the toilet. In their minds, they visualize piles of soiled diapers that will keep them chained to the washing machine all day and night. For some parents, the old-fashioned image of having to boil pans full of diapers to sterilize them hangs over their heads. Yet, none of these images reflect the reality of reusables.

Once you have a baby, you will be doing a load of laundry every day anyway, and including diapers is economical and rarely an inconvenience.

Disposables are still useful for emergencies and for travel, and some parents may prefer them at nighttime. Even better, there are now

HINTS AND TIPS

Try a diaper service

If you can't bear the thought of washing them yourself, consider a diaper service. This service is a growing, and genuinely practical, alternative—especially for mothers who are busy with work or are caring for more than one child.

Diaper services can provide parents with freshly laundered, reusable diapers—and then collect the soiled ones—for roughly the same price as the purchase of disposables.

some varieties that are made from organic constituents that are truly biodegradable and which do not have the highly suspect "super gels" in them.

Nevertheless, there are several advantages to using diapers made from natural fibers.

Economy. Washed carefully, as you would any other item of clothing, cotton diapers should last you through two (or more!) children. Cloth diapers can be washed and reused up to two hundred times and then retired into lint-free rags.

Less diaper rash. The absorbent material in disposables can make a diaper feel dry even when it is wet. Parents may be tempted to leave the baby in the diaper for longer, thus exposing the baby to the ammonia which urine produces as it breaks down. This ammonia can irritate the skin and produce diaper rash.

HIT OR MYTH

Is it important to sterilize everything your baby uses?

Sterilizing baby bottles, toys, diapers, and clothes is completely unnecessary. The types of germs in your home are the kind that you and your family are used to. They are unlikely to produce anything which your baby cannot cope with, particularly if you are breast-feeding and thus passing on some of your own immunity.

In contrast, traces of disinfectant on clothes, bottles, and toys can be harmful to baby's delicate skin and, if ingested, could make the baby sick.

Take the hint from our hospitals, which are supposed to pay closer attention to the process of killing germs than most other environments. Not only do they find it impossible to be completely sterile, but their efforts have contributed to the growth of "superbugs"— bacteria immune to the strongest bleaches, the most powerful antibacterial cleaners, and to antibiotic medicines.

No suspect chemicals. Conventional diapers are bleached using chlorine bleach. Because of this they can off-gas dioxin—a carcinogenic byproduct of the bleaching process. They also contain a super-absorbent "chemical sponge," a gelling material known as sodium polyacrylate. This gel emits an estrogen-like chemical with the potential to reduce future fertility when kept in constant close contact with the testicles. When "super gels" are dry (for instance in a fresh diaper), they are powders. Pediatricians report that it can travel up the urogenital tract of boys and into the vaginas of little girls, where it may cause damage and scarring.

Better use of world resources. According to the 1996 Women's Environmental Network report "Preventing Diaper Waste," using cotton diapers ultimately conserves the earth's resources. Based on five thousand and twenty diaper changes over a two and a half year period, it is estimated that while both systems require similar amounts of fossil fuel energy, disposables use three and a half times the total energy, eight times more non-renewable materials and a staggering ninety times more renewable materials. Disposables produce sixty times more solid waste, and use 20 percent more land for growing the materials used in their manufacture.

Less waste. More than eighteen billion disposable diapers are sold in the U.S. each year, containing some sixty-seven thousand tons of non-biodegradable plastic. Diapers account for around 10 percent of all U.S. household waste. At least one hundred viruses found in feces can survive for over two weeks in rubbish and runoff from a landfill site containing such viruses can contaminate groundwater supplies.

Introducing baby to solids

As a rule of thumb, parents should wait until their babies are six to seven months old before introducing solids. By this time, their systems are mature enough to eat mashed foods. Around this time they are also ready for more vitamins and calories than breast milk can supply. So this is a great time to experiment and help your baby explore and enjoy new tastes and textures.

In general, you should introduce solids a little at a time, perhaps just one meal a day for a week or two. Never try to force a baby to feed. If your baby spits the food out or drools when fed, then they are probably not quite ready for solids. Wait a few more weeks and try again—otherwise solid food becomes associated with tension and trauma for baby—and mess and more work for you.

Introducing some foods too early—particularly dairy and wheat—can cause food intolerance later in life. Babies' intestines are still very porous and this means that large food molecules can get into the blood system, potentially causing allergic reactions. Common signs of food intolerance and allergy include rashes, flushing, runny nose, diarrhea, colic, eczema, crying, breathing problems, and dark rings under the eyes. To avoid this, try introducing new foods according to the following guidelines.

6–9 months
Fresh vegetables (except those belonging to the nightshade family: potato, tomato, egg plant, peppers)
Fresh fruits (except citrus and strawberries)
Dried fruits (unsulfered)
Gluten free grains (brown rice, millet, quinoa, buckwheat)
Beans and pulses
Organic poultry, meat and fish (not shellfish)

9–12 months

Low gluten grains (oats, rye, and barley)

Corn

Nightshade vegetables

Soy products

Finely-ground nuts and seeds

12–24 months

Wheat (bread, pasta, flour)

Dairy products (whole cows' milk, cheese yogurt)

Citrus fruits

Eggs

24 plus months

Shellfish

Strawberries

Fast food for babies

Previously, there was either no organic baby foods to choose from or else you had to go to the health food shop (if there was such as shop in you area) to buy them, but today many supermarket shelves are bursting with organic alternatives for both babies and parents.

If you have a busy lifestyle or are simply not confident in your ability to cook for your baby, the next best thing is preprepared baby foods. Until recently, this meant conventional foods that were made from produce sprayed with pesticides and herbicides. Today, however, organic baby foods account for between 15 and 20 percent of the total baby food market.

Buying organic

Most concerned parents would reason that as long as they are buying organic baby food, then they are giving their child the best. But, when you are shopping, don't buy a jar just because it's organic. There are ingredients in all pre-packaged food that, although natural enough, can have other drawbacks and which you should keep a close look out for.

open→

Nutrition Facts

Serving Size 1 jar

Amount per Serving	
Calories	130
Total Fat	8 g
Sodium	80 mg
Potassium	180 mg
Total Carb.	11 g
Fiber	2 g
Sugars	3 g
Protein	3 g

% Daily Value

Protein 15% • Vitamin A 600%

Vitamin C 0%

Calcium 4% • Iron 4%

• CONTAINS NATURAL VEGETABLE SUGARS ONLY •

Quality Choice

☑ No Added Su...

☑ No Artificial Colors
Flavors or Preser...

PROOF OF PU...

0 522170

DID YOU KNOW?

What's in that jar?

In 1998 a major US study found that nine out of ten children, aged six months to five years, were exposed to thirteen different neurotoxic organophosphate pesticides in the food they ate. Many of these children were consuming quantities of organophosphates at levels that are known to cause damage to the developing brain and nervous system.

In this study, conventionally produced baby food—including apple juice, apple sauce, and meals containing pears and peaches—was one of the main sources of unsafe pesticides.

British researchers have also found multiple pesticide residues in conventional baby food. A 1999 report by the Working Party on Pesticide Residues (WPPR) stated that one in eight—more than 12 percent—of baby food jars containing regular fruit and vegetable baby meals have pesticide residues in them. Of these, nearly one third contained several pesticides known to cause adverse reproductive effects. The WPPR also concluded that because they only tested a limited range of foods, these results were probably an underestimate and that levels of pesticide residues on produce were probably 20 percent higher than reported.

Fillers such as rice starch to thicken watered-down recipes.

Sugar from hidden sources such as fruit juice concentrates and many products that claim "no added sugar" can be just as sugary as those that do not make this claim.

Misleading labeling. For instance, the jar may not actually contain much of the nutritious food advertised on the label. Everything—even the name of a product—gives a clue to what is really in it. For example a lamb and potato casserole will have a minimum of 10 percent lamb in it. But a potato and lamb casserole can contain less then 10 percent meat.

Hollow "healthy choice" claims. There are strict laws governing what can and cannot be put into baby foods. Baby foods which claim "no artificial colors" and "no preservatives" are not necessarily better than those which don't make this claim. Artificial colors and preservatives are not allowed by law in any baby foods. Likewise, there are rules and recommendations governing the amount of salt and the types of flavorings used.

Added vitamins and minerals. Not always a bad thing, but food manufacturers often add vitamins and minerals to foods that are nutrient poor or which have lost their nutrients during processing.

Simple ideas for first foods

Bottles and jars can be useful supplements to a diet based on home-cooked foods, but no baby should rely solely on pre-packaged foods to fulfill nutritional needs.

Fresh food has the advantage of supplying important enzymes and amino acids that are never present in commercially produced foods. From a budget point of view, homemade food is also much cheaper, especially if you are giving your baby the same foods that you are eating each day.

First foods should consist of organic fruits, cereal, and vegetables (introducing protein comes a little later). It is best to introduce new foods one at a time. In the beginning, give your baby a large amount of one single food at mealtime rather than lots of little tastes of different foods. After a month or so, you can begin mixing simple foods for greater variety.

RECIPE

Simple apple purée

Apples are tasty, naturally sweet, and rich in vitamin C.

Put 2 pounds of organic eating apples (peeled and cored) in a pan with 9 fluid ounces of filtered water and bring to boil. Simmer until the fruit is soft. When cooled, purée in a blender to the desired consistency. Pour the mixture into ice cube trays and freeze for use later. To add a little extra flavor you can add a scant pinch of cinnamon to the recipe while you are cooking.

As baby develops, this puree can be added to rice cereal to make a creamy and slightly sweet breakfast cereal

RECIPE

Three fruit purée

A nice little treat for your baby which is rich in essential nutrients. Make this mixture as you need it because bananas don't freeze very well.

Simply mix your apple purée with a very ripe, mashed pear and a little banana. Process all these through a mouli or a sieve and serve.

RECIPE

Butternut squash purée

This subtly flavored orange squash is similar to pumpkin. It is rich in beta-carotene.

All you need is 1 butternut squash. Cut the squash in half, peel, and remove the seeds. Cut the flesh up into small cubes and steam for eight to ten minutes until soft. Purée and use water, formula, or breast milk to adjust the consistency. Freeze for future use.

In general, if a food can be eaten raw—such as bananas, avocado, papaya, or a very ripe pear—then give it raw. Mash these foods or put them through a sieve or a mouli (a small food grinder ideal for making baby foods) when you need them, and you will ensure that baby is getting the most vitamins, minerals enzymes, and fiber from that food. But some "first" foods will have to be cooked and it is very important that you do not use seasonings such as salt, pepper, butter, or sugar.

The best solid food for your baby is the food you make yourself. Keeping a little bit of unseasoned food back from your regular meals and putting this through a blender is the cheapest and easiest way to provide nutritious first foods for your baby.

The easiest way to make cooked foods is to make them in quantity and freeze them in ice cube trays. At six months or so, a single cube defrosted will make an adequate meal for most babies.

HINTS AND TIPS

The nutrients you can't see

One reason why weaning can be difficult is that it does not have the same feel of intimacy that breast-feeding does. Sharing, intimacy, and love are important nutrients that help your child grow.

A child who is stressed out at mealtimes is also less able to absorb nutrients from food. Without these nutrients, baby is more vulnerable to the effects of toxins in the environment. Keeping these new style mealtimes calm and happy means that your baby will learn to enjoy solids and will also be getting all the nutrients needed from them.

RECIPE

Baby oatmeal

For a simple, creamed cereal suitable for babies of age nine to twelve months, start with organic oats.

Grind the oats in a blender or coffee grinder until they are a fine powder.

Mix this with a warm liquid made up of equal amounts of water and formula (or, even better, breast milk) and stir into a smooth gruel. Oats are naturally sweet and rich in iron, so you do not need to add anything else.

RECIPE

Cod and spinach main meal

Cod is a mild fish—high in protein and a good first taste of seafoods.

Steam or oven-cook a fillet of cod and 2 handfulls of spinach in 4 fluid ounces of filtered water. Put in a food processor with 2 ounces of well-cooked brown rice and blend to the right consistency. Freeze and use as needed.

Any vegetable can be made into a simple purée. Because potatoes are a member of the nightshade family, they are best suited to babies that are aged between nine and twelve months. Both zucchini and watercress are iron rich foods. Potatoes are a useful source of calcium.

RECIPE

Purée of courgette and potato with watercress

Steam one large organic potato (peeled and chopped) until nearly tender. Then add one medium zucchini (washed, but keep the skin) and a small handful of chopped watercress leaves, and cook until completely tender. The cooked mixture can then be puréed using water or formula (or breast milk) to adjust the consistency. Freeze to use as needed.

Non-toxic toys

How dangerous are the soft plastic toys that our children, and the generations before them, have been so innocently playing with? According to the international environmental group, Greenpeace, soft PVC toys, particularly those designed to go in the mouth, are potentially very dangerous. They point to scientific evidence showing that those made from PVC, that contain a softening chemical called phthalates, can pose a serious health threat—possibly causing liver, kidney, and testicular damage. Greenpeace has said it would like to see all PVC toys for under-threes removed form the shelves whether they are designed to go in the mouth or not. All over the world, governments and manufacturers are slowly responding to this information.

DID YOU KNOW?

Toxic teething toys

Canada has also added its voice to the growing concern over the use of phthalates in children's toys. In 1999, after a year-long review, the governmental group, Health Canada, concluded that children weighing under eighteen and three-quarter pounds, and who suck on products such as teethers and rattles made with di-isononyl phthalate (DINP) for more than three hours a day, run the risk of liver enlargement or kidney scarring.

In the U.S., a few companies are beginning to phase out the use of phthalates and PVC products intended for the under-threes, but they are still widely available. Parents will need to choose carefully or contact manufacturers for data on product ingredients.

While some argue that it is impossible to determine how much phthalates can migrate from PVC toys into a baby's mouth and into its system, others argue that parents should not be expected to use their children as guinea pigs.

These are not, however, the only hazards that children's toys contain. Lead and cadmium are also used in the manufacture of soft chewy toys, to help stabilize the vinyl. Ingestion of these can result in brain and nervous system damage (in the case of lead) and cancer and kidney disease (in the case of cadmium.)

Recently, there was a major health scare in the U.S. when it was discovered that some crayons (which, as any parent knows, regularly end up in the mouth) contain asbestos. Crayon manufacturers use talc to coat the finished product and talc is frequently contaminated with asbestos.

Other unhealthy toys

There has also been concern expressed in the medical press that the current trend for noisy toys—the ones which squeak, squawk and sing—may be damaging to our children's hearing. According to some scientific reports, squeaky, brightly-colored toys for babies and toy motor vehicles may emit sounds of seventy eight to 108 decibels. When held at arm's length, such toys may reach one 112 decibels. At a child's ear, toy mobile phones may emit one hundred and twenty two decibels and toy weapons may emit as much as one hundred and fifty to one hundred and sixty decibels—well over what it would take to cause damage to children's' delicate ears.

When choosing toys for your baby, consider those that are made from sustainable wood and recycled, unbleached, untreated, chemical free, or organic fabrics. Electronic toys are not suitable for younger children. Several companies now produce such toys and these are becoming increasingly easier to find in stores.

A nice clean baby

Newborn babies are not "dirty." The amount of vernix and blood which covers a newborn baby varies enormously. It is probably fair to say that it is adults, not babies, who prefer the smell of talcum powder and cream. Today, the view is that vernix acts to protect the newborn's sensitive skin during the first days of life and should be left to come off naturally over a period of time. A newborn baby is many times more likely to absorb toxic substances from a toiletry product that an adult, so always use these sparingly.

Even those baby bath products that are extra mild will be too harsh for most babies. Many pediatricians have expressed concern for babies who are exposed to detergents, creams, and oils at a time when their skin is so thin and permeable. Skin reactions to liquid and bar soaps are common.

DID YOU KNOW?

Coming clean

Bubble baths, which strip the skin and mucous membranes of protective oils, are a major cause of urogenital infections in newborns and infants.

Mineral oil does not moisturize the skin. It puts a sticky barrier on top of it that can trap dirt, prevent the skin from breathing, and will eventually strip essential moisture from it.

Talcum powder and cream can actually make your baby dirtier. It can become sticky and unpleasant if your baby becomes overheated, hot, and sweaty. Inhaling talcum powder, which can be contaminated with asbestos, is a cause of respiratory problems in babies.

Baby wipes can contain alcohol that can irritate your baby's skin. Plain water is all that is necessary to clean your baby during diaper changes.

Not all babies enjoy early baths and not all parents find bathing their newborn the relaxing scene it is often made out to be. So why not give yourselves a break. If you want to wash your baby, consider the "top and tail" approach, rinsing the bottom area and face only, with plain water for the first few weeks or more.

Clothing—the organic options

Babies spend a lot of time in playsuits and asleep in their cots. What they wear should be safe but, instead, can often be a continual sources of toxic gases.

Conventional clothes are made from a mixture of natural fibers—such as cotton—which have been sprayed with tons of pesticides and synthetics. Many children's clothes, especially nightwear, are treated with carcinogenic flame retardant.

Natural and organic clothing may be more expensive, and is often only available through mail order. However there are many compelling health and environmental reasons to consider when weighing them up against their more readily available and often cheaper conventional counterparts.

If you are concerned that chemicals in your clothes may be adding significantly to your child's total toxic load, then you need to ask yourself if you can afford not to go natural or organic. There are ways to reduce your risk from conventional bedding.

Dress your baby in organic fibers where possible. Popular choices include cotton, wool, silk, and, more recently, hemp. Reducing toxins in diapers has already been discussed, but T-shirts, sleep and play suits—anything which gets next to your baby's skin can be made that much safer by switching to organic. In general, clothes marked

DID YOU KNOW?

Toxic clothes

In 1977, the flame retardant TRIS (2,3 dibomopropyl) phosphate—a known carcinogen—was finally banned from use in children's sleepwear. At the time of the ban, it was estimated that fifty to sixty million children wore TRIS treated garments. TRIS has been shown to affect kidney, liver, and lung function and to cause mutations in some bacteria. In animal models, it has caused testicular shrinkage and reduced the reproductive capacity of females. Although banned in clothing, TRIS remains a danger to children because it is still used as a flame retardant in polyurethane foam, car seat cushions, and other consumer products.

"flame-resistant" are a low risk. Those marked "flame-retardant" should be avoided because they may be chemically treated.

Look carefully at labels. Many companies—and even environmental organizations—offer clothes, bedding, and changing bags made from unbleached, conventionally-grown cotton. The off-white appearance of the fabric, and the claim of "natural," can make consumers believe they are buying a truly ecological item. Unbleached cotton is only a half solution. It may not contain chlorides but can still contain harmful pesticides.

The useful contacts at the end of this chapter can help you find companies that supply good quality clothing and bedding for your child and for the whole family.

Organic bedding

Remember that bedding and clothing are often made from similar fabrics, so that most of what applies to one, also applies to the other. Bedding is sprayed with the same pesticides and synthetics as clothes and organic goods remain more expensive to buy than conventional bedding.

Look for cotton sheets, pillow cases, and towels made from untreated natural organic fibers. Generally, easy care—or non-iron—fabrics have been treated with formaldehyde. This treatment is designed to remain in the fabric for the lifetime of the product. Again, it's worth looking carefully at the labels when making your purchase to see if the fabric is flame-resistant and truly organic. The most recent evidence suggests that the off-gassing from infant bedding is an important, but often overlooked, possible cause of sudden infant death syndrome (SIDS).

Chlorinated phosphate compound and melamine (the same compound used to coat wooden floors,) are routinely used to treat most polyurethane foam mattresses to make them flame-retardant. Phosphorus is also, reportedly, still used as a fire-retardant in conventional cotton mattresses.

If you use a regular mattress, cover it with several layers of old cotton blankets washed in a unscented detergent or plain baking soda. If you or a kindly relative can sew, make a casing for the crib bumpers out of a heavy barrier cotton cloth that keeps the toxic plasticizers and formaldehyde-stuffing gases to a minimum. Or, start from scratch by making a crib bumper from cotton cloth that is stuffed with organic cotton.

Another option is to avoid the use of cribs altogether and sleep with your baby by your side. Co-sleeping is convenient for breast-feeding and has been shown to lower incidence of SIDS. Pay attention to the fabrics and furniture used in your own bedroom, though.

The vaccination debate

Our ability to deal with everyday toxins is dependent on many things—but most of all on the strength of our immune systems. This is why the debate over routine vaccinations, and their potential effects on children's immune systems, has become an important aspect of the organic debate.

DID YOU KNOW?

Health alert

It's not just vaccines that can assault your child's system. Common over-the-counter drugs—such as cough and cold medicines, and products used to treat conditions such as colic and diaper rash—can also be toxic to young bodies. Often these products are more effective at treating parents' distress then they are at treating simple health problems.

Most childhood illnesses (such as measles, mumps, and rubella) are mild. Nevertheless, babies are being immunized earlier and the long-term effects of this are only just beginning to surface. Many parents are beginning to express concern about the potential long-term effects of immunization and medical research is beginning to add legitimacy to their concerns.

The principle behind vaccination is that a small amount of dead or non-active virus is injected (or in the case of polio, live virus is given by mouth) into the blood stream. The body responds by forming antibodies against the virus. If an individual then comes into contact with the live virus, the body already has a stored surplus of antibodies with which to fight it.

DID YOU KNOW?

Vaccine concerns

• *The vaccine dosage has never been appropriately adjusted to take account of an infant's lower body weight.*

• *Vaccines, as they are manufactured today, contain proteins similar to those found naturally in the human body. Once administered, the body forms antibodies for these proteins. These can eventually result in the malfunctioning of the immune system where these antibodies end up attacking their own system.*

• *Administration of these vaccines actually diminishes the body's natural ability to fight disease.*

• *Some modern vaccines have been shown to contain heavy metals such as mercury and aluminum.*

In contrast to the confidence of health authorities and governments, a very strong lobby against the routine administration of vaccines has emerged.

There are now large amounts of evidence that the program of blanket vaccinations causes other diseases—everything from autism to arthritis. We also know that in some cases disease is not eradicated, but simply by delayed by vaccination. Measles is now an adult disease—causing more harm than it would if it had been allowed to take its course in childhood.

Delaying or deciding against vaccination

Parents who choose to immunize their children should be fully informed and are, on the whole, supported in their choice. The parent who goes along to a doctor's office requesting the full set of injections for their child is unlikely to be met with the question "Are you sure?"

Parents who wish to delay or decline vaccination need extra support. So, whether you decide to immunize your child or not, try to find out all that you can about the vaccines which we currently give our children.

If you choose not to immunize your child, or to delay the decision to vaccinate until a later date, then there are some effective ways of ensuring your child's continued health. Breast-feed your child for as long as possible—your baby's system will not develop its full complement of antibodies until the end of its first year. It is no mere chance that increasingly early immunization mirrors the sharp decline in breast-feeding rates which occurs at two months after birth. Although breast-feeding does not provide immunization against all diseases, certain antibodies, that the mother has, will be passed on to the child. These include diseases which the mother may already have an immunity to, such as tetanus, whooping cough, diphtheria, and polio, as well as other distressing conditions such as typhoid, dysentery, gastroenteritis, flu, and pneumonia.

Some mothers choose to breast-feed their children for six to nine months and then vaccinate. This gives the child's own immune system a chance to become stronger, thus minimizing the possible impact and side effects of the vaccine on your child.

Avoid early contact with other children and places like public swimming pools which are breeding grounds for all kinds of bacteria and viruses. Doing this helps reduce unnecessary early challenges to your baby's undeveloped immune system.

A non-toxic nursery

Many parents energetically enter into preparations for their new babies. These may include turning a spare room into a nursery complete with newly painted walls, fresh carpets, a new crib, blankets, mattresses, and lighting fixtures.

While these preparations may go a long way towards making a room look nice, they may not offer such a warm welcome for your newborn. Instead, they may be exposing your infant to a whole range of toxic chemicals from the volatile organic compounds (VOCs) wafting off fresh paint, to the formaldehyde gas being given off by the carpets, furniture, wallpaper, and even bedding.

But it doesn't have to be that way. Nurseries can be both clean and healthy with a little forethought.

When choosing paint, do it as far as possible in advance of the baby's birth. Use water-based latex paint that has 50 percent less VOCs than alkyd or oil based paints. Some newer brands of paint are even VOC-free. But if you are very concerned about the other potentially toxic ingredients in paint, you can now buy paints made from earth pigments, lime, and a milk derivative called casein. Milk paints come in powdered form and must be mixed with water.

Natural wood furniture is substantially less toxic than that which is made from synthetic materials. Furniture made from pressboard and plastic containers can give off toxic formaldehyde gas.

Synthetic carpets are not only non-biodegradable, they can give off a steady stream of formaldehyde gas for many years. In addition, they may be tainted with around 120 other noxious chemicals. If you chose this option, make sure that you air the room out thoroughly before putting your baby in it. Opt instead for wood floors or natural fiber carpets. Some suppliers sell untreated wool carpets with natural latex and jute backing. These can either be undyed or dyed using organic plant based dyes.

To remove traces of indoor air pollution in the nursery, decorate the room with plenty of green plants such as devils ivy, nephthytis, and spider plants. These have been found to absorb a significant quantity of toxic chemicals.

All cotton bedding has many advantages over synthetics. Being a natural fiber, it is warmer and allows the skin to "breathe." This means that there is less chance of your baby overheating and dehydrating in the night.

Toddler to child...
and beyond

Children grow quickly and, watching their remarkable progress from a helpless baby to a walking and talking individual, it is easy to believe that they are no longer as vulnerable as they were as newborns. To some extent this is true. Your child's immune system has matured—but not fully.

As a child grows, so does the potential for greater exposure to environmental toxins. Starting playgroup, preschool, kindergarten, or school can expose a child to more bacteria, viruses, and allergens than are normally encountered at home. To combat this, parents may start giving their children conventional medicines. Time constraints and "fad" eating may mean resorting to convenience foods. Inside the house there is exposure to electromagnetic fields from televisions and computers. Out of the house there is further exposure to pollutants and, if it is sunny, more chemicals in the form of sunscreens.

Give them organic foods

It may be the most important step you take. In spite of what appears to be a junk food culture, children still eat more fruits and vegetables than adults, consuming up to twelve times as much pesticide residues in the process. In the U.S., it is estimated that three to four million children now have toxic lead levels in their bodies. In addition, junk and convenience foods can be very high in anti-nutrients such as sugar and salt, and hydrogenated fats, coloring, preservatives, and flavors. Putting the emphasis on fresh, organic foods avoids such chemicals.

In addition, make sure that your child gets plenty of variety in their diet. Many children's day-to-day diets are made up of the same types of foods over and over again. This can lead to food allergies and nutritional deficiencies which can alter appetite and weaken the immune system.

Teach your children to drink water. Sodas, fruit juices, and milk top the list of favorite drinks for many children. Equally, some parents feel that they are somehow depriving their children of a "good" drink if they only offer water. But water is necessary for life and is more thirst quenching than any other drink. Adequate amounts of water can also help the body flush out toxins and is necessary to maintain the efficiency of many other bodily functions.

It would be nice to think that our children could get all the nutrients they need from their diets, but this is just not possible. As our world becomes more and more polluted, it is even more important to give you child a daily multivitamin and mineral supplement since a well nourished body is better able to cope with pollution. Many popular brands of children's vitamins only contain a few essentials, such as vitamins A, B, C, D, and E. You may need a trip to the health food shop to find a supplement for children with the full range of nutrients.

Healthy eating

A healthy diet is essential to maintaining your child's good health. But while this is easy to say, it's not always so easy to do. Each week it seems that parents are faced with new and often contradictory nutritional advice. As a result, trying to provide "good" food for your child can be about as easy and as much fun as feeding the lions.

The American Medical Association's Children's Nutrition Study of 1998—which included over seven hundred American parents—highlighted similar problems. Each parent was quizzed as to their personal understanding of "good nutrition" as well as their perceptions of the attitudes and eating habits of their children.

Nearly all of the parents—99 percent—agreed that "it is important for my child to eat

DID YOU KNOW?

So long sodas

In the summer of 2000, research scientist Dr. Roland Griffiths published a report in the Archives of Family Medicine *that was highly critical of the soft drink industry. In it, he cited the parallels between the marketing of nicotine and the marketing of sodas—many of which contain caffeine. Until recently, cigarette companies were still claiming that nicotine was simply a flavor enhancer and not an addictive drug. Soda manufacturers likewise claim that caffeine—present in 70 percent of all sodas—is simply a flavor enhancer.*

Caffeine is an addictive and mood altering drug and one of the most common psychoactive drugs consumed in the world, but most consumers are unaware of its effect.

According to Dr. Griffiths, "Adults and children become physiologically and psychologically dependent on caffeinated soft drinks, experiencing withdrawal symptoms if they stop." He accused the soda industry of loading their drinks up with high amounts of caffeine to keep young customers coming back for more.

nutritious foods." The majority of parents—91 percent—believed it was important to restrict sugar and dietary fat in their children's diets. In spite of this, the rest of the survey showed that children continue to load up on these things. Soft drinks were picked by more parents (27 percent) as their child's "preferred" drink over any other beverage. And those fatty foods—like potato crisps and snacks—were eaten by youngsters nearly five times per week.

A healthy diet is like a jigsaw puzzle—each piece is an important part of the whole picture, and no piece can replace another. From this viewpoint, no food is good or bad in itself. What makes diet good or bad is whether the pieces all fit together. But, over-dependence of junk and convenience foods can lead to unforeseen problems.

Why is my child a picky eater?

All children go through periods where they will only eat *this* and never *that*. But for some children "fad" eating and an apparent addiction to junk foods can easily become a chronic problem.

Children develop a taste for junk food because it is highly flavored with sugar and salt, as well as strong artificial flavorings and flavor enhancers. In a diet where fruits and vegetables are the preferred snack, fiber has the job of slowing down how quickly carbohydrates are digested and released into the bloodstream. In contrast, junk foods tend to be low in fiber so that kids get a quick burst of energy from them (even the savory variety). Even if your child's diet is "well balanced," eating junk foods can work in more subtle ways to compromise health and appetite. Fast foods—particularly kids' favorites like fries, hamburgers, and chicken nuggets—contain free radicals, which are produced when anything is deep fried. Free radicals act like chemical snipers in the body, by damaging whatever tissue or organ they attach to.

Free radicals, combined with the hydrogenated or partially hydrogenated oils that are added to processed baked goods, luncheon meats, and virtually all convenience foods, are very efficient at destroying "good fats"—essential fatty acids—necessary for zinc absorption. Zinc has many functions in the body including regulating appetite control.

In addition, when children are low in zinc, they often have a reduced sense of taste and smell. This may mean that they only respond to foods that contain lots of salt, sugar, artificial flavoring, or flavoring enhancers.

Processed foods like hamburgers and soft drinks are also high in phosphates—chemicals to help carbonation or preserve processed foods. Phosphates also block absorption of zinc as well as calcium and magnesium. High phosphate consumption has also been shown to lead to brittle bones in teens.

DID YOU KNOW?

Sugar and immunity

The average modern diet contains around 5 ounces of sucrose each day. Consuming just 2½ ounces of glucose inhibits the body's ability to produce antibodies to invading organisms. Consuming 3½ ounces of sugar in the form of glucose, fructose, sucrose, honey, or orange juice has been shown to significantly reduce immune system function within less than thirty minutes.

Just two hours after consuming this much sugar, your immune system will be functioning at 50 percent efficiency, and may continue to do so for more than five hours.

This means that the "healthy" fruit juice, claiming to be packed with vitamin C, in reality may be so full of sugar that it renders any added vitamins useless.

Artificial sweeteners such as aspartame are not the answer. They contain a powerful stimulant, phenylalanine, which can hype children up as much as sugar. Furthermore, their long-term safety has never been adequately proven. The only answer is to provide alternative foods and to look out for the hidden sugars in children's drinks and foods, and leave those products for very occasional treats.

Foods to avoid

While advertising and peer pressure play a part in turning kids into picky eaters, sometimes food that is served up with love and good intentions is at the root of dinner time battles at home. Much of what children consume can set up a biochemical reaction that can stop them wanting to eat "good" foods. Among the biggest culprits that are commonly consumed are milk, wheat, and dairy, but also oranges and other citrus and tomatoes (and other members of the nightshade family such as potatoes and peppers).

You might reasonably ask, "If these foods are so popular, and everyone eats them, how bad can the effect be?" Consider what over-consumption of the three most popular foodstuffs can do to a child.

Sugar

From a very early age, many parents unknowingly give their kids so-called "healthy" drinks and foods which, in reality, are loaded with "hidden" sugar in the form of glucose, maltose, dextrose, and fruit juice concentrates. Digestive problems, diarrhea, failure to thrive, chronic congestion, obesity, and lowered immunity top the list of health problems that are linked to the excessive sugar found in fruit juices and other sweet drinks.

Sugar drains essential nutrients from the body. Appetite is controlled in part by the presence of vitamins and minerals in the blood so that when a growing child eats something sweet, which is also high in calories, their caloric requirements are satisfied, but not their nutritional requirements. The brain then sends out a message that the body still needs these missing nutrients. This can result in a vicious circle of overeating, often of the same non-nutritious foods.

Dairy products

Most of us have been brought up to believe that children need to drink milk in order to thrive. Milk is often given to children who won't eat anything else as a way of providing basic nutrition. However, many nutritionists are now challenging the value of milk, saying that over-consumption of cow's milk can lead to food allergies and other problems. For example, milk and dairy products can block iron absorption, with high consumption leading to anemia—a condition that affects a large percentage of today's children. The well-known and recognizable symptoms of anemia are tiredness, fatigue, change in pallor, and lack of stamina. Less well-known are poor appetite and poor growth.

Children that suffer from an iron deficiency have a greater ability to absorb toxic metals, such as lead and cadmium, which not only affect learning and behavior but can block the absorption of other vital minerals, such as zinc. Remember, also, that milk today is laden with pesticides, fertilizers, hormones, farmyard waste, trace metals, and radioactivity. We have no way of knowing what the effect of these products is on a young body.

Wheat

Wheat products such as bread, pasta, cakes, and cereal form the staple of many children's diets from a very early age. Besides being a common allergen, wheat is high in phytates, which bind with calcium, magnesium, and zinc, inhibiting the absorption of these minerals from the intestine. If a child craves wheat products, it's likely that they are low in zinc.

Refined wheat products, such as white bread, cakes, and cookies, have also been robbed of essential B vitamins, including niacin and B6. Deficiencies of thiamin, another B vitamin, and B6 have also been associated with loss of appetite.

Food jags and a decreased appetite are normal during toddlerhood. As your child's growth slows down, appetite will also decline. While it may seem that your child is not eating enough, it is highly unlikely that a child's appetite will decrease to such an extent that their health is compromised. At some point during the preschool years, many children go through another growth spurt. Take advantage of your child's increased appetite at this time to introduce a greater variety of healthier food options based on freshly prepared dishes and unprocessed wholefoods.

HIT OR MYTH

Avoiding the organic junk food trap

Today, more than ever, there are an enormous amount of organic foods that you can give your growing child. But before you buy organic because of what's not in it, consider what is in it as well. A quick look at the supermarket shelves will also confirm that the majority of organic items stocked in any supermarket are convenience foods.

Pre-prepared sauces, burgers, fries, pizza, ice cream, potato chips, peanut butter, jam, sausages, sandwich spread, and chocolate are all big sellers. But it is highly unlikely that any of these foods are substantially more nutritious than their conventional counterparts.

There is still no basic difference in the processing of some organic foods and non-organic foods. Many organic foods are produced using conventional industrial methods and similar types of ingredients, for example, refined flours. They also tend to use preservatives, such as sugar, to such an extent that some organic cookies can be higher in sugar (and fat) than their conventional counterparts. To make healthy choices, get in the habit of reading and comparing labels.

Healthy snacks

There is an argument that children should eat small meals throughout the day because it is better way to maintain health and absorb nutrients, placing less stress on the digestive system. A well-chosen snack can also stave off the extreme hunger which leads to binging on too much of the wrong kinds of foods.

With this in mind, there is room for healthy snacks—whether they be pre-packaged or put together from healthy ingredients—because snacks become an integral part of your child's over-all nutrition. However, instead of turning to pre-packaged snacks, why not a few healthy alternatives?

The key to these snacks is to let your child choose the ingredients and then encourage them to be involved in the preparation.

Veggies and dips. Serve a variety of colorful raw vegetables with a variety of dips to tempt children into eating more.

Fruit by the bowlful. Keep a bowlful of brightly colored seasonal fruits somewhere other than the kitchen. Make it obvious and easy to get to—such as the living room or dining room table. Kids may opt for this rather than walking to the kitchen for something else.

Fruit smoothies. Mix a cup of milk and two or three ice cubes in a blender with a chosen fruit. Soft fruits, such as bananas and strawberries, work best, but part of the fun is to let your child experiment.

The Energy Ball. Mix 1 tablespoon peanut butter, 1 tablespoon nonfat dried milk powder, 1 teaspoon raisins and form into a ball. Roll the mixture in a small handful of crushed sesame or pumpkin seeds, or unsweetened cereal such as muesli, coating generously. This snack is high in calories, but don't fret. Children need more fats in their diets than adults. The fats in this bar are considered "good fats," that is, those that aid the process of growth and metabolism.

Savory cheesy toast. For a savory treat that's much better for them than potato chips, toast a slice or two of bread, spread with unsalted butter. Then sprinkle with parmesan cheese. Eat hot.

Popcorn. An excellent substitute for other less healthy munchies. Made in a hot air type "popper," it needs no oils or other fats. In an otherwise low fat diet, a little melted butter is unlikely to be a dietary disaster. Alternatively, drizzle a little bit of molasses over the popcorn to add to its nutritional vale.

Make it in advance

Sometimes children eat junk foods because that's all that there is in the cupboard. To steer them in the right direction, try making one of these muffin recipes in advance.

RECIPE

Apple muffins

These are sweet and satisfying and contain good sources of vitamins and fiber.

To make 10 muffins:

Preheat the oven to 400°F. Lightly oil ten paper muffin cases.

6 ounces wholewheat flour	**2 fluid ounces/¼ cup vegetable oil**
1 teaspoon baking soda	**2 tablespoons apple juice concentrate**
½ teaspoon ground cinnamon	**8 fluid ounces/1 cup sugar free apple**
3 tablespoons ground flaxseed	**sauce**
1 egg beaten	**2 ounces desiccated unsweetened**
2 ounces melted unsalted butter	**coconut**

Mix the dry ingredients in a large bowl. In another bowl mix the egg, butter, and oil. Then add the apple juice concentrate, applesauce, and coconut and mix thoroughly. Fold the wet ingredients into the dry, and stir briefly until the mixture in moistened (don't over-stir as this can affect the texture of the finished muffin). Spoon the batter into the paper cups, filing each about two thirds full.

Bake for 30 minutes or until lightly brown. These muffins will be slightly moist because of the applesauce.

RECIPE

Veggie muffins

Most people think of muffins as something sweet, but substituting lightly cooked vegetables for fruits can make a really nice savory treat. These muffins are absolutely delicious as a snack or an accompaniment to soup for a light meal.

To make 16 muffins :

3½ ounces squash (or sweet potato)	**2½ ounces sunflower oil, plus extra for greasing**
3½ ounces zucchini grated	**8 ounces cheddar cheese (regular or reduced fat), grated**
9 ounces onions grated	**8 ounces wholewheat flour**
3½ ounces red pepper, finely diced	**1 teaspoon baking soda**
3½ ounces spinach shredded (or broccoli finely chopped)	**4 eggs**
3½ ounces corn fresh or frozen	**salt & pepper to taste**

RECIPE

Preheat the oven to 350°F and lightly oil sixteen paper muffin cases. Steam the squash until tender, mash and set aside. Lightly cook the corn and place in a bowl with the zucchini, onions, red pepper, and spinach. Mix in the oil, grated cheese, and seasoning. Fold in the flour and then the mashed squash.

Beat the eggs until they are frothy and fold them into the mixture. Spoon into the paper cups, filling them about two-thirds full. Bake for 20–25 minutes until lightly brown and risen. The high vegetable content of these muffins make them quite moist.

There are a number of excellent low-fat cookbooks that are available, each with dozens of suggestions for healthy snacks. Investing in one of these can help inspire you. You may even find that making things up in advance becomes an enjoyable part of your weekly routine—a nice way to pass a restful Sunday afternoon.

When making the switch from junk food snacks to healthy snacks, it is important to remember to make changes gradually. This is also good advice for most of the changes needed to lower your family's exposure to toxins. It is unlikely that your children will feel as inspired as you are by the idea of switching to healthier alternatives—at least at first. So, start slowly. Make small changes such as substituting one serving a day of whole wheat or rye bread for the white variety and gradually build from there.

HIT OR MYTH

Preventing cavities

The less time your child needs to spend at the dentist—exposed to mercury vapors and anesthetic drugs—the better. Some parents may worry that snacks such as fruit bars may increase the risk of dental caries. It is true that the longer a food takes to clear from the mouth the more chance it has to set up an "acid attack" on teeth. But research has shown that not all foods are what they appear to be.

For instance, caramels take less time to clear from the mouth that other healthier alternatives. Surprisingly, the worst culprits include bread and cereal products, potato chips, and dried fruits. Providing crunchy items such as sliced apples or carrot sticks alongside snack foods will not only send a good nutritional message to your kids, but eating them will also help clear lingering debris from the teeth.

Also, certain cheeses, such as cheddar, Swiss, and mozzarella stimulate the flow of saliva which helps to clear debris from the mouth—thus the tradition of eating cheese at the end of a meal!

In the end, it's all a balancing act since those children who have poor diets may also end up having teeth which develop poorly. If your child is encouraged to have good dental hygiene early in life, cavities from snack foods are unlikely to be a problem.

Learning healthy eating habits isn't a one-off lesson. It is something that requires persistence on the part of both parent and child, and at school the involvement of education authorities will also help. Remember that what your children eat during their main meals can influence how much they crave other foods during the day.

Cravings for junk foods can be kept in check with planning. Always give your child an adequate breakfast. This does not include sugar cereals or quick energy cereal bars. Remember that a meal does not have to be big to be satisfying. Attention to the nutritional content of the foods that you give your children means that they can get the vitamins and minerals they need without overeating.

Snacks are not bad—they can be a good way of topping up nutrients in a child's diet. You just need to use the foods, such as the above, for nutritionally sound snacks. If your child occasionally has something "junky," then don't worry about it. It's not what your children eats from day-to-day that is important but their overall diet during the course of the week.

Sun safety without (many) chemicals

As much as 80 percent of our lifetime exposure to the sun occurs during childhood. Yet, studies show that less than half of our children regularly use sun protection when outdoors.

Sun exposure and the use of sunscreens is one of the most complex and contradictory areas of child health. On the one hand, exposure to the fresh air and sun is vital for children's health. Sunlight, for example, is an important source of bone building vitamin D. But at the same time, too much sun can raise your child's risk of skin cancer in later life.

Sun creams

Relying on sunscreens as your sole means of protection is also

DID YOU KNOW?

Here comes the sun

The amount of UV radiation received is dependant on many factors. More ultraviolet radiation reaches the earth's surface at higher altitudes and lower altitudes. Many surfaces will reflect UV radiation, for example, sand can reflect up to 25 percent and water can reflect from 1 to 10 percent depending on the time of day.

Clouds do not provide adequate filtration of ultraviolet radiation—up to 80 percent of UV rays can penetrate through a cloud covering. Infrared rays, which give the feeling of warmth, are filtered more efficiently by clouds, and so there is a tendency to stay outdoors longer on cloudy days. This increases the chance of severe sunburns on cloudy days.

fraught with problems because the protection that they offer is never guaranteed and most commercial sunscreens contain many harsh and harmful chemicals that bring their own risks. Among the most harmful are benzophenones, which can cause allergic reactions, and PABAs, which have been shown to form potentially carcinogenic nitrosamines when mixed with other chemicals.

Though many of the ingredients used in sunscreens have been tested individually, studies of the long-term effects of combinations of sunscreen agents, applied liberally over an extended period of time, are rare. It is not uncommon for well-known brand name products to contain three or more sunscreen agents as well as perfumes, insect repellents, and a host of other chemicals besides. Young children can be especially sensitive to this chemical mix.

There are two basic types of creams available on the market today: chemical *sunscreens*, which act by absorbing ultraviolet light, and chemical *sunblocks*, which

DID YOU KNOW?

Label reading

As a general rule, the higher the SPF, the greater the number of chemicals in a sun lotion or cream. This may be a problem for highly allergic individuals. There is also evidence that sunscreens can be absorbed into the body through the skin. If you know that you, or your children, are allergic to certain types of sunscreen, then you have to become a label reader. You may wish to avoid products containing some of the following.

Benzophenones	*Cinnamates*	*Others*
Oxybenzone	Cinoxate	Methyl anthranilate
Dioxybenzone	Ethylhexyl-p-	Digalloyl trioleate
Sulisbenzone	methooxycinnamate	Avobenzone (butyl
	Octocrylene	methoxy-
	Ocytl	dibenzoylmethane)
PABAs	methoxycinnamate	
P-aminobenzoic acid		
ethyl dihydroxypropyl		*Chemical sunblocks*
PABA	*Salicylates*	Titanium dioxide
Padimate O (ocyl	Ethylhexyl salicylate	Red petrolatum
dimethyl PABA)	Homosalate	Zinc oxide
Padimate A	Octyl salicylate	
Glyceryl PABA	Neo-homosalate	

reflect or scatter light in both the visible and UV spectrum. The effectiveness of any sunscreen depends on its UV absorption, its concentration, formulation, and ability to withstand swimming or sweating. But that's not the end of the story.

Recent research in both America and Britain suggests that individuals who use sunscreens may actually be at an increased risk of developing skin cancer. This is because high SPF (sun protection factor) creams give sun lovers a false sense of security that encourages them to venture out during peak periods and to stay out in the sun much longer than would otherwise be considered safe.

Also, while all types of ultraviolet radiation can damage the skin, the SPF factor in your suncream only refers to the degree of UVB protection it provides. Most UVB rays are filtered out by the ozone layer. Those that do get through stimulate the skin's pigment to produce melanin, our natural defense against UV. UVA rays are not filtered out by the ozone layer and penetrate the skin at a deeper level so that they have the potential to cause more skin damage. Gauging UVA protection is a little more difficult, though some creams now put UVA information on their labels.

Sunscreens, such as padimate-O, are thought to absorb harmful UV rays. But once absorbed by the cream this energy has to be discharged somewhere—usually directly onto the skin where it is turned into free radicals which can

HINTS AND TIPS

Natural sunscreens?

Read labels for "natural" and "organic" sunscreens carefully. Usually they are simply the same old ingredients with added plant extracts and oils. Can the addition of these natural ingredients really protect against sunburn? Probably not.

• Aqua, that is water, does not prevent sunburn, as you might guess!

• Glycerin, a fat used in moisturizers to make then feel good and apply more smoothly, has no sun blocking ability.

• Octyl palmitate is a relative of vitamin C. There is no evidence it can provide protection from the sun.

• Retinyl palmitate, also known as pro-vitamin A or pro-retinol, is not proven to provide sun protection.

• Tocopherol acetate, a relative vitamin E shows no evidence it has any effect as a sunscreen.

• Other ingredients, such as, aloe vera, carrot oil, chamomile, borage oil, and avocado oil are used as fillers, stabilizers, or preservatives. They are seldom present in high enough quantities to protect or nourish your skin and none of them have proven sun-blocking ability.

actually increase the risk of skin cancer. The sunblock, titanium dioxide, is also used as a wastewater treatment where its function is to generate free radicals in order to kill organic contaminants.

Experts believe that the breakdown of sunscreens like oxybenzone, when exposed to UV rays, may actually destroy or inhibit the skin's natural defense system against sunlight, leaving it vulnerable to the free radicals produced by sunlight exposure. Free radicals are implicated in skin cancer, premature aging, and other damage to the skin. It is surprising to learn that many suncream ingredients are potentially harmful.

Sunscreens

So what's a parent to do? The only safe recommendation is not to rely on sunscreens as your sole method of protection. Also, avoid applying sunscreens over large parts of the body and over an extended period of time. Studies show that those parents who are most motivated to apply suncreams to their children are those whose children have previously had a severe burn. Certainly, there is nothing like seeing your child in agony from a bad burn to motivate you into being extra safe the next time around. But instead of waiting for that to happen, there are several things that you could do. For instance, limit the time spent outdoors or exposed to the sun between the hours of eleven in the morning and two o'clock in the afternoon.

When your children are in the sun, make sure that they are covered up as much as possible. Consider investing in special sun-protective clothing that can stop UV rays from penetrating to the skin.

Buy hats and sunglasses, and encourage your children to wear them. These are two essentials available in many shops throughout the country. Children should be encouraged to choose their favorites so that they will wear them without fuss when they are outdoors.

Use a special protective tent or umbrella on the beach so that you and the kids have somewhere to sit out of the sun.

Don't scare your children into action with facts and figures about skin cancer. Instead, lead by example. Research into children's voluntary use of suncreams suggests that they follow their parents' lead when it comes to covering up and slopping on the cream.

Playgroups and schools

When your child starts playgroups, nursery, or school, they will be exposed to many more "bugs" than at home. In some ways, this is inevitable and desirable. Every little illness that your child takes during this time provides education for their immune system. In this way your child's body "learns" to cope more effectively with illness.

But school doesn't only bring a whole new set of germs for your child to deal with. It also brings an increase in airborne allergens. While many of us concern ourselves with the educational profile of our children's schools, few take the time to check out its chemical profile. Remember that your child will be spending nearly as many hours at school as you spend at work which means that their atmosphere is important.

DID YOU KNOW?

Back to school

• *Schools concentrate many organisms which can adversely affect your child, among them are dusts, molds, and fungi.*

• *Many of our children go to school in older buildings that have not been well maintained. Windowsills may be damp, walls may be crumbling, and paint may be old and contain lead. Some take their classes in portable buildings that may be damp.*

• *Because heat is expensive, schools increasingly have a policy of heat conservation. However, if you seal a building up and then fill it with people who are breathing and sweating, then you are also encouraging the concentration of molds and toxic chemicals.*

• *The cleaning fluids used in schools can be harsh—both viricidal and bactericidal. Remember that humans are biological and these chemicals are not good for us either.*

• *Years ago, schools would have had woodblock floors, but now some have tough polypropylene type carpets which give off a constant stream of toxic gas.*

• *The materials that children work with can also be suspect. Unless the school is completely computerized, then your child could be using spirit-based glues, fancy paints, and felt tip pens which also give off toxic gases. If you're not convinced that these materials could possibly be toxic, just try sniffing a bottle of correction fluid and see how you feel.*

• *Because of relatively poor ventilation in schools, these things can become as important as allergens in terms of affecting your child's health. If your child has a constant state of sniffles at school, in spite of all your best efforts, suspect airborne allergens. It may be worth your while speaking to the teacher about the chemicals used in the school.*

A healthier approach to illness

It's amazing, but true—at least 95 percent of the ailments to which children are prone are self-limiting. In other words, they will heal by themselves and do not require any medical intervention. In contrast, just-in-case medicine can make symptoms worse and produce a whole range of new and even more debilitating side effects.

When you take your child to the doctor and are told that there's "something going round" or "it's probably a virus," this is not a medical diagnosis but a guess. There is always something "going around." There are viruses in the environment all the time. The possibility that it might be allergies, a run-down immune system, toxic overload, or emotional distress that is making your child susceptible to these bugs is important, and one which your doctor is less well-equipped to answer than you are.

Many parents feel fearful if their child has a rash or a fever. However, the holistic point of view is that these things are necessary and important. Part of organic living is supporting your child through illness, but not pumping them full of chemicals such as those contained in common medications.

Fever Fever "educates" the immune system to respond when needed and is a normal, and even desirable part of childhood. Temperatures up to 102°F don't require action—other than keeping your child hydrated and cool—unless your child is prone to convulsions. Trials have shown that there is no difference between the effect of paracetamol and placebos when it comes to treating fevers. And even though there is evidence that warm sponging can do more to reduce skin temperature than paracetamol, many parents are "not sure" about this treatment—though they continue to be "happy" about administering paracetamol.

Allergies Many childhood illnesses are caused by allergies. These can show themselves in something as obvious as eczema or asthma or chronic complaints like a constant runny nose, a cough, or constipation. It is better for you and your

DID YOU KNOW?

Good medicine?

Research into doctors' prescribing habits suggests that medicines are given mainly to treat the parent's distress and not the child's illness. Medical associations around the world have condemned the practice of prescribing drugs simply because parent's expect the doctors to "do something." In addition to harming physical health, psychologists are beginning to believe that giving drugs for every little illness sets up a dangerous psychological precedent, teaching the child that every problem in life can be solved with a pill or potion. Never accept or expect antibiotics or painkillers for your child unless there is a valid and urgent reason for doing so.

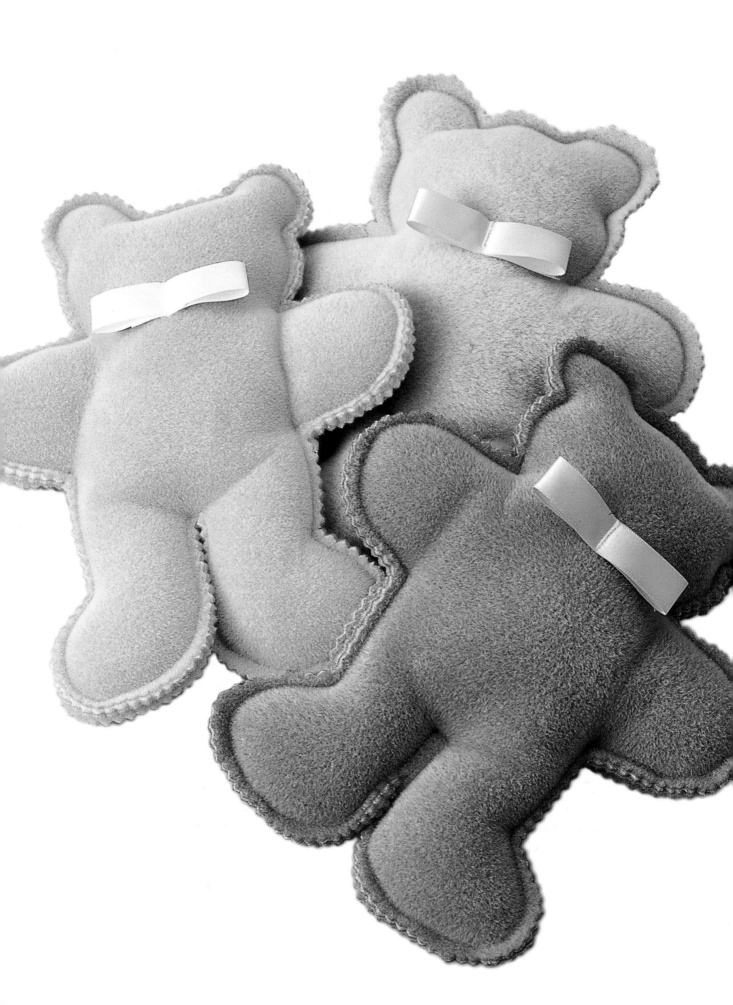

child to rule out these things now. Common dietary allergens include wheat, eggs, cow's milk, peanuts, and peanut oils (used in formula and nipple creams), corn, tomatoes, and food additives such as colorings and preservatives. Environmental allergens can include tobacco smoke, pollen, mold, feathers, dust, cosmetics, perfumes, and soaps.

DID YOU KNOW?

Boo Boo Bear

The Boo Boo Bear ™ is created by Herbs for Hurts Inc., based in Canada. It is a handcrafted warm/cool herbal pack using aromatherapy and herbs, such as chamomile, lavender, and peppermint. Each bear provides gentle, comfort for belly aches, earaches, headaches, or any other "boo boos" that a child may encounter.

Earaches Earaches are painful, can come on quickly, and be very distressing for your child. But they are rarely dangerous. If your child is still breast-feeding, let it suckle freely through the acute phase of the earache. The action of moving its jaw up and down can help to relieve any pressure or build-up in the ear (much like opening your mouth in the pressurized cabin of an airplane to "pop" your ears.) If not, giving them a chewy (non-PVC) toy can be helpful.

Your child is unlikely to need antibiotics unless your doctor can provide evidence of acute bacterial middle ear infection, in which case they should be administered as quickly as possible. Grommets for glue ear are dangerous, producing hardening of the eardrum, chronic perforation, and cysts on the middle ear. Investigating allergies is one of the most positive steps you can take for persistent glue ear.

Coughing Coughing is your child's way of getting rid of phlegm. The use of cough remedies has been shown, in numerous trials, to be useless. Suppressing a cough is not a good idea nor does your child need expectorant—the cough is doing the job it needs to. If your child's throat is scratchy, use a soothing mixture of glycerin or honey and lemon. Once again, investigate environmental and allergic causes of chronic phlegm.

The body electric

As your child gets older, it's not just the obvious dangers that you need to watch out for. Children are entering the electronic age earlier and earlier. They use computers, they sit in front of televisions and radios, and even have their own mobile phones. This use is not a bad thing. Electronics have revolutionized our world.

They have also brought problems. Many scientists believe that overexposure to the electromagnetic fields (EMFs)—generated by electronic goods—is an emerging threat to health. It can cause headaches, digestive complications, and problems with memory and nervous system function. The link between living near power lines and childhood cancer is well established. Increasingly, evidence is suggesting that some of the most frequent users of mobile phones experience chronic problems such as headache, disorientation, and nausea and may be at higher risk of some forms of cancer.

Non-toxic at home

One of the most toxic areas, in which we spend a good deal of our lives, is our home. Chapter 2 of this book explains, in more detail, how to improve your living space to the benefit of both you and your children. How you organize your home is an example to

HINTS AND TIPS

Cutting down the dazzle

No one expects you to give up your electronic goodies, but consider some measures to help limit the risk of exposure to EMFs.

• Make sure your intake of antioxidants—either through food or supplements—is adequate. Vitamins A, C, and E are known to help fight off the damage done by EMFs.

• You can contact your local power company and see if they can come and measure the levels of EMFs in your home. You can then get an idea of which rooms may need reorganizing, for instance, by moving furniture further away from sources of EMFs.

• Encourage your children to adopt the habit of sitting five or six feet away from the television.

• Put an anti-radiation screen on your computer.

• Keep bedrooms free of electronic gadgets. We spend a third of our lives in bed and even after electronic goods are switched off, they continue to generate EMFs. Televisions, stereos, radio alarms, electric blankets, and, for younger children, play ornaments, such as musical light boxes, should be kept away from beds. If this is impossible, try putting at least five feet between electric gadgets and the head of the bed.

• Emphasize to older children that mobile phones are for emergencies only— not for every day talking.

your children who will carry this with them into their adult lives. Rethink storage. Brightly colored plastics in a child's room, such as storage crates, plastic toys, or vinyl wallpaper, give off poisonous gases such as formaldehyde. Consider untreated wood boxes or traditional wooden toy chests to store toys (see The Non-Toxic Nursery earlier in this chapter).

Try to go frangrance free. Fragrances, used in room fresheners, soaps, deodorants, baby wipes, lotions, and cleaning agents contain highly volatile fragrance compounds which have been shown to be allergenic and carcinogenic as well as altering central nervous and immune system function. Using fragrance-free products goes part of the way towards reducing your child's risk of exposure.

Use a nonfluoride toothpaste. Fluoride is only slightly less toxic than lead and more toxic than arsenic, yet we continue to put it in our toothpaste and in our water. We already receive fluoride from other sources: produce grown in soil with a high fluoride content or sprayed with fluoride as a pesticide, "non-stick" coated cooking utensils, and car exhausts and other industrial pollution. It is estimated that our children may be getting between four and twelve times the "safe" dosage per day. Too much fluoride can cause stained, mottled teeth (known as fluorosis) as well as health problems such as fatigue, skin rashes, visual disturbances, stomach problems, headaches, and dizziness.

Looking forward to healthier kids

Good health habits are formed during childhood. These habits have to be learned and, as our world changes, they sometimes have to be relearned.

If you have given your child a good example to follow and a solid foundation by providing adequate nutrition and protection from environmental toxins, you have done the best you can. All that remains is to continue to gently encourage them in this direction.

Almost every child will eat at a fast food hamburger joint at sometime in their lives. When the summer comes, they may have more sodas than you might approve of. And as they grow into teenagers, they may temporarily revolt against the idea of a healthy, non-toxic lifestyle. They may sit to close to the TV, experiment with cigarettes and alcohol, and refuse to go outside on sunny days.

Don't worry. As a parent the best thing you can do is to continue to lead by example and keep the lines of communication open. Include health, ecology, and "green" philosophies as topic for discussion at dinner or on car journeys. Perhaps most importantly make sure your children know they have choices.

One of the most disturbing modern events is the effect of advertising and peer pressure. Children start to believe that they have to eat this food, drink this drink, and buy these clothes to stay "in" and play a certain computer game in order to be "cool." Eventually, a well-supported child will see through such nonsense and, as a parent, you can take pride in the fact that your positive influence has helped contribute to your child's healthy future. It might even contribute to the health of future generations.

HINTS AND TIPS

Eco Kids

Many schools do a great job of teaching children about the environment. But the real learning takes place at home. Respect for the nature and conservation of world resources is an outgrowth of learning conservation on a smaller scale.

Conservation means preserving or saving things. While it is commonly used in relation to the environment, children can be taught the value of conserving both material and spiritual goods. These can include objects such as clothes, furniture, and buildings, food, and money, as well as friendships and other important relationships, energy, and physical and mental health.

A child who is taught the value of conserving things which are real and concrete in their life will have less trouble understanding the value of conserving things which seem more remote like rainforests and sources fossil fuel.

Everyday activities that can bring conservation into focus for your child might include:

• Adopting an animal at the local zoo.

• Getting together with friends and cleaning up litter in your local area.

• Planting trees or other greenery in school or the local park.

• Helping with recycling activities at home and at school.

• Learning more about historic buildings and places in your local community and making sure these are preserved for future generations to appreciate.

10 steps to
an organic family

1. Before conception, both you and your partner should start to lead an organic and more healthy life: add organic food to your diet, let your home breathe "naturally" by using low-toxin household products, and reconsider how many toiletries you use each day.

2. After baby is born, breast-feed for as long as possible—it's the best "medicine" in the world.

3. Limit the number of toiletries used on your baby. Water will clean most things adequately. Instead of harsh baby wipes, try carrying a wet washcloth (flannel) in a plastic bag to deal with sticky faces and hands.

4. When it's time to wean, make sure you give your baby fresh organic foods or, if time does not allow, organically preprepared foods.

5. Learn more about complementary therapies and use these in preference to conventional medicine for everyday ailments.

6. If you already have a family, don't force too many changes on the family at once. Start small and feel your way through what works for all of you. Every little step you take is a step closer to a toxic-free lifestyle.

7. Limit time in front of the television and computer. Instead, encourage your child to trade a bit of virtual reality for actual reality, preferably outdoors in the fresh air.

8. Begin to expand your commitment to an organic lifestyle beyond foods and into other commonly used items such as bedding, toiletries, and household cleaners

9. Lead by example. If you take care of yourself and show respect for the environment, then your children will receive a powerful message that this is the correct way to behave.

10. Believe that you can make a difference to your child's, and your own, health.

Resource material

You will be able to find much of the resource material for improving your everyday living environment in the previous three chapters—particularly in chapter two. However, here are some resources that are particular to mother and baby.

The Ecomall
web: www.ecomall.com
"Earth's Largest Environmental Shopping Center." On their site you can find green products that are good for people and the environment. The site also features information on the wider aspects of conservation.

Nirvana Safe Haven
3441 Golden Rain Road, Suite 3
Walnut Creek, CA 94595
Tel: (800) 968-9355 or (925) 472 8868
Fax: (925) 938-9019
e-mail: daliya@nontoxic.com
web: www.nontoxic.com
A range of goods for a healthier home. They offer safe non toxic goods such as organic cotton and organic wool mattresses, organic wool pads, organic wool comforters, and organic wool pillows.

The Green People
web: www.greenpeople.com
Not to be confused with the UK company, this site provides a searchable database of eco-friendly products including organic food, pet supplies, baby products, beauty products, home improvement, hemp, organic cotton, health products, and recycled products.

Clothing, Diapers and Bedding

Greenbabies
Tel: (914) 524-7906 or (800) 603-7508.
e-mail: mail@greenbabies.com
web: www.greenbabies.com
Catalog features 100 percent organic cotton clothing for children newborn through seven years. All their colors and pigments are nontoxic and low-impact on the environment.

A Happy Planet
PMB # 71
2261 Market St, San Francisco
CA 94114
Tel: (888) 946-4277 (toll free in the U.S.)
Fax: (415) 821-2770

e-mail: info@ahappyplanet.com or orders@ahappyplanet.com
web: www.ahappyplanet.com
Earth-friendly products for safe homes and sustainable living, including 100 percent organically grown cotton underwear, T-shirts, leggings, socks, pants, sweaters, and sweatshirts, for adults and children.

California Organic Clothing Company
Tel: (323) 727-0001
e-mail: steward@organiccottonandhemp.com
web: www.organiccottonandhemp.com
For a range of organic cotton, hemp, and recycled textiles

Cottonfield
PO Box 1386 , Brookline, MA 02446
Toll free: (888) 954-1551
Phone: (617) 713-2744
Fax: (617) 232-3796
e-mail: cottonfield@cottonfieldllc.com
web: http://www.cottonfieldllc.com
Comfortable, simple, and stylish organic and natural fiber clothing for men and women.

Earth Baby
2312 Northeast 85th Street, Suite C
Seattle, WA 98115
Tel: (877) 375-3600 (toll free in the U.S.) or (206) 729-9600
Fax: (206) 729 1800
e-mail: mail@earthbaby.com
web: www.earthbaby.com
Organic cotton nursing bras, maternity lingerie, hemp baby bags, slings, and herbs can all be supplied by this company. Their website also features lots of interesting reading material.

Ecobaby Organics
332 Coogan Way, El Cajon
CA 92020
Tel: 888-ECOBABY
Fax: (619) 562-0199
Email: dottie@ecobaby.com
web: www.ecobaby.com
A huge selection of organic clothes and bedding for

adults and children, as well as diapers. They also have a large range of other natural goods including bath accessories. Visit their site for a range of natural parenting articles as well.

Maggie's Functional Organics
1955 Pauline Blvd
Suite 100A
Ann Arbor
MI 48103
Tel: (800) 609-8593
e-mail: maggies@organicclothes.com
web: www.organicclothes.com
A line of beautifully basic, comfortable clothing, accessories, housewares and, most recently, bedding! All items are as environmentally sustainable as possible and most are organic.

Uncle Zach's Earth Friendly
PO Box 1655 , Portland
OR 97207
Phone: (503) 248-1837
Fax: (503) 274-1060
e-mail: uzachs@teleport.com
web: http://www.unclezachs.com
Naturally safe and organic clothing and accessories for men, women, and children.

Under the Nile
5792 Dichondra Place, Newark
CA. 94560
Tel: (800) 883-4402 (toll free in the U.S.)/(510) 797-2793
Fax: (510) 742-1345
web: www.underthenile.com
Specializing in certified organic cotton clothing and toys for children made from Egyptian cotton. Their colorful line features underwear as well as other basics.

What's Hempenin Baby
e-mail: diaper@babyhemp.com
web: http://www.babyhemp.com
Specializing in hemp based clothing for mothers and babies. The range includes Hempers ™ hemp diapers and a range of comfortable hemp clothing.

Birth and Parenting Organizations

CIMS
Coalition for Improving Maternity Services
2120 L Street NW, Suite 400
Washington, DC 20037
Tel: (202) 478-6136
Web: www.motherfriendly.org
Umbrella organization for many professional groups concerned with maternity care. Their main aim is to promote evidence-based, mother-friendly maternity care.

International Childbirth Education Association (ICEA)
PO Box 20048, Minneapolis
MN 55420
Web: www.icea.org
An organization—with over seven thousand members from forty-two countries—that unites those who believe in freedom of choice based on knowledge of alternatives in family-centered maternity and newborn care.

Le Leche League1400
North Meacham Road, Schaumburg
IL 61073-4049
Tel: 847 519 7730
Web: www.lalecheleague.org
A leading source of breast-feeding information and support. Through the LLL, a mother can talk to other breastfeeding mothers, have access to the latest research on breast-feeding, and seek help with breast-feeding problems form experienced counselors.

Lamaze International
1200 19th Street NW, Suite 300
Washington, DC 20036-2422
Tel: (202) 857-1128
Web: www.lamaze-childbirth.com
Since 1960, this group has promoted the idea that the ideal birth experience is one where the mother is awake, aware, and supported by family and friends, with no maternal/infant separation after birth. They run ante-natal classes throughout the world to support mothers who believe in this idea.

The Bradley Method of Natural Childbirth
Box 5224, Sherman Oaks
CA 91413-5224
Tel: (800) 4 A BIRTH
Web: www.bradleybirth.com
Also known as the American Academy of Husband Coached Childbirth, this group supports the concept of natural pregnancy and birth and place particular emphasis on the active participation of the husband as a birth "coach."

Index